10650015

Civil Wars

PUBLISHING FOR THE WORLD
125 Years

THE JOHNS HOPKINS UNIVERSITY PRESS

Civil Wars

American Novelists and Manners,
1880–1940

Susan Goodman

The Johns Hopkins University Press
Baltimore and London

© 2003 The Johns Hopkins University Press
All rights reserved. Published 2003
Printed in the United States of America on acid-free paper
9 8 7 6 5 4 3 2 1

The Johns Hopkins University Press
2715 North Charles Street
Baltimore, Maryland 21218-4363
www.press.jhu.edu

Library of Congress Cataloging-in-Publication Data
Goodman, Susan.
    Civil wars : American novelists and manners, 1880–1940 /
Susan Goodman.
       p. cm.
Includes bibliographical references and index.
    ISBN 0-8018-6824-6 (hardcover : alk. paper)
       1. American fiction — 20th century — History and criticism.
2. Manners and customs in literature. 3. Literature and society —
United States — History — 20th century. 4. Literature and society —
United States — History — 19th century. 5. American fiction — 19th
century — History and criticism. I. Title.
PS374.M33 G66 2003
2002008123

A catalog record for this book is available from the British Library.

To Carl

The manners, *the manners:*
where and what are they, and what have they to tell?

HENRY JAMES, *The American Scene*

Contents

Preface   *xi*

Acknowledgments   *xvii*

Introduction: American Novelists and Manners   1

1   William Dean Howells: The Lessons of a Master   13

2   Henry James: The Final Paradox of Manners   39

3   Edith Wharton: A Backward Glance   60

4   Willa Cather: "After 1922 or Thereabout"   83

5   Ellen Glasgow: A Social History of America   104

6   Jessie Fauset: The Etiquette of Passing   130

    Conclusion: Excursives   150

Notes   *157*

Selected Bibliography   *179*

Index   *191*

Preface

"The Vanderbilt entertainment was just what you say," Edith Wharton wrote to a friend in 1902. "For a novelist gathering documents for an American novel, it was all the more valuable, alas!"[1] The sigh of that last "alas," which unites Wharton with her correspondent (also a member of the class that the Vanderbilts and "their kind" supplanted), points directly to the topic of my book: the relationship between manners and American fiction in the last decades of the nineteenth century to the Second World War.

To Wharton, the Vanderbilts offered a vast field for social speculation, which she hoped to turn to her advantage. She found them absorbing because, unlike her parents and the "old" New Yorkers, they made a spectacle of consumption. If it takes radical social change "to set a writer in motion,"[2] the advent of the multimillionaires promised a new epoch and a fiction to match. Wharton did not assume that the Vanderbilts *were* America. She did think their manners a piece in the larger puzzle of how America imagined itself, which is to say, how its writers defined their work. How could she not? Contrary to the widespread conviction, advanced by Alexis de Tocqueville in the nineteenth century and Lionel Trilling in the twentieth, that the United States has neither the rich past nor the stratification of classes required to produce a novelist of manners, its writers have always tied the subject of national identity to the norms of everyday life.

The "American novel" is my subject here, and the American novel at a particular period in its history. And my premise throughout the following chapters is that the emphasis on manners and the importance of novels of manners can be seen, perhaps should be seen, as a defining quality in our literature. That is my premise, but of course it is complicated in a number of ways. Wharton, for example, who was a voracious reader and a lifelong student of fiction, refused to

---

1. Letter of Edith Wharton to Sara Norton, Sept. 1, 1902, in Susan Goodman, *Edith Wharton's Women: Friends and Rivals* (Hanover: University Press of New England, 1990), 34.
2. Henry James, "Hawthorne," in *Henry James: Literary Criticism*, ed. Leon Edel (New York: Library of America, 1984), 1:320.

recognize a substantive distinction between novels and novels of manners. Their history seemed basically the same, from Greek and chivalric predecessors to the intrigues of the Italian *novelle* and other continental models, to social treatises and conduct books by novelists like Maria Edgeworth. Wharton's remark about the Vanderbilts may remind us that manners have been the great subject for Western novelists since Samuel Richardson set Mr. B. in pursuit of Pamela. My aim, then, is not to show that novels of manners are an American invention or that all American novels amount to novels of manners. Nor is it to assign a particular novel to one category or the other. Instead, I hope to show that the emphasis on manners in American fiction around the turn of the twentieth century at once typifies a major preoccupation of American novelists and offers ways of understanding later developments.

This brings me to the whole vexed question of definition, for manners, as well as novels of manners, have meant different things to writers in different countries and at different times. To be sure, manners concern patterns of speech, gesture, decoration, and dress; they also go beyond modes of behavior to include the complexities of human experience. Their confirmation of a society's boundaries and possibly its authority permit awareness of underlying social structures and cultural differences.

The writers in this study—William Dean Howells, Henry James, Edith Wharton, Willa Cather, Ellen Glasgow, and Jessie Fauset—embraced the protean nature of manners and of novel writing. Not surprisingly, the vacillations they attributed to manners seemed akin to the historical process itself. Howells, for example, saw the best of fiction rivaling historical narrative, and Ellen Glasgow conceived her books as social history. They were not alone. Among all of the novelists I discuss, the topic of social relations converged with a renewed passion for history.

Novelists grew to think about fiction as a version of history, but history reformulated to express the needs and the anxieties of their own worlds, in which women, workers, immigrants, and African Americans demanded more power. When James surveyed "the American Scene" in 1907, he objected to the influx of immigrants. Glasgow spoke "the first word ever uttered in Virginia in favor of votes for women,"[3] and Fauset edited the official magazine of the NAACP. Living in an era characterized by xenophobia, labor strikes, racial and religious divisions, and tensions between the sexes, they recorded the behavior of middle-

3. Ellen Glasgow, *The Woman Within* (New York: Harcourt, Brace, 1954), 185.

class America as it responded to such movements as Reconstruction, the western march, and the urbanization of American life. It may have been inevitable that writers who came to maturity in the years after the Civil War, or those who lived through the First World War and saw another war looming, would come to think manners more fluid than fixed. By design or default, manners contained their own social dynamic, an ever-alternating balance between beliefs and assumptions embedded in the culture and those emerging.

As we might expect, scholarship has followed where the novelists have led. Since the 1960s, there has been at least an indirect interest in the topic of manners — witness Roland Barthes's examination of Japanese society or French fashions, Michel Foucault's analysis of mental institutions and prisons, and Patricia Meyer Spacks's meditation on gossip. Filmmakers intrigued with past cultures have translated books by Willa Cather, Henry James, and Edith Wharton to the screen. The allure of Wharton's *The Age of Innocence* comes from a form that depends on specific, historical moments when codes of conduct, once the sign of social or political supremacy, retain an imaginative appeal. It is odd, if not paradoxical, that while the form has become more culturally central, critics continue to think about it in a conventional way, almost wholly, that is, as a reflection of upper-class excesses in past times.

Recent critical emphasis on "cultural studies," on the social construction of identity, and a "subject's" position in history — not to mention considerations of the novel itself — all have bearing on manners. James Tuttleton has written persuasively about selected writers (*The Novel of Manners in America*, 1972); Amy Kaplan, about the realistic novel (*The Social Construction of Realism*, 1988); and Nancy Bentley, the intersection of fiction and anthropological theories (*The Ethnography of Manners: Hawthorne, James, and Wharton*, 1995), but there is nothing directly approaching the focus of my book. I present the novel of manners as an evolving form, responsive to the persistent recomposition of American classes and culture and crucial to an understanding of American literary history. Let me explain at the outset that my purpose is not to decide the debate sparked by Trilling's influential essay on novels of manners — a debate that has always been less historical and analytical than political; nor do I borrow theoretical frameworks from other disciplines and apply them to the study of manners. My approach, at once more specific and comprehensive, is to look at manners as they were defined, discussed, and fictionalized by one specific cluster of writers at various stages in their careers.

A word must be said about my choice of authors and texts. Among any number of pertinent authors, I have selected novelists who consciously and publicly wrestled with the idea of manners and their implications for fiction. Wharton, for example, began her career with *The Decoration of Houses* (1897), a practical manual for middle-class householders who felt anxious about what constituted "good taste." A decade later, James wrote a series of articles on the speech and manners of American women. And Cather argued in her influential essay "The Novel *Démeublé*" (1936) that writers do not make fictional worlds believable by simply stuffing them with material details. Such discussions, whether in reviews, essays, correspondence, or books of travel, are especially pertinent to an author's fictional treatment of how society conducts itself, and I have not hesitated to make use of them.

Despite including well-known texts, such as Howells's *The Rise of Silas Lapham*, I have purposely chosen not to revisit others, notably James's splendid portrait of Isabel Archer. The reason for each decision rests with the individual author. Howells is known today, if at all, for that single title, whereas James's *Portrait* has defined and helped to "caricature" the novel of manners for generations. In other words, students familiar with *The Portrait of a Lady* often view it as the main, sometimes the only template. My aim differs. I focus on books that illustrate the elasticity of a form that dissimilar writers have manipulated for their own purposes. I end my chapter on Howells, for example, by examining *An Imperative Duty*, a novel written after the Haymarket Riot left him disillusioned with American justice; with James, I am interested, among other works, in the manuscripts he could never bring himself to complete after the bombing of Rheims.

The structure of my book remains largely chronological. It begins with Howells and proceeds with individual chapters on James, Wharton, Cather, Glasgow, and Fauset. Because I consider this study more an extended essay than a treatise, I have tried to suggest a pattern of recurrent concerns and themes, from discussions of civilization, especially in the face of the First World War, to questions about race, nationality, and place, which I see (in the fashion of Lewis Carroll's Red Queen) working backward and forward. Each of my chapters incorporates these themes with distinct emphases; the chapters on Howells, Cather, and Fauset, for example, highlighting, in turn, questions of class, history, and race.

I ask readers to understand the spirit of this study, which takes broad social issues and specific matters of definition and attempts to explore them through the workings of related yet diverse literary works. No doubt there can be definitions that link Wharton with Glasgow, for example, or Howells with Fauset, and where possible, I move toward definition. Still, it remains obvious that the books themselves cry for a more encompassing approach, so that a simple thesis — like Lionel Trilling's — encourages rather than reduces aesthetic misunderstanding. Although my title, *Civil Wars*, may seem to suggest the critical disagreements mentioned, it refers to the conflicts writers of this era assumed between the classes and the masses, civilization and chaos.

In a sense, this book works from the inside out, from archival materials and literary texts, but also from and within the worlds that American novels of manners operate. I see it as unimportant that another student of the field can assert, say, that Cather did not write novels of manners. I would reply by showing how Cather (or James or Wharton) began with an understanding of American literature *as* an assessment of its manners and thought the categorization of books an unfortunate necessity for marketing. I grant that it may be impossible to define something as prevalent and as fluctuating as manners. James tried, and if he and the other writers I discuss were only partly successful, it was because they refused to have human behavior — or their life's work — reduced to formulas.

Although I do address the shifting and sometimes idiosyncratic nature of definitions, I have sought, above all, to demonstrate that novels of manners are central to American literature; that how they were read at the turn of the twentieth century has been lost to most contemporary readers; and that these novels speak in a large cultural way about who and what "composes" America.

Acknowledgments

William Dean Howells admired his father for having a friendly eye. This is not to say that he ignored the more brutal or unpleasant aspects of life, but if an unfriendly eye can be said to miss the best in any prospect, his eye focused on the "warm heart of humanity." I begin with Howells's tribute to his father because it captures my own feelings about the many people who have helped me with this book.

First, let me thank Jerome Loving for reading this (and past) manuscripts, as well as those friends and colleagues who have made my work easier and my life better: Lawrence D. Stewart, Fleda Brown, Jerry Beasley, Leo Lemay, Ellen Pifer, Drury Pifer, Richard Zipser, Ulrike Diedenhofen, Ed Folsom, Mary Suzanne Schriber, Willis G. Regier, Jackson Bryer, Linda Wagner-Martin, Maureen Murphy, June Hanson, Cynthia Griffin Wolff, and Charles Robinson. In addition, I have received much help from librarians at the Morris Library, University of Delaware, the Alderman Library, University of Virginia, the Houghton Library, Harvard University, the Harry Ransom Center, University of Texas, and the Huntington Library, San Marino, California. Roger Stoddard, curator of the Howells Collection at Harvard, and Cally Gurley, curator of the Women Writers Collection, the Abplanap Library, University of New England, provided invaluable assistance. William White Howells and the Houghton Library have graciously granted me permission to quote from unpublished material, as has the Alderman Library. My work with various collections was aided by a General University Research Grant from the University of Delaware, the Dorothy M. Healy Visiting Professorship (University of New England), and the William Dean Howells Memorial Fellowship in American Literature (Houghton Library).

I have benefited from the wisdom of a not-so-patient circle of listeners — Arthur Balderacchi, Ted Weesner, Janet Schofield, and Arthur and Celeste Dimambro. And as always, I remain extraordinarily fortunate for having had the wisdom and encouragement of my husband, Carl Dawson.

Acknowledgments

William Dean Howells admired his father for having a friendly eye. This is not to say that he ignored the more brutal or unpleasant aspects of life, but if an unfriendly eye can be said to miss the best in any prospect, his eye focused on the "warm heart of humanity." I begin with Howells's tribute to his father because it captures my own feelings about the many people who have helped me with this book.

First, let me thank Jerome Loving for reading this (and past) manuscripts, as well as those friends and colleagues who have made my work easier and my life better: Lawrence D. Stewart, Fleda Brown, Jerry Beasley, Leo Lemay, Ellen Pifer, Drury Pifer, Richard Zipser, Ulrike Diedenhofen, Ed Folsom, Mary Suzanne Schriber, Willis G. Regier, Jackson Bryer, Linda Wagner-Martin, Maureen Murphy, June Hanson, Cynthia Griffin Wolff, and Charles Robinson. In addition, I have received much help from librarians at the Morris Library, University of Delaware, the Alderman Library, University of Virginia, the Houghton Library, Harvard University, the Harry Ransom Center, University of Texas, and the Huntington Library, San Marino, California. Roger Stoddard, curator of the Howells Collection at Harvard, and Cally Gurley, curator of the Women Writers Collection, the Abplanap Library, University of New England, provided invaluable assistance. William White Howells and the Houghton Library have graciously granted me permission to quote from unpublished material, as has the Alderman Library. My work with various collections was aided by a General University Research Grant from the University of Delaware, the Dorothy M. Healy Visiting Professorship (University of New England), and the William Dean Howells Memorial Fellowship in American Literature (Houghton Library).

I have benefited from the wisdom of a not-so-patient circle of listeners — Arthur Balderacchi, Ted Weesner, Janet Schofield, and Arthur and Celeste Dimambro. And as always, I remain extraordinarily fortunate for having had the wisdom and encouragement of my husband, Carl Dawson.

American Novelists and Manners

> Manners are what vex or soothe, corrupt or purify, exalt or debase, barbarize or refine us, by a constant, steady, uniform, insensible operation, like that of the air we breathe in. They give their whole form and color to our lives. According to their quality, they aid morals, they supply laws, or they totally destroy them.   EDMUND BURKE, *Letters on a Regicide Peace*

When Henry James (1843–1916) said that we cannot know a culture until we know its manners, he merely stated conventional wisdom. No matter that Edith Wharton (1862–1937) resented being seen as a "masculine" Henry James, that Jessie Fauset (1882–1961) suffered from unflattering comparisons to Wharton, that Ellen Glasgow (1873–1945) thought William Dean Howells (1837–1920) dull and Willa Cather (1873–1947) unreadable. These writers agreed that the secret to any society, its variable crosscurrents of sympathy and strife, lay in its manners.

From Edmund Burke to Roland Barthes, people have tried to make sense of civilization through its rituals, but at no time has this been more true than in the turn-of-the-century United States. The Civil War had accented regional and racial differences, which campaigns for economic parity and social equality did little to correct. As the twentieth century approached, millennial anxiety, heightened by the Spanish-American War of 1898, fueled long-standing debates about national definition and direction, in which men often seemed to line up against women, whites against blacks, entrenched generations of Americans against recent immigrants, and "haves" against "have-nots." People hoped that shared codes of behavior would help to impose order on the growing welter of art and industry, science and government, that they called "civilization."

Discussions of manners permeated every aspect of both American life and American letters. William Dean Howells and Ellen Glasgow considered themselves to be biographers of life in the sense that they chronicled the impact of social transitions, while Edith Wharton's main theme could be interpreted as the tension between individual desire and society's need for discipline.[1] "There is no such thing as an isolated man or woman," Madame Merle tells Isabel Archer in James's *The Portrait of a Lady* (1881); "we are each of us made up of a cluster of appurtenances. What do you call one's self? Where does it begin? Where does it end? It overflows into everything that belongs to us—and then it flows back again."[2] According to both Madame Merle and her author, manners present a set of complex interrelationships that, given an increasingly relativistic universe, call for finer discrimination.

Expatriates like James and Wharton did not discover the relevance of manners in exile so much as concentrate on a topic it seemed almost impossible to ignore. The late nineteenth century was an age that believed anatomy to be destiny, an age when the fictional detective Sherlock Holmes (auguring the methods of the real-life detective, Sigmund Freud) discovered the histories of his clients in their mannerisms. "[O]ne's house, one's furniture, one's clothes, the books one reads, the company one keeps" (*Portrait of a Lady*, 397–98)—these expressed the self not only to novelists but also to scientists according to the "silent laws" of genetics and natural correspondences.[3] If Henry James saw manners as the dominant feature of fiction, his brother William argued a direct connection between manners and human psychology; counting to ten *did* dissipate anger, and whistling in the dark *could* make one feel less alone.[4] People looked for evidence of their own worth or preeminence in the set of a jaw, the sweep of a cheekbone, the shape of the eyes and skull, duly cataloged in the *Human Dictionary*.[5] Ordinary citizens believed that the practice of polite behavior could lead to lasting changes in character, and they routinely studied manners to know themselves and others.

Whether or not late-nineteenth-century readers had a greater passion for self-improvement than preceding generations, theirs manifested itself in the proliferation of culture clubs and women's groups dedicated, for example, to the betterment of public health or the beautification of city thoroughfares. Always popular, etiquette manuals gained ever greater importance as the cultures of home and business overlapped. The demographics of nineteenth-century America, with its roving populations in search of higher wages and social opportunities, expanded this already huge market. Technological advances in typesetting, bookbinding, papermaking, and transportation had made etiquette guides available to an ever-increasing reading public.[6] On hand for reference in middle-class households, advice books challenged the supremacy of the family Bible. Readers believed that polite behavior produced an immediate return in augmented wages and status. As long as they could dream of belonging to the Astor Four Hundred, it did not matter to them that manners reinforced traditional class divisions. "Tell me thy Manners and I'll tell thy Fortune," one almanac writer promised.[7] With a little luck, it seemed that anyone with sufficient drive could rise from shoeshiner to millionaire.

Advice on friendships, prohibitions against gossip, rules for spinsters, and etiquette for small towns and villages, once the province of almanacs and ladies' magazines such as *Godey's*, found their way into the more "highbrow" pages of the *Atlantic, Lippincott's*, and *Putnam's*. At the beginning of the nineteenth century, Sir Walter Scott had complained that scarcely a subject — journalism, literature, or politics — escaped being viewed from the angle of "the manners or want of manners peculiar to Americans."[8] By 1885, manners manuals became so ubiquitous that Howells lampooned them in *The Rise of Silas Lapham* for telling readers "not to eat with their knives, and above all not to pick their teeth with their forks — a thing which . . . no lady or gentleman ever did."[9] By 1923, the writers of manners manuals could read Howells and laugh all the way to the bank. That year alone, Emily Post's *Etiquette* sold an estimated one million copies.

In an odd but understandable way, manners manuals or etiquette books obliquely legitimized the novel of manners, and vice versa. More than one unsophisticated reader was said to have sought a guide to high society in Wharton's *The House of Mirth* (1905), which in turn articulated (by Lily Bart's negative example) polite behavior for unmarried women. A mix of history and autobiographical anecdote, manners manuals included examples of other cultures, notably French and English, in their definitions of and prescriptions for better living. Hypotheses about religion, empire, femininity, and family framed practical as well as aesthetic advice. Mrs. Beeton's *Book of Household Management* (1861) remained a perennial favorite, as did the Beecher sisters' impossibly titled tome *The American Woman's Home or, Principles of Domestic Science; Being a Guide to the Formation and Maintenance of Economical, Healthful, Beautiful, and Christian Homes* (1869). Biographies that preceded the text of manners manuals announced their authors' social and moral standing. As Sarah Josepha Hale, the editor of *Godey's*, and Catharine Maria Sedgwick, the popular historical novelist, knew, they provided an occasion to influence the tastes and values of a growing middle class.

In a society still perceived to be divided into separate spheres for men and women, manners manuals helped to justify the extension of women's influence beyond the home. Women did not own the copyright on manners manuals, but whether written by men or the president-general of the Daughters of the American Revolution, these books promulgated certain views about class and gender, which their advocacy of women's education and legal enfranchisement covertly undermined. In this way, they employed rhetorical strategies not dissimilar to those of novelists of manners or the so-called domestic novelists whom writers of Glasgow's generation grew up reading:

> Women's profession embraces the care and nursing of the body in the critical periods of infancy and sickness [Catherine Beecher and Harriet Stowe wrote after the Civil War], the training of the human mind in the most impressible period of childhood, the instruction and control of servants, and most of the government and economies of the family state. These duties of woman are as sacred and important as any ordained to man; and yet no such advantages for preparation have been accorded to her.[10]

Glasgow put it more sardonically in *Virginia* (1913), her portrait of the vanishing southern lady, when she wrote that "the less a girl knew about life, the better prepared she was to deal with it."[11]

Not above playing the southern belle herself, Glasgow knew that the public liked to hear about the family portraits hanging in her drawing room and the Chippendale furniture that survived the War between the States. By making fetishes of cultural practices, such as the paying of morning calls, manners manuals further fixed class mythologies in the popular imagination. An anecdote in *Correct Social Usage* (1906), a book written by eighteen "distinguished" authors on good form, style, and deportment (and published by the New York Society of Self-Culture), exposes the class snobbery that gave manners manuals and novels of manners their appeal. A family who had owned a shirt factory painted an armorial design on their carriage. "What was it," someone asked, "a shirt pendant and a washerwoman rampant?"[12] The shock of recognition — in this case, getting the joke — draws the audience into an act of exclusion, which paradoxically unites them with their class. Novels of manners contain a comparable dynamic when they align readers with principles they would normally disdain. The tension of books, including Wharton's *The Age of Innocence* (1920) and Fauset's *The Chinaberry Tree* (1931), comes from the loving presentation of practices about which their narrators feel ambivalent. Readers remember silk-stockinged footmen, the smell of Turkish coffee, or the blaze of a dozen Jacqueminot roses, details that help to explain why novels of manners are often considered nostalgic and why critics tend to see their authors, despite their widely varying creeds, as both conservative and quickly outmoded.

Novels of manners obviously rely on facts of material culture to communicate an entire envelope of culture, the intangible assumptions and inferences that make a particular society itself. By the turn of the century, they could also rely on something more — a whole network of interdisciplinary connections. If manners could not be fully considered without taking into account their importance to other fields, the same holds true for novels of manners. They seemed to contain a built-in "dialogic" (to borrow Mikhail Bakhtin's well-known term), because readers approached them from a variety of perspectives influenced by their reading in other genres. To give just one example, people read such novels against and alongside their understanding of manners drawn from travel literature. In the nineteenth century, the market for travel literature had ballooned, as more and more middle-class Americans took advantage of improvements in transportation and favorable rates of exchange. By the 1880s, as *Scribner's Monthly* announced, all Americans had become "by nature 'Passionate Pilgrims'" (Mott, 3:258).

As the writers in this study realized, travel books are themselves studies in manners, and Howells's *Roman Holidays and Others* (1908), James's *Italian Hours* (1909), and Wharton's *Italian Gardens and Villas* (1905) — not to forget Fauset's reporting of the Pan-African conferences — use manners much as their eighteenth-century counterparts had — to communicate and critique what they thought to be common moral concerns. A generic equivalent of the novel of manners, travel books tend to address how people and nations conduct their lives, and they usually work by comparison. Typical chapter titles included "The Social Instinct" (a key to character), "Intelligence" (usually of the quick- or slow-witted variety), "Morality" (taken more lightly in Europe than the United States), and "Women" (their "place"). Writers routinely predicted that an increased understanding of another country would make readers more appreciative of their own, and, like many sightseers, they tried to account for the unsettling sensation of being stranded between two worlds.

The feeling of displacement, which both novels of manners and travel literature capture, partly accounts for their ambivalent tone. When told from the first person, travel memoirs frequently showcase the drama of personal consciousness that especially intrigued a travel writer like Henry James. Novels of manners work by appearing to endorse what they ultimately reject, and travel literature conveys a comparable and similarly contradictory impulse, which expresses itself in moves toward merger and separation. For example, the great Japanologist Ernest Fenollosa foresaw a marriage between East and West, with the West perhaps the slightly dominant partner. The astronomer Percival Lowell sought an ideal society — first in Japan, viewed as the France of the East, and then on Mars, where he imagined a higher and superior version of his own Brahmin

Boston. And the travel writer Bayard Taylor adopted an Arab burnoose and a turban before his translation of *Faust* allowed him to be an acceptable candidate for a ministry to Germany. From one perspective, Taylor made a career of acquiring and shedding identities. This man, who began by reporting on the manners of California miners, panhandlers, and legislators attending the would-be state's first constitutional convention, also wrote short stories set in Russia (after a year as secretary of the United States' legation in Saint Petersburg), along with novels of literary life in contemporary New York City.

The title of Taylor's California book, *El Dorado: Adventures in the Path of Empire* (1850), which weds history, myth, and politics, again suggests that studies of manners could not be separated—indeed they accrued significance—from their dialogue with other fields. The highly technical vocabulary that thwarts such dialogue in the twenty-first century had few equivalents for the gifted and widely read amateurs who defined emergent fields in the nineteenth century and whose research tended toward the inclusion of topics now divided into distinct specialties. Charles Darwin was one of those early pioneers. Forever identified with theories of evolution, Darwin also applied those theories to the study of manners—in an effort to determine whether the expression of emotions was "universal" (the same among Polynesians, Maoris, Aymara Indians, Britons, and Americans, for instance) or tied to specific historical or cultural situations.[13] Darwin concluded that three principles largely determined expression: inheritance (affected by will and intention); our instinctive recognition of expression in others, which bears on the unity of the human races; and evolution, or successive acquirement. He had sought to offer a natural explanation of phenomena that appeared to undermine his theory that species are immutable, and, as we might expect, other writers used his findings for their own ends, whether to advance or to debunk cultural hierarchies. Writers of manners manuals, who felt in need of a scientific framework, borrowed Darwin's theories to perpetuate or challenge generalizations that Europeans were more "civilized" than non-Europeans, say, or that the rich were morally fitter than the poor.

Although Darwin might have liked to disown pseudoscientific uses of his work, they provided grist for writers like Wharton, who played on the title of Darwin's 1871 book on sex and selection when titling her short-story collection *The Descent of Man* (1904). Cultural stereotypes naturally provided a point of reference for those admirers of Honoré de Balzac's history of French social life. Children of their time, James, Cather, Glasgow, and Fauset all composed "types out of a combination of homogeneous characteristics" (to quote Balzac's self-description).[14] James's *The American* (1877), Cather's *O Pioneers!* (1913), Glasgow's *Romance of a Plain Man* (1909), and Fauset's *Comedy: American Style* (1933) chronicle the principal incidents of an era as well as the individuals who epitomize it.

Cosmopolites in spirit, these writers could not think about eras or manners except in an international context, and here they differ from many so-called naturalist writers of the period — notably, Rebecca Harding Davis, Frank Norris, and Theodore Dreiser, who focused less on changes within the middle class than the hereditary and environmental forces assailing it from without. James settled permanently in England after a brief flirtation with France; Wharton lived in Paris longer than she lived in Lenox, Massachusetts; and Fauset, for many years a teacher of French, studied at the Sorbonne.

The idea of France, which had been part of the American imagination since Benjamin Franklin's time, blossomed in the nineteenth century with the publication of John S. C. Abbott's history of Napoleon Bonaparte — a serial so popular that in the early 1850s it saved *Harper's* from bankruptcy. France occupied a special place in American affection for its pageantry, dubious morals, and flirtations with democracy. With England, France provided a measure of American manners. In 1872, *Frank Leslie's Lady's Magazine* carried a series of illustrations, supposedly depicted by the European press, that spoofed American manners, the wearing of Bloomers, for example, or displaying the spittoon as a parlor ornament.[15] From *Parisian Sights and French Principles Seen Through American Spectacles* (1852) to Richard Harding Davis's *About Paris* (1895) and *My Parisian Year* (1912) subtitled *A Woman's Point of View*, writers assumed that France had much to teach the rest of the world about living. Novelists who considered manners their stock in trade might be excused an occasional lament for "the sanctities of tradition, the claims of slowly acquired convictions and slowly formed precedents" that a nation like France seemed to typify.[16] Howells, disillusioned by the Haymarket Riot and the jingoism of the Spanish-American War, actually thought France more democratic than his own country,[17] while Cather considered it the birthplace of civilization. As Cather said: "Most things come from France, chefs and salads, gowns and bonnets, dolls and music boxes, plays and players, scientists and inventors, sculptors and painters, novelists and poets. It is a very little country, this France, and yet if it were to take a landslide in the channel some day there would not be much creative power of any sort left in the world."[18] Not surprisingly, interest in France reached its apex during the First World War, creating a market for Wharton's *French Ways and Their Meaning* (1919) and W. C.

Brownell's hastily reissued *French Traits: An Essay in Comparative Criticism* (1888; 1919), aimed at justifying American participation.

Americans admired English letters nearly as much as the French art of living, but they bristled at any signs of assumed superiority. Arnold's 1883–84 tour of the United States, for instance, rekindled smoldering resentments and debates about manners, notably his own imported affectations. Arnold's lectures struck many in his audiences as a renewed effort at colonization. His recitation of long, untranslated passages from ancient Greek seemed to represent everything antithetical to democratic concepts of culture. For Walt Whitman, such a man, a veritable excess of "delicacy" and "prettiness,"[19] could never understand the United States. And, though it may not have worked in Arnold's case, perhaps this is the point — that travel teaches us most about ourselves.

Like Arnold, European tourists came with certain prejudices, and many expected to find any country that called itself a democracy more social than one that did not. Those who had envisioned an ideal republic evolving from the practice of polite behavior — what Ralph Waldo Emerson summarized as good manners, lucrative labor, and public action — inevitably came away disappointed. "Observers of American manners have always been in a great hurry," Howells wrote, "and so we have fallen under heavier condemnation than we might if our visitors could have taken time to look into our morals. . . . [H]ad [these] been studied as tokens of our manners, we might now be famed for being the politest of the civilized peoples, instead of the rudest."[20]

To foreigners, American democracy appeared to place undue importance on the individual. Philosophers such as Herbert Spencer reiterated Burke's premise that government owes much of its stability to a mannerly populace.[21] The free mingling of classes in railroad stations and hotel lobbies, the courting of unchaperoned couples in the Boston Commons, stood at odds with traditional systems of civility, dependent upon the endorsement of rigid class hierarchies (Kasson, 58). Without definite, fixed rules and punishments, its people would remain primitive, their society chaotic, and their literature second-rate. As the editors of *Correct Social Usage* phrased it, America was "ignorant of the best way to express itself" (24–25), and the uniformity of its manners, its general distrust of social conventions and groups, gave writers little to work with. This was the challenge, and novelists who shared Glasgow's concern with change or Cather's fascination with things not spoken, honored the material at hand.

Those who saw no variety of manners in the United States forgot that since its colonization, the New World had served as a laboratory for investigating human behavior. As John Smith's accounts of native peoples and St. Jean de Crèvecoeur's resounding question — "What is an American?" — suggest, the secret of identity seemed to reside in questions of civilization or the lack of it. Alexis de Tocqueville, Frances Trollope, and Matthew Arnold all attributed America's amorphous definition to its poverty of manners, and later critics have merely repeated or extended their observation. Few nations could match the United States for its scientific advances, Tocqueville asserted, or for its dearth of great writers, poets, and artists. The literature of a nation is largely "subordinate to its social state and its political constitution," he writes in *Democracy* (1835; first U.S. edition, 1838), and a heredity ruling class aids the transmission of a coherent national literature.[22] This is assuming, as writers like James and Cather did not, that there is a coherent national culture.

More than a century later, Lionel Trilling echoed Tocqueville in his influential essay "Manners, Morals, and the Novel" (1947). In America, he wrote, novelists have a difficult time "searching out reality," because there is neither a "sufficiency of means for the display of a variety of manners," nor "enough complication of appearance to make the job interesting."[23] While Tocqueville thought that democracy could yield a literature free from conventional rules (and predicted the rise of the "business novel" in a society where money distinguished people more than manners), Trilling claimed that "the real basis of the novel has never existed — that is, the tension between a middle class and an aristocracy which brings manners into observable relief as the living representation of ideals and the living comment on ideas."[24] James had already bemoaned this state of affairs with his long list of American deficiencies that ends with a sly burlesque of British values: "No sovereign, no court, no personal loyalty, no aristocracy, no church, no clergy, no army, no diplomatic service, no country gentlemen . . . no pictures, no political society, no sporting class — no Epsom nor Ascot!"[25] But as James intimates, this is not the whole story. Some of Trilling's favorite writers — James, Wharton, and Howells — should have persuaded him that the dynamic nature of cultural forces defied definition. He did after all like to quote W. H. Auden's remark that "a real book reads us," or, as the writers in this study would say, that literature drives society to confront its social reality.[26]

Notwithstanding the astuteness of Trilling's analysis, not only do manners exist in American life, they have been and remain the primary focus of American fiction. Novelists merely extended their location to Vermont farmhouses, Indian camps, and all-black towns, these social spheres more various than even such a perceptive observer as Tocqueville could have imagined. In the decades leading up to the First World War, the influx of immigrants caused concern that American tradition, "even with notable modifications," could not maintain "its continuous American identity."[27] Such thinking seemed almost unpatriotic, especially for those who consider change to be at the heart of American identity. The paradox highlights the nature of this country's cultural struggles, its "civil wars." America *was* a nation of immigrants; the debate had to do with the numbers of immigrants coming from non-European countries and their probable impact on social life and politics. The old claims of tradition, or the behaviors that passed for it, appeared to be losing their authority, and change carried the threat of forfeiture as well as opportunities for novelists investigating social fields.

It should be self-evident that any perceived lack of manners has only served to feed interest in the topic, for the novelist's task is to see presences where others see absences. The drama or the *donnée* of the American novel of manners lay in *not* knowing one's place. "I think to be an American is an excellent preparation for culture," James asserted as a young man, because it allows a writer to be a kind of practicing historian, "to pick and choose and assimilate."[28]

James's remark undercuts another common assumption about American writers in keeping with Tocqueville's immediate — and except for his running comparison with European aristocracies — largely ahistorical depiction of American democracy. Contrary to popular mythology, American writers wanted to be embedded in, rather than emancipated from, history.[29] Speaking about his American friend Henry James, Joseph Conrad wrote, "Fiction is history, human history, or it is nothing."[30] By the turn of the century, distinctions between historians and fiction writers were frequently blurred. James thought that both had the same goal, "to represent and illustrate the . . . actions of men"; where they differed was in emphasis or "proportion."[31] Many novelists considered themselves to be historians to the degree that they preserved human experience. At the same time, they questioned the construction of history by fictionalizing primary sources, such as travelogues, diary entries, or recently discovered letters.

The great storytelling historians of the nineteenth century, Francis Parkman, William Prescott, and George Bancroft, may not have been novelists, but they began by writing poetry or fiction and considered their work part of the greater tradition of belles lettres. Plot and character development assumed a new importance in an age when almost every gentleman's library had a leather-bound set of Sir Walter Scott's historical novels. Henry Adams, known for his revisionist historical perspective, was himself a novelist of manners. His satiric look at the social politics of "democracy" (*Democracy: An American Novel* was the title of his

1908 work) underscores the connection that he and other historians supposed between manners and the broader culture.

The historicizing of fiction and the fictionalizing of history resulted partly from attacks leveled at novelists for sentimentalism, and historians for elitism. Historians began to assume the intimate voice of novels narrated in the first person; and novelists (for example, Glasgow and Cather) asserted their authority as historians. History provided the framework and the subject of many novels of manners. Wharton admired the work of George Santayana, while Glasgow and Hamlin Garland openly acknowledged their debt to the German philosopher Johann Fichte, who saw human life almost wholly in terms of history. To many novelists, history supplied a theoretical raison d'être. The now sufficiently distant past became "usable" in various and sometimes contradictory ways. As Nathaniel Hawthorne argued at midcentury, it brought the historical process as much as the obfuscations of the present into clearer focus. For later writers, caught between the poles of Darwinism and entropy (popularly viewed as progress or decay), this also meant a reformulation of the past. No longer a self-contained and transferrable entity, the past acquired significance from its instability, its suspect parameters, methods, and conclusions,[32] and novelists tested their characters under "the impact of change" as much as against established standards.[33] To them, manners appeared convertible and above all responsive to an evolving culture. Writers like Glasgow who wanted to convey a psychological or spiritual dimension of human existence, or those like Cather interested in form, extended the parameters of the novel of manners.

In James's time, no less than our own, people of course contested the nature of reality. American culture was never of a piece or easily defined. As James himself recognized on his 1904 return to the United States, it consisted of cultures within cultures. The formulas of art must be by definition dependent upon things unstable — on tastes, beliefs, theories — that change over time, and the novel of manners, like any novel, is a living, constantly developing form. Among other things, Howells extended its parameters to include middle class family life; James, the encroachment of modernity; Wharton, the commodification of an increasingly international culture; Cather, the lives of indigenous peoples; Glasgow, the rural poor; and Fauset, African Americans. Writing against European stereotypes of an untutored American exuberance and American myths of cultural homogeneity, they altered the way in which the novel of manners attended to matters of class, now a matter of race as well as gender, of politics and principles, social mobility and inherited position. Their "aristocracy" included patricians of Wall Street, whose social futures rose and fell with the day's market, and uncategorizable women like Wharton's Countess Olenska or Fauset's Angela Murray. Authors like James and Wharton who recognized a full range of fictional forms were drawn to the novel of manners not least for its elasticity. Redefining the scope and subject matter of realistic novels of manners to include elements of biography, history, and romance, they extended its domain beyond strict verisimilitude.

If the novelists in this study show us anything, it is that the novel of manners is only a distant cousin to the "novel of society," which Vladimir Nabokov dismisses for ignoring the "inner texture" of life.[34] Writers as different as James and Fauset confirm that it belongs to no special class, race, region, or perspective, whether that of "Woolett" or "Harlem." Regardless that their versions of "America" differed, the subjects of this book produced a new vision of America—one they may not have expected or necessarily approved. Together they created in fiction what Balzac claimed no historian had yet attempted, a history of manners. That "history" forms part of a comprehensive and unacknowledged tradition of manners in American letters, woven and interwoven of other traditions, which have crossed genres and disciplines without losing their individual identities. What I want to argue is that the novel of manners stretches back to the beginnings of our national literature and continues today largely because a handful of writers at the turn of the last century successfully altered the form to meet the needs of their particular time and place.

CHAPTER ONE

William Dean Howells

The Lessons of a Master

You had grown master, by insidious practices best known to yourself, of a
method so easy and so natural, so marked with the personal element of your
humor and the play, not less personal, of your sympathy, that the critic kept
coming on its secret connection with the grace of letters much as Fenimore
Cooper's Leatherstocking . . . comes in the forest on the subtle tracks of Indian braves.   HENRY JAMES, "A Letter to Mr. Howells"

I am a coward and all kinds of a tacit liar — not because I don't love the truth,
heaven knows, but because I'm afraid to tell it very often.
    LETTER OF WILLIAM DEAN HOWELLS TO S. WEIR MITCHELL

I

Perhaps no other writer has influenced American letters as much as William
Dean Howells (1837–1920) or been so fully forgotten by the novel-reading
public he helped to shape. At twenty-three, with some poems and a campaign
biography of Abraham Lincoln to his credit, this self-educated Midwesterner
made a pilgrimage to Boston, then the literary capital of the United States. There
he met James Russell Lowell, Nathaniel Hawthorne, Ralph Waldo Emerson, and
Oliver Wendell Holmes. Lowell invited him to dinner at the Parker House,
which Holmes jokingly proclaimed a version of the apostolic succession. Time
proved him nothing less than clairvoyant. Howells succeeded Lowell and James
T. Fields to the editor's chair of the *Atlantic Monthly* (1871–81) before moving to
New York and *Harper's* in 1885.

The stewardship of the most respected magazines of his day gave Howells tre-
mendous power. Not only did he sway the tastes, values, and mores of a growing
middle-class readership, he also brokered literary reputations. Apart from paying
well, serialization in the *Atlantic* or *Harper's* created a market for book publication
and conferred immediate legitimacy. So did a review by the editor. "Such an

encomium from such a source!" is how Charles Chesnutt phrased it when Howells launched his career with a favorable review of *The Conjure Woman* (1899).[1] As
Chesnutt knew, Howells possessed an almost unassailable authority, and over
three decades of exercising in equal measure ruthlessness and charm, he shaped a
canon of American literature that stretched far into the twentieth century.

It is hard to imagine what American culture as well as American literature
might have become without Howells, who made both more inclusive and less
provincial. He introduced American readers to the work of Thomas Hardy,
Émile Zola, Leo Tolstoy, Henrik Ibsen, Björnstjerne Björnson, and Ivan Turgenev, and he championed Henry James when others dismissed him as unreadable
and unpatriotic for settling in Europe. Howells remained a fierce enemy of
sentimental fiction, though not of female "scribblers," and promoted the careers
of regional writers, many of them women. He brought the perspective of African
Americans, such as Chesnutt and Paul Laurence Dunbar, into the literary mainstream, arguing, sometimes like a man possessed, that American fiction needed
an infusion of "real" life or the very subjects polite society ignored.[2] Looking
back to his early years at the *Atlantic*, he explained that the magazine had become
southern, midwestern, and far-western in its sympathies without ceasing to be
Bostonian at heart. He himself had been much of the reason.

Ironically, Howells's small-town Ohio background and his work for country
newspapers, including his father's own *Ashtabula Sentinel*, gave him a cultural
perspective that was at once national and international. The story of Howells's
childhood reads like an encapsulated history of nineteenth-century America,
with its changing demographics, the collapse of the family farm, experiments
with communal living, stands against slavery, and the rise of the middle class.
Where else save the West of American legend could the son of a man defined by
his deficiencies — not a "very good poet, not a very good farmer, not a very good
printer, [and] not a very good editor" — ever dream of becoming a consul to
Venice or the first president of the American Academy of Arts and Letters?[3]

The subject of manners naturally interested a man intent on bettering his own
fortunes and who as a boy had lived on the edge of poverty and respectability.
Howells did not know what to say about a man who refused to consider "the
things that make for prosperity."[4] And his father did not. William Cooper, a
radical in politics, a Swedenborgian by religion, and a failure by habit, had his
ten-year-old son setting a thousand ems of type a day, and could barely keep his
eight children adequately clothed and fed. The year that Howells turned thirteen, his family, destitute and with no prospects on the horizon, retreated to the

wilderness of Eureka Mills on the Little Miami River. Much as Americans might mythologize log cabins as outposts of civilization, these primitive dwellings, surrounded by primeval forests, did produce new visions of democracy and one of America's most literate writers. W. D. Howells always had "prosperity" in mind, married "above" his station, wrote enough books to feed several families (as at least three of his siblings could testify), and went on to become as wealthy perhaps as he was famous. Like Benjamin Franklin, he followed a regimen of self-improvement that would make him a "gentleman," someone "known and respected the moment he is seen" for his "unaffected pride of self . . . tempered with courtesy."[5]

In the many places the Howells family lived (Martin's Ferry, Hamilton, Dayton, Ashtabula, Jefferson, Columbus, and Eureka Mills), they were a class unto themselves. Howells's father employed three journeymen, a boy apprentice, and several girl compositors, but he and his sons also worked with the people he hired. While Howells saw through middle-class trimmings, or "bric-à-brac Jamescracks" as he called them,[6] he also yearned for what they represented, the unassailable respectability that came with financial stability. He never worshipped money for its own sake, *and* he never denied its importance. Few people were more aware of or amused by his uncertain social status than Howells himself, who enjoyed the advantages of a class he could not wholly sanction. Howells never entirely resolved his own ambivalence about the groups he liked to call the masses and the classes.[7] As long as both existed, he felt that he could "never be at home anywhere in the world" (*Literature and Life*, 35). To some extent, he remained a feted outsider in the insular world of Harvard-educated Boston, never losing his midwesterner's skepticism about standards and behavior stereotyped as "eastern" (self-consciously intellectual or arty). In "Literary Boston As I Knew It," he remembers his sense of failure when he expressed something "native" to those who accepted only Boston theories and Boston criticisms,[8] which to Howells seemed "Puritanical" or outmoded and sterile.

It should come as no surprise that Howells found most intriguing those times and places where behavior remained indeterminately on the social margin. He brought a unique perspective to the novel when American society was redefining its attitudes about class, a term that became part of the popular lexicon in the early 1900s. Andrew Jackson's presidency (1829–37), which ended in the year of Howells's birth, had inaugurated a new era, symbolized geographically by the building of the Baltimore and Ohio Railroad, and politically by the formation of the Working Men's Party of Philadelphia, a precursor of organized labor. Not only did the United States have to respond to forces from without, particularly waves of European immigrants, it confronted forces from within, when, for example, members of the working urban class made their way into the ranks of businessmen and industrial capitalists. Then, too, the definition of "class" as largely economic became amended by considerations such as the status accorded certain professionals, the descendants of patrician families, or those who accrued public honors. Howells's fiction examines how these and other socioeconomic changes result in what would appear to be contradictory responses: a stricter stratification of classes coupled with a weakening of standards of conduct and social hierarchies. Democracy seemed to Howells at a crucial stage in its history, offering, on the one hand, the promise of true equality; on the other, oligarchy or even anarchy.

Howells's revisioning of the American novel cannot be separated from his understanding of social realism. A Marxist might argue that social and economic forces determined Howells's concept of realism, and in part Howells himself would have agreed. But he refused to see the world from one, limiting perspective. "America is so big and the life here has so many sides," he told an interviewer in 1898, "that a writer can't synthesize it."[9] The conditions of his life, not least of all his Swedenborgian upbringing, made him acutely aware of the tenuous nature of reality. To a Swedenborgian like Howells's father, individual acts of perception make any reality possible, for they reveal a world of inner and outer correspondences. Howells was not a Swedenborgian, yet he did believe people individually responsible for their actions. This affects his view of the possibilities of fiction and the accountability of the artist.

According to Howells's code, anyone who believed that fiction could change people's lives had a civic obligation to tell the "truth," which naturally differed from writer to writer. This may help to explain his wide-ranging generosity, his admiration for fiction as different as Rebecca Harding Davis's *Life in the Iron Mills* (1861) or Stephen Crane's *Maggie: A Girl of the Streets* (1893), and his close friendships with two very different men and writers, Mark Twain and Henry James.

Howells's own books, especially those written after the 1870s, simultaneously salute and deplore the instability of modern life. Their subject is — to borrow from T. S. Eliot's "The Hollow Men" — the shadow that falls between the idea and the reality, that intermediate world of conscience between the emotion and the response. Howells not only wrote about the deepening "sense of unreality" at the heart of his era's middle class life,[10] he embodied it, having suffered from attacks of intense and extended anxiety as an adolescent. During these periods, he became convinced that he had contracted hydrophobia or rabies. Though his symptoms lessened after his marriage in 1862, they never fully disappeared. Whether Howells looked outward or inward, he saw forces, social and hereditary, beyond his control.

Howells believed in those favorite nineteenth-century shibboleths, honor and duty. More than anything, he believed in work. "If you can't do all you want to, at present," he advised a younger brother, "don't give up trying to do something. There's a way out of everything. I think hopelessness is about as bad as atheism."[11] He was to need his own advice. Many times, notably after the death of his oldest daughter Winifred in 1889, hopelessness seemed his one reality. Yet Howells chose to emphasize moments of recuperation, as opposed to homogeneity, not because he shied away from truth or lacked courage but because he saw no other alternative.

Howells differs from previous novelists in two evident ways: He emphasized the political and commercial significance of manners; and he assumed their ability to bestow cultural authority. He understood that the tipping of a hat brim might betray an entire system of power. Manners granted a kind of moral sway that those belonging to the "wrong" class had to earn. They placed one in relationship to a whole set of values that Howells himself questioned without abandoning.

When Howells wrested the novel of manners from the upper class (and took the capital *S* out of society), he operated on the principle that nothing was too common or paltry a subject for fiction. Critics thought his work plotless, it so replicated the eventless rhythms, the humdrum artlessness of daily life. "In defiance of novelistic convention, which asked for elaborate plots, for heroes and crises," his stories seemed to transcend form or tell themselves. Foreshadowing the fiction of Willa Cather, they leave readers with "an impression of outlines not filled in." Howells was a playwright as well as a novelist, and as such he tried to realize "a middle form between narrative and drama, which may be developed into something very pleasant to the reader, and convenient to the fictionalist."[12] The same might be said of his novels, with their resistance to linear plotting, limited characters, and suppressed action. He didn't want "much world, or effect of it," in his fictions,[13] yet how many other writers could make a country picnic carry the social weight of an Academy dinner given by a celebrated Faubourg hostess? Domestic details absorbed his attention. In weekly Sunday letters to his family, he sang the praises of potato cakes, English walnuts, and apricots, and argued the pros and cons of different models of furnaces. Here is a man who, finding the private world of family and friends no less fascinating than the public world of business and politics, belies nineteenth-century stereotypes about gender.[14] Howells did not recognize separate spheres for men and women. Though he could be chauvinistic, he also encouraged his female relatives to pursue careers in literature and the arts. Later writers may have thought his fiction too domesticated or too feminine. A compulsive writer, Howells naturally wrote about everything he knew, and he remained faithful to reality rather than to literary conventions, even those of the realism he popularized.

By expanding the definition of "manners" to include its most unassuming, even vulgar forms, Howells hoped to communicate the entire prospect of American life, or what his friend Henry James described as "our whole democratic light and shade."[15] Anyone who wants to "trace American 'society' in its formative process," advised Thomas Wentworth Higginson in 1880, "must go to Howells. . . . he alone shows you the essential forces in action."[16] Those forces include large cultural patterns and class shifts, from labor unrest in *A Hazard of New Fortunes* (1890) to interracial marriage in *An Imperative Duty* (1891). More personally, they reflect trends in the production and consumption of literature that self-consciously critique Howells's own position as his country's quintessential man of letters.

In an ironic twist of fate, Howells became a victim of his own success. He had hoped to mentor "the whole family" of younger writers—his title for a novel that contained chapters by himself ("The Father") and other well-known authors of his day, including Elizabeth Stuart Phelps ("The Married Daughter"), Henry James ("The Son-In-Law"), and Mary Wilkins Freeman ("The Old-Maid Aunt").[17] Alas (to repeat Wharton), succeeding generations of realists thought his daring hopelessly old-fashioned. No matter that he had exhorted them to expose the "dark places of the soul, the filthy and squalid places of society, high and low" ("Novel-Writing and Novel-Reading," 228), he had become identified with a Victorian gentility bordering on prudishness. Even as old a friend as Wharton accused him of an "incurable moral timidity which again and again checked him on the verge of a masterpiece."[18] Considering the magnitude of his own competitiveness, James remained unwaveringly loyal. He may have harbored private doubts about the "grasping" quality or the depth of Howells's mind, but never his courage or moral resolution.

Howells's dismissal was perhaps inevitable, a case of "the hungry generations" gobbling their elders.[19] It also had something to do with questions of manners.

Howells became identified with patrician standards of polite behavior, his books fit reading for young ladies in need of instruction. Howells did voice concerns about the content of fiction, and so did Edith Wharton, Ellen Glasgow, and Jessie Fauset. For him, the problem of aesthetics went beyond matters of sex or personal squeamishness. In fact, Howells, who called himself Victorian in his preference for decency, believed shame to be good in the sense that it kept one honest. "The style is the man," he wrote, for words cannot disguise the "manner of man" within.[20]

Today Howells, who wrote over a hundred books, is most remembered for a single novel, *The Rise of Silas Lapham* (1885). Yet Thomas Higginson's assessment of Howells's contribution to American letters remains as true at the turn of the twenty-first century as it did a century ago. Before James's "Daisy Miller," Howells had studied the "American girl" in Europe and the conflict between distinct cultures. His focus on the middle class, its prejudices and politics, its morals and manners, allowed him to survey a changing American population from its rural and urban poor to its gilded millionaires. "Stroke by stroke and book by book" (James, 561), this historian of culture appraised the character of his compatriots.

To Howells, manners meant those thoughts and actions that make nations as well as individuals "humanly, spiritually" themselves.[21] He viewed forms in conduct like those in art: "They alone can express manners; and they are built slowly, painfully, from the thought, the experience, of the whole race."[22] But, as we might expect of someone who wrote professionally for seventy years, his use of manners falls into several phases. In Howells's early books, manners supplied a quick sketch, an easily translatable shorthand for summarizing people and places. He had a telling eye for details of behavior that abound in travel writing and memoir, including his own fictionalized travelogue *Their Wedding Journey* (1872) and books such as *Venetian Life* (1866), *Literary Friends and Acquaintance* (1900), *London Films* (1905), and *Roman Holidays and Others* (1908). In an early novel like *A Foregone Conclusion* (1875), Howells used manners largely for comic purposes. His American ingenue, Florida Vervain, misinterprets the intentions of her Italian tutor because he is a priest. She cannot decide what is more appalling: that this agnostic hears confession, that he occasionally wears street clothes and smokes a cigar, or (the foregone conclusion) that he loves her.

In the novels that followed, Howells began to weave manners more integrally into the structure of the stories themselves. Apart from providing the social texture or felt background of "special civilizations,"[23] they expressed various interpretative communities. Their dramatic fusion of private lives and collective historical experiences made it possible to tell the related histories of individuals and institutions. This realization led to the books that many critics consider Howells's finest: *A Modern Instance* (1882), *The Rise of Silas Lapham*, and *A Hazard of New Fortunes*. In these books, Howells suggests that institutions, such as the press (his focus in *A Modern Instance* and *Hazard of New Fortunes*), largely define, rather than reflect, their societies (though the dynamic works in the opposite direction as well), and that etiquette or the marketing of class is big business *(The Rise of Silas Lapham)*. He conceptualized the role and influence of institutions very differently from his contemporaries. Instead of being, as conventional wisdom argued, leviathans of conservatism, they registered and responded to societal changes before the people they supposedly served.[24] Above all, he saw class itself as an institution, so pervasive and enigmatic that many Americans erroneously celebrated its absence.

Howells wrote at his best, as he said of Honoré de Balzac, "under the burden of traditions," which he helped American fiction to cast off.[25] The manners of the poor and middle class had at least as much to say about American society than those of their so-called "betters." Although he thought manners only a partial expression of the self, he felt that they could train the heart to goodness. He hoped, without fully believing, that manners might function as a call-to-arms, that readers would feel impelled to live by the "civil" truths they discovered through fiction.

II

In *A Modern Instance*, which chronicles the courtship, marriage, and divorce of Marcia Gaylord and Bartley Hubbard, Howells examines how the media adversely influences notions of personal and national identity. The title of the novel emphasizes the idiosyncratic nature of the Hubbard case but also a larger cultural malaise that Howells blames on the media through his characterization of Hubbard, a deplorably smart and conscienceless journalist who is too much show and too little substance.

Of Howells's many characters, Hubbard may be the most Dickensian. "I admired other authors more"; Howells remembered about his boyhood passion for Charles Dickens, "but when it came to a question of trying to do something in fiction I was compelled as by a law of nature, to do it at least partially in his way" (*Literary Passions*, 71). Howells respected Dickens for the breadth and depth of his work, which he saw as nothing less than a treatise on humanity itself. Although most readers may not consider Dickens's characters "deep," to Howells they represented the movement of social and moral moods. By moods, he meant the "vital truths" (*Literary Passions*, 74) that lay beyond superficial realities.

From Dickens's *Our Mutual Friend* (1865), Howells most likely borrowed the idea of veneering so central to his conception of Hubbard. Hubbard is a social parvenu, the orphaned son of indigent parents educated beyond his station. His work as a journalist, which gives him access to classes from which his background would normally exclude him, positions him between the classes and the masses. He illustrates a process of veneering that crosses class lines and augurs a world in which there remains no discernable difference between appearance and reality. Yet Howells, as he himself noted, only partially went Dickens's way. *A Modern Instance* is most his own in its criticism of the economic forces that Hubbard represents.

Howells saw the press as a major instrument of cultural transformation, which in the hands of a Bartley Hubbard reduces individuals and classes alike to a ubiquitous and regrettable norm.[26] As a reporter for the *Events*, Hubbard presumes to speak for the general populace in articles that bear titles like "Confessions of an Average American." Fundamentally a thief, he profits from publishing the anecdotes of a friend who intended to write his own life story. Hubbard's style marks a cultural shift — the modern instance — in which banner headlines stop reflecting and start determining people's notions of themselves and of society. "Both Legs Frozen to the Knees" begins his article on Maine loggers,[27] the headline substituting the part for the whole and literally severing character from its embodiment. In Hubbard's world, headlines have the power to legitimize and in turn generate practices previously disdained. News becomes advertisement when Hubbard tries to sell the idea of Equity, Maine, his wife's hometown, as next season's chic resort. Foreshadowing Edith Wharton's *The Custom of the Country* (1913) and John Dos Passos's trilogy *U.S.A.* (1938), *A Modern Instance* anticipates a time when people will consult the tabloids to know how they feel and think.

Howells defines the veneering of America in two ways. The first, ironically, concerns the classes becoming the masses. The power (and danger) of the press lay in its ability to bring together audiences or classes previously thought distinct. Howells, who would have preferred the masses to become the equal of the classes in taste and education, held popular culture accountable for the inversion of this exchange. Hubbard's dream is to create a newspaper that every class will have to read. He would begin by catering to the rabble first, then politicians, those interested in fashion and society, finance, sports, and finally book-reviews. Howells worried that sensationalism would win out (or had already), that taste would exist apart from conviction and that packaging would matter more than content. To him, the United States risked becoming a nation of Bartley Hubbards: men who live on a diet of junk news, who literally grow fat (as Hubbard does over the course of the novel) on "gross" effect rather than substance (*Modern Instance*, 304, 438).

Howells's second concern about the veneering of America has to do with a general lowering of moral standards. People like the Hubbards can be too free. They need the forces of habit to act rightly. Yet Howells remains ambivalent about an alternative. On the one hand, he suggests a redefinition of the upper class. On the other, he expresses anxiety about its absorption into the larger culture. That anxiety can be seen in the characterization of Ben Halleck, an upper-class Bostonian who is crippled by a childhood accident and his secret passion for Marcia, which spans her marriage, Hubbard's desertion, her divorce, and widowhood. At the same time, Howells criticizes the moral smugness of this class through his depiction of the attorney Eustace Atherton, who tells Halleck that under no circumstances should he think of marrying Marcia. Howells's portrayal of Atherton so enraged Robert Louis Stevenson — himself the second husband of a divorced woman — that he severed his friendship with Howells. Howells had no quarrel with divorce as such — a point Stevenson later acknowledged by regretting his outburst.[28]

Despite his ambivalence about the upper class, Howells wants little to do with the intermediate class Hubbard represents. It seems a divine form of poetic justice, for example, when Hubbard becomes both victim and subject of the chromo-journalism he advocates. Marcia learns of his divorce suit from its announcement in a country paper, and of his murder from an article that recalls his own purple prose. The novel itself ends inconclusively. Will Halleck give up the ministry to marry Marcia? Would she feel still bound to Hubbard? Howells's refusal to resolve these questions reflects his focus on the evolution of contemporary culture and his noncompliance with literary convention. A book that remains "true" to life by chronicling process can have no definitive end, even the conventional one of marriage.

As we might expect, Howells's analysis of American society originates from his own insecurity about class. Like most people, he had mixed feelings about "ancestor worship." He poked fun at aristocratic titles without failing to mention them and complained about his wife's "geneologizing" while taking pride in her discoveries. When Howells first visited James Russell Lowell, he confided that he had tried hard to believe himself a literary descendant of Sir James Howell. (Lowell took out a volume of "Howell's" *Familiar Letters* to show his young guest the error of any family connection based on the spelling of their last names.) Later in life, Howells couldn't resist telling his grandson that a Howel had once ruled part of Brittany, though such stories, as Howells himself knew, form the stuff of historical romance.

To some extent, Bartley Hubbard serves as a kind of evil alter ego, and he reappears (like a bad penny) in other novels, notably *The Rise of Silas Lapham* and *The Quality of Mercy* (1892), the story of a crime brought about by inequities in the socioeconomic order. In *A Modern Instance*, money and corporate concerns drive the news. From his own experience, Howells knew that aesthetics tend to take a back seat to printer's costs, especially in an age that considers "the dollar . . . the measure of every value, the stamp of every success" (*Hazard of New Fortunes*, 173). As a young editor of the *Cincinnati Gazette*, he sought the favor of local politicians, who later recommended his father as a consulate to Canada. In the 1870s (as at any time), scarcely a publisher did not feel the pull between scruples and profits. The front pages of many newspapers routinely carried society gossip about heiresses, run-away marriages, financial reverses, and suicides of prominent citizens, typically without context or continuity. People could not get enough details about Henry Ward Beecher's adulterous affair with Mrs. Tilton, though it would take several more decades before Theodore Roosevelt, incensed by David Graham Phillips's 1902 *Cosmopolitan* article entitled "Treason in the Senate," coined the term "yellow journalism."[29] As a free-lance journalist, Howells was not above writing his own sensational account of New Orleans, with its orgies of drinking, lewd women, and pickpockets straight from Dickens. And certainly *A Modern Instance* capitalizes on a subject that had become too topical to ignore. Articles in the *Century* and the *New Englander*, for example, routinely deplored the rising rate of divorce at the same time that women's rights activists like Elizabeth Cady Stanton were advocating for more liberal divorce laws.[30] By his own account, Howells could not bear to face the school of reality he associated with journalism (a nice admission from someone so closely tied to American realism).

Howells realized that a hereditary aristocracy often reigns over the intersecting worlds of art, politics, and finance. As an employee of the *Atlantic*, he encountered another aristocracy, who required that he uphold a vague set of ethics proclaimed to be "the American idea." The editors stated their purpose as endeavoring "to keep in view that moral element which transcends all persons and parties and which alone makes the basis of a true and lasting national prosperity. It will not rank itself with any sect of anties [disgruntled protestors or fringe groups], but with that body of men which is in favor of Freedom, National Progress, and Honor, whether public or private" (Mott, 2:499). This mission statement, which reads like the *Atlantic's* version of manifest destiny, assumes both a homogeneous America (something that Howells himself doubted) and a causal relationship between public morals and national prosperity.

Perhaps it is no coincidence that much of Howells's fiction explores these same relationships from a more skeptical perspective. To Howells, art was anything but benign. Too often "propaganda" masqueraded as "art," while art imposed its own set of values. For Howells questions of art could not be separated from those of civilization, defined in *A Modern Instance* as an "implanted" constant "treasured from generation to generation" (*Modern Instance*, 417). This definition presents a problem. It offers a theory of human development seemingly independent of socioeconomic conditions. In *A Modern Instance* and *A Hazard of New Fortunes*, Howells reckons the price of decency, if not civilization, at a few thousand a year — a salary Howells's own father did not realize until late in life. This amount might have kept Bartley Hubbard a complacent husband, while it allows Basil Marsh, the editor of a literary magazine in *A Hazard New Fortunes*, the luxury of having principles.

Howells neither could nor wanted to deny his own connivance in the selling of capitalism, which made esoteric magazines and the comfortable lives of his family viable. *A Hazard of New Fortunes* suggests that little separates "arty" magazines from insurance company newsletters or, for that matter, *Harper's* from its notorious sister, *Woodhull & Caflin's Weekly*. Both magazines had social agendas, whether supporting or decrying the status quo. Every month *Harper's* made its courtly bow, wrote one critic; and, with bent head and unimpeachable toilet, whispered smoothly, 'No offence, I hope' " (Mott, 2:392). In contrast, *Woodhull & Caflin's Weekly* stood for "Progress! Free Thought! Untrammeled Lives!" — free love and women's rights (Mott, 3:358, 445). *Harper's* endorsement of middle-class values and *Woodhull & Caflin's* self-conscious unorthodoxy were equally prescriptive in their appeal to targeted markets.

Any editor walks a moral tightrope, and Howells proved no exception. In a world that covertly endorsed a policy of *quid pro quo*, he received as many advantages as he bestowed. If delicacy precluded "his admitting any mention of himself, whether for praise or blame within his own pages," serialization of his novels augmented his income, not to mention his reputation by keeping his work almost constantly before the public. Howells's celebrity hurt him in unexpected ways. It took a brave reviewer to refuse his work or to offer the honest criticism any artist needs. His leading literary contemporaries were also his contributors, and for them to discuss his work openly amounted to "debating the character of one's habitual host."[31]

Whatever his misgivings about the power of the press, literary endeavor in general, or his role of cultural warden, Howells sometimes practiced a more benign version of the "chromo-morality" he criticizes in Bartley Hubbard.[32] "After fifty years of optimistic content with 'civilization,' " he wrote Henry James in 1888, "and its ability to come out all right in the end, I now abhor it, and feel that it is coming out all wrong . . . unless it bases itself anew on a real equality. Meantime, I wear a fur-lined overcoat and live in all the luxury my money can buy."[33]

III

Howells embodies a peculiarly American ambivalence toward prosperity and social distinction, and it is precisely this ambivalence that propels his most famous novel of manners, *The Rise of Silas Lapham*. Readers of novels of manners often covet what they feel they should despise. The act of reading permits what should be contradictory, the intimacy of participation and the distance for criticism. Readers stand in and outside but also above, a position that approximates Howells's relation to his Boston neighbors and the publishing world at large. *Silas Lapham* replicates the nature of this displacement, while focusing on the assimilation of the rising middle class.[34]

Although this novel and *A Modern Instance* are seldom paired, *The Rise of Silas Lapham*, by analyzing etiquette itself, continues Howells's critique of the veneering of America. The mediated rules of etiquette underscore the contractual basis of a society that mythologizes its own bill of rights as nonnegotiable or unaffected by social circumstances. Differences between "good taste" and "moral scruples" gripped Howells because they hailed new phases (moral, psychological, aesthetic, political) of American culture. Too often, he implies, rules of civility are used to support moral disengagement. The Coreys ought to be "nice," Lapham tells his wife; they have "never done anything else."[35] Howells blames the failure of American democracy on a class-based system of social divisions legitimized by laws of "natural selection."[36] The rigidity of these divisions can be inferred from the Boston witticism that the Cabots only talk to the Lowells and the Lowells only to God.

To Howells, etiquette has its own economy; that is, it is a business, as much a product as is Lapham's Persis Paint (named for his wife) or Bromfield Corey's gentlemanly attempts at making portraiture pay. Paint or painting, manners or manner, each activity glosses the gulf between superficial and inherent qualities. The focus of etiquette on cosmetics ignores the intricacies of human behavior and tacitly furthers the interests of a soulless capitalism, in which money solely "prizes and honors itself" (*Hazard of New Fortunes*, 279).

According to Howells, etiquette works in two, equally corrupt directions. It holds the promise of a more democratic society, while maintaining class divisions based on interest, ambition, vanity, and folly. The upper-class Coreys pride themselves on their probity and ignorance of business, but their social dealings have an implicit fiscal scale. They want to repay the Laphams for nursing Mrs. Corey on an ill-fated vacation and for taking their son, Tom, into business. They do so with a family dinner, an assemblage of cousins and in-laws by marriage, that gives the appearance of society without its endorsement. "We don't really care what business a man is in," Mr. Corey explains, as he paves a way for his son's marriage to the Lapham millions, "so it is large enough, and he doesn't advertise offensively" (*Silas Lapham*, 102). His wife knows that society does not always abide by the same rule. Her promotion of Colonel Lapham to "General" illustrates society's process of refining and merchandising raw material like the Laphams themselves. Social stratagems such as the Coreys's necessitate "a thousand little lies a day" (*April Hopes*, 18). The Laphams fare little better. Their attempts to buy a son-in-law effectively estrange their two daughters. Above all, such efforts teach them their place by removing them from Nankeen Square and returning them to their Vermont homestead.

In the world of Howells's novel, manners are anything but static. The writers of etiquette books respond to changes in the marketplace — the rise of a new mercantile class of entrepreneurs, for example — no less than editors like Hubbard. Howells's emphasis on process, the inheritance, destablization, and manufacture of manners, recalls William James's belief that truth happens to an idea: "Its verity *is* in fact an event, a process: the process namely of its verifying itself."[37] The same postulate applies to rules of etiquette, which appear to reflect while also imposing social norms. Howells called etiquette a "manufactory" of virtuous behavior that tended to remove people from visceral feeling.[38] As an old socialist tells the editor of *Every Other Week*, "You have to see it, hear it, smell it, taste it, or, you forget it" (*Hazard of New Fortunes*, 190). Inherited codes of behavior lend themselves to hierarchical constructions of the world. They divide and distance. Yet change does not necessarily entail a constructive process of succession or the freeing of individual will. Life becomes a spectacle to those who want to deny their own complicity; to those who anesthetize themselves against life to "forget death" (*Hazard of New Fortunes*, 62). Howells deprecates what he sees as a national inclination toward voyeurism, rather than involvement, which characterizes Boston Brahmins such as Bromfield Corey or artists and editors such as Bartley Hubbard, Basil Marsh, and, by extension, himself.

For Howells, so-called news pieces such as Bartley Hubbard's "Solid Men of Boston" series epitomize the commodification of human behavior usually associated with etiquette manuals. Featured in both *A Modern Instance* and *The Rise of Silas Lapham*, Hubbard's series represents the transformation of ordinary businessmen into celebrities, the voice not of the people but of special interests. These profiles, which glamorize the accumulation of capital, pander to those in power. Worse, they divert the attention of "the masses" from the socioeconomic issues affecting them. Hubbard's article on Lapham trivializes, by turning to commercial use, the very things that give Lapham's life and work its meaning: his memory of his father's discovery of the paint ("deep in the heart of the virgin forests of Vermont, far up toward the line of Canadian snows") and his relationship with his wife, "born to honour the name of American Woman" (*Silas Lapham*, 20, 21).[39] Hubbard's exploitation of Lapham's Civil War record, his republicanism, and his "colossal fortune" reinforce national chauvinism and mark the beginning of his subject's as well as the country's reversals.

In Howells's analysis, Lapham is not simply a victim. He cannot resist, for instance, the opportunity to advertise both himself and his paint, slapped over rocks and other natural formations as if the countryside were a giant personal billboard. "The landscape," he thinks, "was made for man, and not man for the landscape" (*Silas Lapham*, 15). Such desecration reflects a schism in both Lapham's own nature and the culture as a whole. It foreshadows Cather's argument with America and Wallace Stegner's crusade for the environment.[40] Lapham may suspect that Hubbard had his fun with him; nevertheless, he believes what he reads, and the paper's erroneous depiction of him as a modern Midas spurs him to greater vanities. The article similarly alters Lapham's commerce with others, whom he self-consciously assumes have read the interview and inflated his worth. To Howells, Lapham's transformation from private citizen to local celebrity marks a historical shift in the ways in which people define both the "self" and "privacy" when private and public interests overlap.[41]

Silas Lapham may be Howells's most cynical novel. While morality implies a code of behavior that should exist independently of economics, it owes its existence to untried prosperity. *Business ethics* becomes an oxymoron as Lapham's empire flounders, but so do those ethics dear to Beacon Hill. Lapham's tragedy partly results from his taking the Coreys and their friends, whose respect he hopes to win through economic abjection, at their own valuation. He believes they are what they say they believe. Lapham does not understand that the Coreys owe their superior disinterest to inherited income (the few thousand a year needed for principles). The only way Lapham can be a gentleman, the product of generations of bequeathed wealth, is to beggar himself. In a sense, etiquette defeats him. Howells differs from writers like Theodore Dreiser or Booth Tarkington who made their tycoons almost willfully scornful of social niceties. The inability of Howells's characters, indeed their final disinclination, to separate home and business comments ironically on the gentrifying of American culture.

The plot of the novel hinges on an escalating series of moral decisions that become downright suicidal.[42] Lapham's failure provides Brahmin Boston an almost decadent, aesthetic pleasure. His immediate problems stem from his trying to right a wrong most business ethicists would have trouble untangling. Lapham lends money to his former partner, an unscrupulous man named Rogers, and takes several mills as collateral. He does this to please his wife, who has never felt right about his buying Rogers out (at more than his shares were worth) just before striking it really big. Lapham has never trusted Rogers, and for good reason. The mills are worth far less than Rogers leads him to believe. Lapham realizes that the railroad, by refusing to transport the goods of rival purchasers, can set its own price.

The only way that Lapham can recoup his investment is to sell the mills to scam artists working for a legitimate association of English philanthropists. At first, the situation appears fairly clear cut: Lapham must and does disclose what he knows about the devaluation of the mills. But when the mills are to become part of a charitable, utopian experiment, rather than a money-making operation, his responsibility becomes less plain. The pecuniary value of the mills may be ancillary to the would-be colonists' goal of social reformation. Lapham sees the problem solely from a "morally" fiscal perspective that—depending on one's point of view—may ignore other responsibilities and options, such as warning the English philanthropists and negotiating directly with them. Lapham, by confessing the extent of his reverses to his lone, would-be partner, retains the mills and wrecks whatever other chances he has to salvage his company. People like the Coreys publicly applaud his behavior; privately, they thank God for returning the Laphams to Vermont. The Coreys' discriminations are lost on Lapham, who believes that the price of a painting determines its artistic value. In retrospect, he has little understanding of his experience or the forces that drove it, though its "price" gives readers an index of its worth. "I don't know if I should always say it paid," he tells his minister, "but if I done it, and the thing was to do over again, right in the same way, I guess I should have to do it" (*Silas Lapham*, 365).

Howells's vision of existence links it to social circumstances that seldom reflect "good sense and — right ideas" (*Silas Lapham*, 138). In fact, he subverts the notion of Lapham's "rise" by presenting it in dollars and cents — the one way that Lapham himself would have previously credited it.[43] The novel's ethical economy puts the world of robber barons and con men on a par with old India merchants, on whose profits the Coreys still dine. Lapham so equates any personal profit with moral transgression that he makes a fetish of gentlemanly behavior ("the mere husk of well-dressed culture and good manners") romanticized in etiquette books and sentimental novels like *Tears, Idle Tears*.[44] Lapham's niceties seem fruitless given Howells's analysis of a marketplace, which has invaded the private, spiritual lives of all his characters and whose very language shapes their consciousness of their own being. The novel's economy of ethics does not support its "economy of pain," a philosophy articulated by the Coreys' minister, which advocates the strictest containment of suffering.

The Civil War, which forms the immediate past of the novel, reminds us of the dangers of a culture disciplining "personal feeling to custom." Such a culture creates an individual whose innermost feelings exist "apart from the ritual of society." At the same time, ritual paradoxically gives expression to the very feelings an individual knows as his or her own.[45] The novel ends with a marriage between Tom Corey and Penelope Lapham, and the couple's future remains at best ambiguous. For an indeterminate number of years, they expect to live in Mexico and South America. According to Howells, the Coreys and the Laphams, with their distinct ethical systems, might as well belong to different races. Penelope, that "little, black, odd creature" (*Silas Lapham*, 264), with her strange way of saying what she thinks, will forever be a stranger to the Coreys, who hope that "[a]s she's quite unformed, socially . . . there is a chance that she will form herself on the Spanish manner . . . and that when she comes back she will have the charm of not olives, perhaps, but *tortillas*, whatever they are: something strange and foreign even if it's borrowed" (*Silas Lapham*, 360). This thinking reflects the Coreys's provincialism as much as it suggests the rigidity of American civilization, which, despite its democratic ideals, has difficulty accommodating difference. Howells's criticism of the Coreys underscores their cultural myopia. Which of our beliefs, our customs and principles, he asks, are not in some way "borrowed"? The assumption by the Coreys that their manners and mores have an unchanging value, that time can indeed stand still, already relegates them to the past; they cannot remove themselves from what Howells considered to be the "economic chance-world" (*Hazard of New Fortunes*, 436) in which we live.

Howells denies his readers any moral smugness. There is no nostalgic recapitulation at the end of *Silas Lapham* as there is in Wharton's *The Age of Innocence* (1920), for example, when Newland Archer hugs his failure closer than the woman he once loved. While Wharton reinstitutes the novel's opening hierarchy, Howells creates a novelistic version of a Venn diagram that brings the seemingly incompatible worlds of the Coreys and Laphams into conjunction. Doing so, he might be said to "westernize" the novel of manners by collapsing its central stratification of classes and ending with his hero and heroine lighting out for new territories.

IV

When Howells thought about manners, he could not separate them from issues of class and race. *An Imperative Duty*, the story of a woman who discovers her African heritage, looks at the process of veneering from an especially American perspective. One of the first novels to address directly the place of African Americans in American society, it presents race as a function of class and manners, rather than biology, which was typically invoked to protect the hereditary rights of a besieged class.

Howells considered identity to be largely a matter of social construction. "What I hate," he told a friend, "is this dreary fumbling about my own identity, in which I detect myself at odd times. It seems sometimes as if it were somebody else, and I sometimes wish it were. But it will have to go on, and I must get what help I can out of the fact that it always *has* gone on."[46] His characters often question whether they have any real selves, for they seem to be what people make them, "and a different person to each."[47] In such a world, the usual markers of identity appear unstable, even manufactured.

Howells would not have denied that race could be a more visible marker than others. Yet everything in his background prepared him to see it as less than skin deep. The Howellses were a staunchly antislavery family. "If I were not your son," Howells told his father, "I would desire to be Old John Brown's — God bless him!"[48] In 1860, on his legendary trip to Boston, he sent a letter to an Ohio newspaper boldly asserting the propriety of interracial marriages.[49] That same year, he published "The Pilot's Story," a poem that dramatizes the suicide of a mulatto woman whose lover sells her to repay a gambling debt.[50] Almost fifty years later, he signed the petition that led to the founding of the NAACP.

Despite his great sympathy for and support of African Americans, Howells had, like many liberals of his time (and our own), areas of blindness. When he thought a stereotype was positive, he failed to see its racist nature. For example, he believed that "colored Americans . . . seem really to love good manners, though perhaps they sometimes value them beyond good morals" (*Editor's Study*, 318). This statement, which partly belies Howells's "general" comments about the causal relationship between manners and morality, suggests that he made certain assumptions about behavior, perhaps character, according to race. His introduction, for example, to Paul Laurence Dunbar's *Lyrics of Lowly Life* highlights both his good intentions and his prejudices. Prophesizing the end of racial hostility and prejudice through art, Howells interprets Dunbar's achievement as proof that his "primitive" race has attained "civilization."[51] Howells made a point of saying that he praised Dunbar for his art and not for reasons of race or class, yet he prefaced his remarks with a biographical sketch of Dunbar stressing his African ancestry and his work as an elevator operator. "There is a precious difference of temperament between the races which it would be a great pity ever to lose," he wrote, "and . . . this is best preserved and most charmingly suggested by Mr. Dunbar in those pieces of his where he studies the moods and traits of his race in their own accents of English" ("Introduction," 13–14). Following Howells's lead, other editors judged Dunbar's dialect poems (which represented only a fraction of his work, not to mention of the black experience) the most "authentic."[52]

Although Dunbar felt indebted to Howells, he resented (as did later writers like Countee Cullen) not being able to market his more traditional poems.[53] To this extent, Howells defined what constituted "black" art. He claimed to use a

Platonic standard when in fact he used a standard deviation, the degree to which African-American artists departed from the content and speech of their peers. *An Imperative Duty* incorporates the paradigm of benign paternalism that characterizes Howells's relationship with Dunbar, and like Mark Twain's *Puddn'head Wilson* (1894) or William Faulkner's *Light in August* (1932), it comes perilously close to endorsing racist stereotypes. Unapologetically capitalizing on the "thrilling" (*Imperative Duty*, 38) possibility of sex between whites and blacks, *An Imperative Duty* helped to create a market for fiction, especially turn-of-the-century African American fiction, that included characters of "mixed blood."[54]

With *An Imperative Duty*, Howells hoped to show that first and foremost race was less important than class. What distinguishes Howells's novel is that it is told, unlike most other African-American stories of passing, such as Frances Harper's *Iola Leroy* (1892), from a "white" perspective. The heroine, Rhoda Aldgate, never thinks herself anything save white until her aunt reveals the secret of her mother's parentage. To the dismay of many readers today, Howells looks at the question of race as if it were a set of neurasthenic symptoms to be cured by removal to a more felicitous clime. And this is exactly the prescription of his protagonist Dr. Olney, a specialist in nervous disorders who marries Rhoda and whisks her off to Rome, where she is admired for looking more Italian than the Italians.

Howells's metaphor anticipates W. E. B. Du Bois's borrowing of William James's term "double-consciousness."[55] James used the phrase to describe the condition of schizophrenics, and Du Bois extended it to include the experience of being black in the United States: "It is a peculiar sensation, this double-consciousness, this sense of always looking at one's self through the eyes of others, of measuring one's soul by the tape of a world that looks on in amused contempt and pity. One ever feels his two-ness, — an American, a Negro; two souls, two thoughts, two unreconciled strivings, two warring ideals in one dark body, whose dogged strength alone keeps it from being torn asunder."[56] This is exactly what Rhoda feels when she learns her history and wants to escape. As an expatriate, she will live her life in "translation," a word that Howells uses to suggest simultaneous acts of interpretation, conversion, and metamorphosis.

Howells refused to accept the idea of inherited racial characteristics. He thought, like Du Bois, that general prejudice against African Americans came from their having been slaves; in other words, racial prejudice had more to do with assumptions about class, rather than color. Nonetheless, *An Imperative Duty* seems to endorse a racial hierarchy that places whites above blacks. "Sooner or later," Dr. Olney argues, our race must absorb the colored race; and I believe that it will obliterate not only its color, but its qualities. The tame man, the civilized man, is stronger than the wild man; and I believe that in those cases within any one race where there are very strong ancestral proclivities on one side especially toward evil, they will die out before the good tendencies on the other side, for much the same reason, that is, because vice is savage and virtue is civilized.[57]

Olney's statement reveals the novel's racial hierarchy. His theory of racial absorption in terms of class assumes that the white race can assimilate the black and still retain its defining characteristics — in this case, color, rectitude, and culture. Through Olney, Howells raises without answering one of the central questions of Ralph Ellison's *The Invisible Man* (1951): how many drops of black paint can a vat of white paint absorb?

The tension in Howells's novel comes from the related belief that sinister, atavistic tendencies or inherited mannerisms may assert themselves at any time or in succeeding generations. Rhoda's aunt, for example, starts to hear her niece's voice as *"black"* (*Imperative Duty*, 37), her love of ease and pleasure as racial legacies. Howells argues that racial coding rests primarily on manner and perception.[58] Unlike Henry James, Howells does not welcome knowledge in and of itself. From his point of view, knowledge can readjust the very terms of one's being. Rhoda, for example, actually seems to appear darker "as if the fact of her mother's race had remanded her to its primordial hue in touching her consciousness" (*Imperative Duty*, 51). Race becomes, in this way, a function of the imagination.

Howells clearly thinks that environment has a greater influence on identity than heredity, the circumstances of Rhoda's upbringing determining her "whiteness." Rhoda blames her aunt for not telling her the facts of her birth from the moment she could speak or understand her first word: "You let me pass myself off on myself and every one else, for what I wasn't" (*Imperative Duty*, 50). Without such duplicity, she could have grown up "knowing it, and trying to bear it" (*Imperative Duty*, 75), yet her class determined that she would develop as she did. And to a large extent, class must be blamed for Rhoda's own latent racism.

Rhoda's attitudes about race change after her aunt's revelation. Once fascinated by African Americans, she now finds them repulsive: "She never knew before how hideous they were, with their flat wide-nostriled noses, their out-rolled thick lips, their mobile, bulging eyes set near together, their retreating chins and foreheads, and their smooth, shining skin; they seemed burlesques of humanity, worse than apes" (*Imperative Duty*, 58). Her response, which focuses entirely on appearance rather than manner or character, is a form of self-revulsion. Rhoda thinks the women worse than the men; the lightest-skinned "mixed bloods" most odious of all (*Imperative Duty*, 64). In a sense, she becomes the subject of her previous condescension as she is forced to see a concealed part of herself. She intuits what it is to be in the other's skin, while ironically occupying her own more fully. Howells's dramatization of Rhoda's consciousness fittingly emphasizes the exterior. Her attempts to find her mother's people, to help them so that she can love them, are from her author's point of view misguided to the point of being ludicrous. She could never be other than a tourist in black neighborhoods.

To Howells, attitudes about race remain strictly a matter of feeling, not fact, though feelings can be difficult to contain and be affected by social imperatives.[59] Howells deflates the climax of his novel by making a potentially tragic moment comic. When Olney asks Rhoda to be his wife, she histrionically proclaims: "I am a negress!" Already possessing that knowledge, he laughs outright: "Well, not a very black one. Besides, what of it, if I love you" (*Imperative Duty*, 94). Although the marriage plot "absorbs" Howells's critique of America's unhealthy feelings about race, the point that race should not matter remains. It is perhaps more disturbing that Howells has his novel's most entitled character determine the nature of racial identity or "feeling," which returns Rhoda to the class she never really left. "If you must give your life to the improvement of any particular race," Olney tells her, "give it to mine" (*Imperative Duty*, 97). The quotation, which suggests the suppression of Rhoda's dual heritage, if not her singularity, ironically leaves her impaired, not cured.

An Imperative Duty could have been called *There Is Confusion* — the title of Jessie Fauset's 1924 novel about racial definition. Rhoda's "secret" makes her feel a "sense of guilty deceit" (*Imperative Duty*, 101), which Dr. Olney humorously cures with the reminder that fifteen-sixteenths of her heredity comes from slave-holders. He argues that Rhoda's shame comes from these ancestors as much as her mother's. Suggesting that the United States has no place for people who think like the Olneys, Howells disrupts a myth of seamless assimilation. His critique of contemporary laws against miscegenation places him ahead of his time. As late as 1926, New York was riveted with the Rhinelander divorce case, which hinged on questions of intermarriage, racial purity, and inheritance rights. Leonard Rhinelander demanded a divorce on the grounds that his wife, Alice Jones, hid her African-American heritage. In the course of the trial, the jury examined Mrs. Rhinelander's body, naked to the waist, to determine whether her husband could have perceived her antecedents. He prevailed, as much from class and custom as the legal merits of his suit. She received a monetary settlement.[60]

Howells's title *An Imperative Duty* begs the question "What is our duty?" Rhoda's aunt supposes she must tell the "truth" whatever the consequences, while Olney detests "any crazy claim upon conscience" that enforces an "aimless act of self-sacrifice" (*Imperative Duty*, 101). Howells leaves definitions of "truth" to his readers, though his title carries its own imperative in a nation whose people continued (and continue) to be divided by questions of "blood."

V

William Dean Howells never tired of what he called the "social spectacle" (*Imperative Duty*, 19). Favoring social patterns and exceptions over meditations on consciousness, he expanded the parameters — to some extent, the definition — of the novel of manners to include the ongoing incorporation of the middle class. He outlined his own aesthetic for the novel in an 1899 lecture entitled "Novel-Writing and Novel-Reading: An Impersonal Explanation." Significantly, for later writers such as Wharton, Cather, Glasgow, and Fauset, he championed the "historical form" because it "documents" the persistent recomposition of society itself. Howells delivered his lecture in small Midwestern towns and on university campuses. Sometimes more than a thousand people gathered to hear him. It is hard to imagine that world now. Citizens from a cross-section of the community assembled in high-ceilinged school auditoriums and overheated sitting rooms eager to meet the man they thought a messenger of American letters. Unable to refuse people's hospitality, he spent endless hours socializing but essentially politicking for a national literature that would reflect the lives of his audience. The kindness of well-meaning people, some of whom traveled hours in search of "culture," nearly "killed" him.[61] It was all so extraordinary and fine and exhausting.

Howells's actual lecture was much like the "dean" of American literature himself: self-deprecatingly humorous and slightly erudite. He saw novels falling loosely into three forms, or "main sorts": the autobiographical, the biographical, and the historical. The autobiographical novel, told from a single point of view as if it were the author's own, he said dramatizes — in the tradition of Charles Dickens's *David Copperfield* — individual consciousness. The biographical novel varies by having a central figure, such as James's Roderick Hudson, reporting every fact and feeling. The third form, the historical, is the slipperiest and, according to

Howells, the "greatest." Not to be confused with the "historical novel" or "romance," which Howells disparaged for masking "the facts of the odious present,"[62] it refers to any novel that presents a series of events as though they were "real history." The narrator might present that history in two ways, either from original records, as "a certain passage in the real life of the *race* is known to the historian" ("Novel-Writing and Novel-Reading," 230; emphasis mine), or from lived experience. This form, at once narrative and dramatic, gives individual lives a greater historical significance. Howells thought Tolstoy alone had mastered the contradictions of this form, which he saw encompassing novels as different as Harriet Beecher Stowe's *Uncle Tom's Cabin* and Nathaniel Hawthorne's *The Scarlet Letter.* Many of his own novels might also be said to fall into this category, for they register sweeping changes in American society, including the selling of spiritualism in *The Undiscovered Country* (1880) and the rise of a new rural middle class in *The Landlord at Lion's Head* (1897).

Well aware of the socioeconomic dimension of literature, Howells hoped that his own contribution would be a democratizing force. Fiction was to his mind more "real" than history, and of course it had a decidedly historical dimension.[63] Almost inevitably, any blurring of history and fiction presents problems, as we can see by the controversies that books such as Twain's *Adventures of Huckleberry Finn* (1885) or William Styron's *The Confessions of Nat Turner* (1967) generate. Critics have denounced Twain's use of dialect and Styron's sources, not to mention Styron's adoption — some would say theft — of Turner's voice.[64] In his lecture, Howells acknowledges that readers have different standards of "truth" for history and fiction: "[T]he historian has got the facts from some one who witnessed them," he explains; "but the novelist employing the historic form has no proof of them; he gives his word alone for them" ("Novel-Writing and Novel-Reading," 230). Whatever its disadvantages, the beauty of the historical form lay precisely in its gangly, "splay-footed" shapelessness, which to Howells allowed the fullest expression of the inner complexities and "outer entirety" of life ("Novel-Writing and Novel-Reading," 231).

In his "social history" of the United States, comprised of novels like *A Modern Instance, The Rise of Silas Lapham*, and *An Imperative Duty*, Howells cultivated an authorial stance of distant yet empathic omniscience. He spoke to Americans in the process of deciding how they defined themselves and for what they stood. He had no easy remedy for the problems he observed, though he tended toward a view that combined William James's philosophy of pragmatism with Josiah Royce's Hegelian idealism. "We are all but dust," Howells quoted in an 1886

review of Royce's *History of California*, "save as this social order gives us life."
Howells may have seen the trajectory of his own career in the following quotation from Royce:

> When we think it our instrument, our plaything, and make our private fortunes the
> one object, then this social order rapidly becomes vile to us. . . . But if we turn again
> and serve the social order, and not merely ourselves, we soon find that what we are
> serving is simply our own highest spiritual destiny in bodily form.[65]

On the occasion of Howells's seventy-fifth birthday, Henry James wrote a
tribute for the *North American Review*, directly addressed to Howells himself: You
knew and felt "the *real* affair of the American case and character better than I," he
granted. "You had learned them earlier and more intimately."[66] James was not the
only novelist to profit by the Howells example. The most respected women
writers at the turn of the century, Wharton, Glasgow, and Cather, created their
own so-called novels of manners, social histories, or histories of manners, which
incorporated Howells's understanding of the novelist's role in analyzing, if not
promoting, changes in the existing order.

When Howells acknowledged the amorphous nature of the historical form of
the novel, he accepted the destabilizing conditions that its relationship to history
dictate. He believed that the wonder and glory of art resides in its resistance to
formula.[67] The plasticity of the historical form allows the dramatization of multi-
ply competing forces — the tension between the idiosyncratic and the archetypal,
characteristic of contemporary writers such as Leslie Silko and Maxine Hong
Kingston, for example, or the ambivalence of a writer such as F. Scott Fitzgerald,
who both loved and hated the jazz-age generation. It particularly lends itself to
the representation of a society in transition, a fact that partly explains its appeal
for writers alert to the encroachments of modernism and the contending forces
of assimilation and segregation.

Howells thought of history as both a record of events and a prophecy for the
future. He did not doubt that human nature and motives remained relatively
constant; whenever the strong could take advantage of the weak, they would. To
him, the difference between the spirit of the past and the spirit of the present had
to do with the rhetoric of ideals and ends.[68] He may have felt, as he told a young
friend, that life had passed him by,[69] but he had seldom failed to immerse himself
in it. Maybe it does not matter "so much what you do" as long as it is done
with Howells's "unfailing, testifying truth." Howells himself knew authors to be
"largely a matter of fashion, like this style of bonnet, or that shape of gown"

(*Literature and Life*, 33). Nonetheless, he must have found it comforting to be told by his peers in the American Academy of Arts and Letters that his "day should be as long as his country's history." At the time they most needed it, he had given them the assurance that American life held "the material of an adequate American art."[70] Future readers can remain hopeful that Henry James's prediction will continue to hold fast: that Howells's abiding engagement with the truth will keep him from ever being fully neglected.[71]

CHAPTER TWO

Henry James

The Final Paradox of Manners

It is a blow to think that our great Henry should be *au fond*, only a Howells!

LETTER OF EDITH WHARTON TO GAILLARD LAPSLEY

Europe had been romantic years before, because she was different from America; wherefore America would now be romantic because she was different from Europe.　　　HENRY JAMES, *The American Scene*

I

The fall of 1904, Henry James (1843–1916) returned to the United States after an absence of twenty years. Ostensibly he planned to visit family and friends, to look after his literary property. At least as important, he hoped to garner the kind of material details, including the ways in which Americans ate their eggs, that readers of travel literature craved. In fact, his voyage home gave James the opportunity, through a process of recognition and rejection, to take his own measure as an American writer. He felt driven, as he explained to William Dean Howells, "pathetically and tragically," by a fervor of nostalgia.[1] Before he grew too old, he wanted to see America, to taste its air, to loll on a hillside in the manner of his youth. Perhaps Howells's advice to a mutual friend still lingered in his mind: "It doesn't so much matter what you do — but live. . . . I haven't done so — and now I'm old. . . . You have time. . . . Live!"[2] James had said much the same thing to Edith Wharton several years before his transatlantic adventure, advising her to take hold of her "American Subject" as of life itself and let it pull her where it would.[3]

Friends predicted that James would hate everything he saw in the United States, and they knew their man. He missed what he thought confident of finding and found what he had never imagined: skyscrapers, streetcars, featureless highways, league-long bridges, and houses that proclaimed their cost. His past assaulted him at every turn in remembered sights, half-heard sounds, and faintly

familiar smells, while the changes, and above all "the bignesses," seemed engulf-
ing.[4] The contrasts that had launched his creative boat and made his reputation
with "Daisy Miller" (1878) now left him marooned and gasping for breath. Too
raw, too chaotic, America also proved too much,[5] and though James tried to take
it bit by bit, or region by region, it defied categorization. His usual ways of
ordering and evaluating experience proved inadequate as competing impressions
cancelled one another, rendering America a vast negation.

As he soon recognized, James had entered both another country and a new
era — an era that, having broken away from the orthodoxies of his youth, celebrated its present. Not only did his experience change his thinking about manners generally, as evidenced by *The American Scene* (1907), it also had a profound
effect on the form of his last, unfinished novels, *The Sense of the Past* (1917) and
The Ivory Tower (1917). The paradox that James encountered in the United
States — a society of excesses that seemed defined by its voids — threatened to
make his understanding of fiction anachronistic. During the First World War,
the invasion of Belgium and the bombing of France roused his determination to
make a stand for the values he associated with "civilization." Yet the problem
remained: How could he, a novelist who came to maturity in the nineteenth
century, respond to the cultural upheavals epitomized by the Great War?

In a world distrustful, even bereft, of tradition and increasingly antagonist
toward concepts like "honor" and "duty," James had to find a way to make history
as well as manners matter. He did this not by minimizing social context, as
in his last completed novel, *The Golden Bowl* (1904), but by amplifying it. He
achieved his desired effect in two ways: First, he reversed the perspective usually
associated with the historical form of the novel. Instead of commenting on the
present through the past, James commented on the past through the present,
establishing (as in *The Sense of the Past*) a point of reference needed for dialogue.
Second, he combined (as in *The Ivory Tower*) elements associated with very different fictional forms; notably, the romance and the realistic novel. Through
intertextual allusion, he restored significance to defunct or fading worlds such as
the Newport of his youth or the London of his early manhood. What originally
began as a crisis for James ended as an experimental investigation of the parameters of the novel of manners, which, in his hands, synchronously embraced the
historical and the ahistorical by way of the psychological.

James's solution differs markedly from Howells's brand of realism, with its
implicit call for civic or political action to bridge inequitable socioeconomic

divides or its continued dependence on observable detail. James relies upon fictional form itself and largely subjective, epiphanic moments when "truth," intimate and infinite, bursts forth to free readers from the paralysis of everyday life. His late, posthumously published fiction offers a conduit between time and place and the multiple selves that to literary modernists like Virginia Woolf or William Butler Yeats constitute human identity.

James characterized himself in retrospect as "a foredoomed student of manners."[6] As a cultural critic, he had envisioned himself in the tradition of Alexis de Tocqueville and Matthew Arnold, whose methods he associated with a "free play of mind."[7] He wanted to comment on the organization of American society in the context of other civilizations, paying attention to customs, speech, manners, and the sexes. To highlight sectional differences, he organized *The American Scene* around places rather than topics. Individual chapters focus on New England, Newport, Boston, Concord and Salem, Philadelphia, Baltimore, Washington, Richmond, and Florida, with four separate chapters on New York—perhaps a tacit wish that the United States still conformed to maps from an earlier century. We might expect that since James concentrates on place, *The American Scene* would be crowded with physical description. Instead, he crams it full of abstractions, as if words like *newnesses*, for example, could corral the gangly monster of contemporary life. Wharton remembers James bewailing his inability to use the "material" of modern American life. In *The Golden Bowl*, he failed, in her opinion, to realize either the financier Adam Verver or the "concrete reality" of his American City. The same sense of unreality, of places divorced from history, of people from their surroundings, hovers over *The American Scene*.[8]

James's reading of Tocqueville and Arnold aside, he could not have known how to prepare himself for his own emotional response to America, a country with wildly heterogenous manners. Mistaking his subject, he forgot that the real protagonist of any first-person narrative is the narrator himself, with his prejudices, prevarications, compromises, and idiosyncracies. Despite its title, *The American Scene* has almost nothing to do with an identifiable culture, even granting that it can exist apart from James's fancy. It has everything to do with the evolution of James's thinking about perception. The quality of his mind not only imbues the whole show with meaning, it *is* the whole show. What he feels determines what he sees. Whether directly recognized or not, there is no objective reality except the psychological. The book's drama comes from James's projection of his feelings onto another body, in this case America itself. Only as a recording instrument, a kind of emotional seismograph, can he maintain the comfortable fiction of artistic disengagement discussed in his prefaces and re- futed by the protagonists of his last novels.

In *The American Scene*, James assumes certain "truths" about society that his own ambivalence paradoxically sabotages. He presents his recollections as "truth," or evidence of an undisputed standard, which reverses the usual process of knowing and then remembering. This causes him to oscillate between arbi- trary and changing points that signal what he recalls and what he presently encounters or "knows." When James returns to Fresh Pond, for example, he finds it part of a "Park System" whose newly sprouted golf links and tennis lawns sound "the eternal American note" —

> the note of the gregarious, the concentric, and pervaded moreover by the rustle of petticoats too distinguishable from any garment-hem of the sacred nine. The dese- crated, the destroyed resort had favoured, save on rare feast-days, the single stroll, or at worst the double, dedicated to shared literary secrets; which was why I almost angrily missed, among the ruins, what I had mainly gone back to recover — some echo of the dreams of youth, the titles of tales, the communities of friendship, the sympathies and patiences, in fine, of dear W. D. H[owells]. (*American Scene*, 414–15)

James's objection to contemporary life concerns its commercialism and feminiza- tion ("the rustle of petticoats"). Before him, he sees the erasure of his youth and the values that have sustained his adulthood; the predestined decline or reevalua- tion of his life work. James assumes a world he never shared with Howells. "One queer thing about Harry James," Howells's wife Elinor told her sister-in-law, "is though we've been *intimate* with him so long we do not know him a bit better than the first time we met him."[9] As James's commemoration of Howells in *The American Scene* hints, James tacitly agreed with critics who thought Howells's fiction too feminine and too "social," by which they meant "superficial" — while Howells, having grown more political himself, thought that James had retired "to his own interior to ruminate the morsels of his fellow-man which he captures in his consciousness of things outside."[10]

Howells's analysis of James summarizes James's response in *The American Scene*. The versatility that allows manners to perform several, sometimes conflict- ing functions suddenly makes them appear disturbingly subjective. No wonder that James decides — within the space of his opening ten pages — "that in such conditions there couldn't *be* any manners to speak of" (*American Scene*, 364) — a pronouncement that makes the commotion of his American "scene" complete.

James backs himself into his personal "jolly corner" (words he used to title a subsequent story of repatriation). The system of signs that he wants to impose on his "fictive nation" cannot survive the process of his close scrutiny.[11] Their apparent randomness makes him question the logic of his thought. It is one thing to accept the shifting nature of perception as the author looks at the scene before him from different windows in his own house of fiction; it is another for him to topple the hierarchies that have given his point of view their privilege. James's title grants the fluid nature of seeing in its suggestion of the past (the seen); contemporary locales (sites); and the present view (or to use James's word, the "spectacle"). As this wordplay highlights, he surveys manners that seem indigenous to place, material circumstances, and national types against the measure of a mythologized Europe known to him through literature, painting, and his own experience.

In *The American Scene*, James attempts to objectify fleeting sensations by giving them a fixed form through language. Because the object usually matches neither memory nor the continual stream of immediate experience, he confuses sensation, which is evolving, "with its permanent external object."[12] Perception becomes an act of appropriation that demands a commensurate act of dispossession. James sees signs severed from some living reference or root and wants to restore them to a prior state. Yet, the architecture of America, speaking to him with one voice, resists: "We are only installments, symbols, stopgaps . . . we have nothing to do with continuity, responsibility, transmission" (*American Scene*, 365). To put it simply, James feels out of step with a new and fractured time and, therefore, with himself. Words cannot express the sense of continual process, which seems embedded in these things themselves.

All this may be seen as James's intuition of "modernism." The gross changes he observed in contemporary American life resulted in his suffering a series of "vastations" (the Swedenborgian term his father used to describe a frightening dissolution of self). Henry Senior attributed his breakdown to an invisible presence whose fetid character seemed to poison the very air he breathed. A similar panic stalks James throughout the pages of *The American Scene*. Resembling his protagonist in "The Jolly Corner" (1908), he tracks the man he might have become. What if he had made a colossal mistake, drained the wrong cup to its dregs? Torn between acknowledgement and denial, James pays, like every expatriate, with his person.[13] The ways in which he organized his life became suspect, for America revealed a ghost encamped in what had been his own safe house: Who is the horror, he wondered: the one who renounced or the one who remained?

"America" came as near to silencing James as anything could. Yet its value lay in the fear itself. According to Albert Camus — another writer fascinated by themes of displacement, or what the French call *depaysment* (a queasiness of soul in a strange place) — "It is the fact that, at a certain moment, when we are so far from our own country . . . , we are seized by a vague fear, and an instinctive desire to go back to the protection of old habits. This is the most obvious benefit of travel. At the moment, we are feverish but also porous, so that the slightest touch makes us quiver to the depths of our being." Camus concludes that we travel finally for culture, because travel allows us "the experience of our most intimate sense."[14] This premise proved both true and untrue for James, who began to doubt the powers of discernment and assimilation upon which his art depended. He believed that every great artist has a kind of double intelligence, which is both moral and aesthetic. No good novel, he argued in "The Art of Fiction" (1884), can come from a superficial mind.[15] Truth grows from unflinching honesty, and sympathy from penetration. To him, the real represents the things that could not possibly remain hidden from the artist's perception. The impenetrability of the American scene left James stammering into an existentialist void. No matter where he looked, he could not find what he needed: a "moral touchstone" — a referent that would assure the integrity of his life and his work. Given these conditions, he defined his relationship to American culture agonistically. What other choice did he, a man who had made a high art of quivering, have? He could rediscover America or reinvent himself, and in his last fiction, he attempts both.

James's dilemma involves the whole question of manners — their definition, intention, and perception. It extends to questions of civilization and history, themselves dependent upon the study of manners. America's dearth of settled standards undercuts James's sense not only of himself but also of historical chronology and time. The present does not seem to arise from the past in the usual way. Visiting his brother William in New Hampshire, he contemplates Mount Chocorua:

> the "high-perched cone of Chocorua, which rears itself, all granite, over a huge interposing shoulder, quite with the *allure* of a minor Matterhorn — everywhere legible was the hard little historic record of agricultural failure and defeat. It had to

pass for the historic background, that traceable truth that a stout human experiment had been tried, had broken down. One was in presence, everywhere, of the refusal to consent to history. (*American Scene*, 373).

What has always seemed to be a train of fixed points on a line of human progression derails. The refusal to consent to history in a sense negates history by breaking the spell of a common narrative or shared practices.

In America, manners seem to have a life of their own. It's almost as if they stand there waiting to have their stories told before echoing Bartleby's "I prefer not to." James imagines them, or his "impressions" of them, as "artless, unconscious, unshamed, at the very gates of Appearance; they might, verily, have been there, in their plenitude, at the call of some procession of drums and banners — the principal facts of the case being collected along our passage, to my fancy, quite as if they had been principal citizens" (*American Scene*, 361). To reassert order, James institutes an "architectonic" scale of manners that promises to yield what the manners of Hoboken or Harvard, New York or Washington, "connote" (*American Scene*, 362): "The huge new houses, up and down, looked over their smart, short lawns as with a certain familiar prominence in their profiles, which was borne out by the accent, loud, assertive, yet benevolent withal, with which they confessed to their extreme expensiveness. 'Oh, yes; we were awfully dear, for what we are and for what we do'" (*American Scene*, 362). Testaments to their observer's sensibility, they wait for James to give them significance.

It seems curious that the author of *The American* (1877), *The Portrait of a Lady* (1881), and *The Ambassadors* (1903) — books that explore types — should see in the United States so few, apart from businessmen, New Bostonians, and "summer girls." James's almost exclusive focus on the material facade, which screens elusive (rather than allusive) ghostly presences, seems a judgment in itself, a way of gouging "an interest *out* of the vacancy" (*American Scene*, 366). "I am nothing, I am nothing, nothing!" Washington whispers from every door and window, though James feels it peopled by Henry Adams, John La Farge, and Augustus Saint-Gaudens.[16] James ascribes this vacancy to the promiscuous or public nature of American life, which values action over reflection. "Constituted relations" (*American Scene*, 364), upon which the social and domestic order rest, demand privacy.[17] He found — foreshadowing Theodore Dreiser's *An American Tragedy* (1925) — so little privacy in the United States that he located its social and aesthetic ideal in the modern hotel, a vast way station for transients wealthy enough to pay the tax.

To borrow Gertrude Stein's phrase, James came back to America and found no "there there." While he felt compelled to lie at every stop by commemorating for his hosts the charm of their home city, he thought its culture faddish and disposable. America displayed its wealth to him, and little else.[18] Liberating mechanical appliances—stoves, typewriters, sewing machines, washing machines—merely set people whirling like solitary dynamos in a social maelstrom. James looked in vain for the signs of cultural transmission that he had found in Europe and eulogized in *A Little Tour of France* (1900), *English Hours* (1905), and *Italian Hours* (1909)—the latter two, collections of previously published essays. James sees a direct correlation between the isolation of these places, "enclosed and ordered and subject to the continuity of life,"[19] and his ability to extract their history.

Where the majority sees no need for any tastes, habits, or traditions other than their own, there can be no drama, no progression of history. "It takes," says James, "an endless amount of history to make even a little tradition, and an endless amount of tradition to make even a little taste" (*American Scene*, 495). And taste, as his father used to say, is "a blessed comprehensive name for many of the things deepest in us."[20] Whatever James observed of "history" in the United States seemed nothing more than "a colossal recipe for the *creation* of arrears" (*American Scene*, 735)—whether Ye Olde Mills and turreted storefronts or something as sacred as Civil War mementoes commemorating the "original vanity and fatuity" (*American Scene*, 660) of the slave-owning South.

These reconstructed or commercial pasts desecrated the landscape and the memory of "other" Americans, especially native peoples, to whom James pays tribute in the last section of *The American Scene*. This section, published in the United Kingdom but not in the United States, provides an addendum to received history as well as an admonition. Sequentially headed "The Last Regret," "The Last Question," and "The Last Answer," the section rails against the aesthetic monotony that Americans have chosen for their future: "If I were one of the painted savages you have dispossessed," he writes, "or even some tough reactionary trying to emulate him, what you are making would doubtless impress me more than what you are leaving unmade; . . . and I should owe you my grudge for every disfigurement and every violence, for every wound with which you have caused the face of the land to bleed" (*American Scene*, 734). Although James acknowledged that money could provide a kind of "short-cut" to culture, he still insisted that there was no substitute "for troublesome history" and "the immitigable process of time" (*American Scene*, 366). Contrary to other commentators, James saw manners growing from conflict, from conditions that possibly require concealment and diplomacy, even prevarication, to survive. To him, they relayed a siren's song of dark, concealed spaces in the self. They tacitly acknowledged the deep division between the multiple public roles people perform and the multiple people they see themselves to be.

This might lead us to presume that James, who saw nothing except contention in America, might surprise its history; instead he wonders, "*[w]ere* there any secrets at all, or had the outward blankness, the quantity of absence, as it were, in the air, its inward equivalent as well?" (*American Scene*, 392). For James, America lacked the right kind of history, the intrigue we might associate with Elizabethan England, say, or eighteenth-century France. Nevertheless, it seems strange that James had so little sympathy for the South. Richmond, the capital of the Confederacy, looked to him (much as it looked to a foreigner like Dickens) simply blank, its past a product of mistaken ideals. James felt sorry for the South, bound by provincial heritage, its "hundred mistakes and make-believes, suppressions and prevarications" (*American Scene*, 663). He refused to recognize its history in the spirit he recognized as that of the Medicis, perhaps because their evils had supported Donatello, Brunelleschi, Ghiberti, and della Robbia.

The American Scene finally shows James unable to resolve his conflicting impulses toward cultural isolation and integration. On the one hand, he appreciates any change in "social sameness" (*American Scene*, 442), which reduces everything to a suitable average. On the other, he seeks an infusion of "Color" (*American Scene*, 462), if it comes from Europe (Italy excepted!). James objects to the "huge national *pot au feu* . . . [to] the introduction of fresh — of perpetually fresh so far it isn't perpetually stale — foreign matter into our heterogeneous system" (*American Scene*, 408). As these contradictions suggest, James both protested and applauded what he called the "white-washing" of America.

As a young man, James could not have imagined the profound effect that immigrants would have on American culture, especially its language, which he felt increasingly called upon to protect against barbarian corruptions. America clearly looked and acted differently than he remembered. By 1900, for example, the Immigration Bureau reported that of the year's 361,000 immigrants to the United States, one-fifth were from Britain, the Scandinavian countries, Germany, and Finland; one-tenth were Jews; and more than half were Roman Catholics. Although blacks made up only one-ninth of the population, a shift in demographics made their presence more visible along the eastern seaboard.[21] James had to account for the ways these differences implicitly demanded a reordering of social hierarchies. He made a distinction, for instance, between African Americans, whose rights he defended, and the new immigrants, who made him uneasy. In *The American Scene*, he singles out W. E. B. Du Bois for special praise, not just because William James had taught him at Harvard,[22] but because Du Bois's belief in a Talented Tenth echoed James's own wish, expressed in the preface to "Lady Barbarina," for "some eventual sublime consensus of the educated": "There," James announced, "in the dauntless fusions to come — is the personal drama of the future" (*Art of the Novel*, 203).

Unlike W. C. Brownell, an editor and critic sympathetic to James, he did not champion the differentiation of races, which (according to Brownell) made Americans the world's most aristocratic democrats.[23] On the contrary, James felt that tradition flourished best in homogeneous and stable societies that produced a collection of detached and socially conservative cosmopolites like himself. In a section of *The American Scene* headed "The Eclipse of Manners," he sounds more like a eugenicist than a travel writer. James hopes that after the United States has absorbed many of its ethnically diverse new members, the European elements will again rise to the surface.

James's vision of a new democracy is itself paradoxical, for although praising the egalitarian principles of the country club, he identifies manners with patterns of intercourse — intellectual, moral, emotional, sensual, social, and political — that benefit the general population. In America, he had to concede the claim of the alien, which, in turn, highlighted his own foreignness — an occurrence that may explain his sympathy for groups like Native Americans. The racial hodge-podge made it impossible to attach any meaning to a peculiarly "American" character defined historically by metamorphosis. He groped in vain for both a theory of civilization and a language that could express the "ethnic synthesis" he called the "Accent of the Future." He feared that language would not be "English — in any sense for which there is an existing literary measure" (*American Scene*, 471). A people need a common language to impart a coherent sense of culture, he argued.[24] They need a "national stamp." James had once thought its lack was an "excellent preparation for culture";[25] now culture itself seemed the only preparation for culture.

II

Whatever else it did, James's trip to America convinced him that the multitude had become a "mob," with no sympathy for the linguistic and literary tradition he represented. During his stay, the *New York Times* routinely published letters criticizing the decadent nature of his novels and the denseness of his prose. One writer reported that of the thousand people who belonged to his book club, only thirty had ever read a James novel, and the others had no plans to do so. Remarks like these reinforced James's aversion to the general reading public, whose admiration he simultaneously craved and disdained. As early as 1872, he had informed his brother William that "the multitude has absolutely no taste — none at least that a thinking man is bound to defer to. To write for the few who have is doubtless to lose money — but I am not afraid of starving."[26] This is the same man who dreamed of writing a "hit" play and being freed forever from financial worries. "I am not sure," Edith Wharton remembered,

> that Henry James had not secretly dreamed of being a "best-seller" in the days when that odd form of literary fame was at its height; at any rate he certainly suffered all his life — and more and more as time went on — from the lack of recognition among the very readers who had most warmly welcomed his early novels. He could not understand why the success achieved by "Daisy Miller" and "The Portrait of a Lady" should be denied to the great novels of his maturity. (*Backward Glance*, 191–92)

After the turn of the century, James could no longer deny that the world of his fiction struck the majority of readers as insularly hybrid. He probably suspected his friends of wondering how the author of *The Portrait of a Lady* could have written the later novels.[27] Wharton thought he had no choice, being "qualified by nature and situation" to observe the vanishing types that had belonged to old America or to their more picturesque counterparts in Europe. And James seems to have agreed. Acutely conscious of his imaginative limitations, he "bewailed" his inability to turn his observations about the American scene to artistic advantage (*Backward Glance*, 176).

James's American reception may help to account for the almost reactionary tone of a series of articles he published in *Harper's Bazar* on the manners and speech of American women. The subject was not original to James. It had been popular at least since the 1870s. In less than a dozen years, for example, the *Galaxy* printed more than 450 pages on correct usage and diction.[28] Responding to this market, James's called the first of his articles, which grew from a lecture that he had given to the graduating class of Bryn Mawr on the sacredness of the spoken word, "The Speech of American Women." Divided into four parts, his extended essay ran from November 1906 to February 1907. After a month's hiatus, "The Manners of American Women," also in four parts, appeared through

July. Five months later (December 1907), Scribner's began issuing the volumes of the New York edition. His worst misgivings coming true, James felt a kind of " 'lettered' anguish" (*American Scene*, 470). The nonresponse, he told his agent, turned out to be a greater disappointment than any he could have anticipated.

James's articles can be read as a last-ditch effort to defend an artistic vision that the process of writing *The American Scene* had unnervingly subverted. On the one hand, they seek to impose an order, to contain an audience that challenges him to a new understanding of the world and its fictional representation. In this, they are "antimodern" (to use T. J. Jackson Lears's term), and maybe even antiwomen, since James sounds like an exasperated uncle lecturing a recalcitrant niece for attending too many meetings of her "culture club."[29] On the other hand, they acknowledge a world, largely self-created, inherently relational, and known to us through individual as well as shared perceptions.

It should come as no surprise (given his remarks about "petticoats" in *The American Scene*) that James holds women largely responsible for America's lack of manners and culture — though he does also blame men for devoting themselves to the stock exchange and the football field. In James's estimation, a "woman-made" society (*American Scene*, 639) hardly deserves the name — a prejudice that did not stop him from publishing his articles in a lowbrow "ladies' " magazine like *Harper's Bazar*, known for feature columns (such as "Diets for Invalids") and gossip from England and Washington.

James argues a direct connection between manners and morals and morals and civilization: "The interest of tone is the interest of manners," he writes, "and the interest of manners is the interest of morals, and the interest of morals is the interest of civilization."[30] He characterizes the American woman much as he had Isabel Archer at the beginning of *The Portrait of a Lady:* she is heroically obtuse and insensible to the kind of subtleties that constitute older civilizations. The "object of prey and patronage,"[31] she exists independent of society, having neither stages nor probations to satisfy. As a result, she has none of the patina that a society rich in antecedent conditions can supply. Her poverty of manner is most apparent to James in her speech, which lacks the principles of selection and comparison that he valued. Without considered speech, he argues, there can be no real thought — merely advertisement.

Although the meaning of speech is open to interpretation, in social circumstances it can often work to suppress dissent, thereby advancing a norm for civilized behavior. According to James, speech gives form to human relations. When automatic ("Our Speech," 22), it composes part of a long civilizing tradition that imbues life with grace and poetry. For him, the most common colloquial statements articulate the nature of public life and the history of the national character. Writers who wanted to convey contemporary culture could not ignore alterations of common vocabulary, usage, or syntax, and expatriated writers felt at an understandable disadvantage. Their plight was not just a function of exile. Intellectuals in general bemoaned the deterioration of proper speech and traditional values, resulting from rapid changes in the makeup of their societies and the world at large.[32] James argued not against change as such—to highlight another apparent paradox—but for a more all-embracing democracy and for a consistent position toward manners themselves. The suppression of cultural transitions that comes from having a nonapproach to manners, he wrote, results in the disconnectedness of groups and whole classes.

As the installments of his articles on manners proceed, James's rage gathers momentum. If the social record writes itself in the manners of American women, James read that record as rapacious. "What," he asks, "*would* be the civilization, what in other words would be the manners, of a lady who, surrounded at breakfast, at luncheon, at dinner, by a couple of dozen or so of small saucers of the most violently heterogeneous food, should proceed to exhaust the contents by a process of incoherent and indiscriminate spooning?"[33] Impudent and coarse, the American woman, whom he continued to parody in the stories that form *The Finer Grain* (1910), is more than anything illiterate. Whatever else compelled James, his pronouncements about speech cannot be wholly separated from his concerns about audience, the ubiquitous "she," whom he identified with the American reading public and who appeared to have lost interest in James himself.

James's ideal American reader would belong (as he previously suggested in *The American Scene*) to a small group of people who, possessing acute consciences, recognized "importance" greater than their own. What he desires is a population "*trained*" to finer discriminations.[34] What he continues to get are the very readers he chastises in *Harper's Bazar,* for around this time he also chose to participate in another project for the magazine, the writing of a serially authored novel—James and eleven others would each write a chapter—that ran from December 1907 to November 1908. James's characterization of the son-in-law, Charles Edward, caught between pleasing his mother and wife, humorously comments on the artistic soul trapped in a family of philistines.[35]

The *Harper's Bazar* articles show James at a crucial juncture in his career. At his most extreme, he seems to endorse a totalitarian land of letters that preserves social, civil, and conversational discipline by restraining bedizened, gum-chewing "little girls" like his own Daisy Miller: "In societies other than ours the male privilege of correction springs, and quite logically, from the social fact that the male is the member of society primarily acting and administering and primarily listened to—whereby his education, his speech, his tone, his standards and connections, his general 'competence' . . . color the whole air, react upon his companion and establish for her the principal relation she recognizes."[36] More dispassionately, James argues that manners have their own physics requiring losses to be made up. There had to be an artistic facility for the working of any social form, no matter how elastic or resistant. Still, the question remained, what.

As a "historian of fine consciences,"[37] James had always depended upon manners to function in much the same way as "master-plots." Their assignment of values, their very predictability, gave his readers a framework of generated responses, which he could then anticipate and manipulate. In early novels such as *Roderick Hudson* (1875) and *The American*, he incorporated a formulaic set of national characteristics that he reversed or collapsed in later novels, notably *The Wings of the Dove* (1902), *The Ambassadors*, and *The Golden Bowl*.

In James's fiction, manners work by inference, construction, and divination to advance the plot. His best known scenes of recognition emerge from points of manners. When Isabel Archer sees her husband seated in the presence of Madame Merle, for example, she divines through inference their intimate history: "Their relative position, their absorbed mutual gaze, struck her as something detected."[38] Assailed by this vision, Isabel comes to understand the character of the man she has married. More, she understands her own folly for taking this vulgar adventurer on his own terms as "the first gentleman in Europe" (*Portrait of a Lady*, 348). In *The Ambassadors*, Lambert Strether resists a similar awakening to the knowledge that Chad Newsome and Madame de Vionnet are lovers. He constructs his own "truth" of their "virtuous attachment" from suppositions accepted and denied, from contradictory interpretations and outright fabrications: "He had heard of old, only what he *could* then hear; what he could do now was to think of three months ago as a point in the far past. All voices had grown thicker and meant more things; they crowded on him as he moved about—it was the way they sounded together that wouldn't let him be still."[39] As with Isabel, the process of discerning new measures exposes the parameters of his own loss. When the dictates and proportions of manners change, so do the very terms and conditions of thought (*Ambassadors*, 196).

James recognized the various things (from curios to the remembered accents of youth) that provide the "*human fringes* we necessarily trail after us through life" (*Backward Glance*, 191). Ironically, considering his articles on American women, these symbols of manners had become less and less important in his later fiction — so much so that Wharton accused him of suspending *The Golden Bowl*'s main characters in a void. Despite his suggestive title, James had written a novel of manners in which there appeared to be no direct connection between characters and a larger social world. This happens partly because the setting has a physical, stable reality, while its characters fluctuate in reaction to one another.[40] James often thought of the first half of a novel acting "as the state or theatre for the second half" (*Art of the Novel*, 86). In *The Golden Bowl*, he stages and then dispenses with the material trappings of the novel of manners, paving the way for Cather's theory of the modern novel expressed in "The Novel *Démeublé*" (1936). Ironically, this "void" makes the centrality of manners, which govern, reflect, and sometimes determine the sum of human psychology, more apparent. "That was my problem . . . and my *gageure*," James remembered, "to play the small handful of values really for all they were worth" (*Art of the Novel*, 330–31). Personality becomes for James — and later for F. Scott Fitzgerald — an unbroken "series of successful gestures."[41] His serial characterization of self assimilates the thinking of his brother William, who saw in human nature the writing of an ever-unfolding autobiography, which chance and change affect.[42]

III

In the latter part of his life, James struggled even to finish a piece of fiction. Like many writers, he wondered how he could talk about the past and present when each seemed jeopardized by the horror of the First World War. After the war, other writers solved the problem structurally, though they retained James's stylized meditations on consciousness. Virginia Woolf, Ernest Hemingway, Willa Cather, and Ellen Glasgow literally cleave their novels into pieces. Woolf divides life before and after the war with the "Time Passing" section of *To the Lighthouse* (1927); Hemingway uses intruded, italicized chapters between the short stories that constitute *In Our Time* (1925); Cather suspends her metanarrative to include a character's diary in *The Professor's House* (1925); and Glasgow bridges the Civil War and the First World War through memory in "The Deep Past" chapter of *The Sheltered Life* (1932). Writing without the comfort of distance, the very, very late James saw life less in terms of division than co-existence, the opposite of his response in *The American Scene* or his *Harper's Bazar* articles. For him, as for those who followed him between the First and Second World

Wars, boundaries became more mutable, whether between nations, selves, time, or fictional forms.

Four years before his visit to the United States, James had started and abandoned *The Sense of the Past*. Nine years later, in 1909, he made notes for *The Ivory Tower*. In the summer of 1914, he returned to both manuscripts, hoping that the concentration required for writing would offer an escape of sorts from present realities. James's immediate challenge lay in recuperating, if not reinventing, the novel of manners for readers living through a period of catastrophic change — changes so great that the facts of daily existence made all prior assumptions about civilization inadequate. Given such conditions, the act of writing seems heroic and the incompleteness of James's manuscripts perhaps inevitable.

In a merely titular way, *The Sense of the Past* turns on William James's belief that history dates from and is altered through the intervention of individual lives. Its hero, an American named Ralph Pendrel, literally steps into history, exchanging places with a double who thrived nearly a century before in 1820 London. The reverse of James's 1904–5 journey, the situation pits an established set of manners against those in transition. Cleverly exploiting the popularity of historical romances, he makes any escape from the present hopeless and surprisingly undesirable.

James conceived the tale along the lines of his most famous ghost story, "The Turn of the Screw" (1898). When Howells had suggested he write a fifty-thousand-word story that contained "an international ghost," he wondered if his manuscript of *The Sense of the Past* might serve.[43] James wanted to create a "quasi-Turn-of-Screw effect," as it gradually dawns on Pendrel that he has become imprisoned in a particular "form of the Past" for which he is "so intimately and secretly wrong."[44] Like "The Turn of the Screw," the story might be seen as a "Gothic" of manners; that is, one in which manners become mysteriously uninterpretable and characters find themselves operating in accidentally intersecting realities. As a result, identity becomes incidental and behavior disembodied from the personality it supposedly expresses.

Where "The Turn of the Screw" explores a breakdown in manners that leads to transgressions against children,[45] *The Sense of the Past* explores trespasses that make it impossible to resume a prior life. James ends by condemning the very kind of "consecrated English tradition" (*American Scene*, 470) he had advocated in *The American Scene* and that now appeared unresponsive to current conditions. Once Pendrel enters the past, the surrounding universe barely intrudes, and this designed absence contributes to the book's claustrophobic atmosphere. Pendrel, the author of "An Essay in the Aid of History," believes that he can penetrate the past because it is codified and therefore subject to mastery. Instead, he finds that the tone and manners (which James advocated in his *Harper's Bazar* articles) are no less philistine than those of the future. Manners grow intimately from culture, James argues again but with a different conclusion; they cannot and should not be imposed. Out of step with the past and with a present continuing in his absence, Pendrel risks losing a sense of who he ever was.

James both acknowledges and resists the social construction of identity that Howells explored in *An Imperative Duty*. Whether a reflection on his method, the nature of human identity, or the writing of history, the novel emphasizes the risks of reifying a past that by definition must remain fluid. Pendrel had hoped "to cultivate some *better* sense of the past" (*Sense of the Past*, 101; emphasis mine), not to prove, as he succeeds in doing, the falsity of his own life. More opportunistic and less empathic than he supposes, Pendrel initially enjoys the freedom that his doubleness bestows. Part of that freedom, which involves violations of trust and hospitality, is moral. Pendrel has few scruples about withholding information from his alter ego, and he ravishes the consciousness of the young woman who helps him regain his former life. Pendrel's self-deception indicates his compromised identity. Before leaving, he tells the American ambassador in London, "I really believe I ought to be tracked, to be subject to identification, to have an eye kept on me" (*Sense of the Past*, 106-7). Pendrel, the artist, "that queer monster," as James called himself (Edel, 690), intuits that he is in danger and also dangerous. His infiltration of the past, which might or might not change the present, has insidious implications.

Unable to count on his genius, his natural taste, the inexhaustible sensibility that has always saved him, Pendrel learns the risk of creative immersion. He follows his "sense" at the expense of other "truths" or ways of knowing. Danger lies, as the novel's Jekyll-and-Hyde plot intimates, in a method that becomes overly introspective, self-referential, and narcissistic. Functioning like a secret agent, Pendrel increasingly fears exposure. He worries that his double can observe him, whereas he cannot observe his double; and that a friend of the family, an effete connoisseur, who represents the perverse extension of James's own aesthetic conceits, will intuit his impersonation. To this extent, *The Sense of the Past* echoes the artistic impotence underlying *The American Scene*: the psychological predicament reveals a hero divided from himself. At the same time, James suggests, through Pendrel's recovery, that history can be approached only through "sense" or inspiration, not so-called facts. More significantly perhaps, James sides with

America, the place to which Pendrel imaginatively returns through his expected marriage to a Euro-phobic woman aptly named Aurora. As in much of his early fiction, James warns against too intimate a communion between past and present. Knowledge can rob someone like Pendrel of the innocence (it may be ignorance) he needs to meet an unknowable future with courage. It seems oddly fitting that James returned to this novel after writing *A Small Boy and Others* (1913) and *Notes of a Son and Brother* (1914), memoirs that might be said to violate the past in the sense that they rewrite it. Not only did James combine events to give his narrative coherence; he also revised letters from his father and brother to make them more readable: "I did instinctively regard it at last as all my truth, to do what I would with" (Edel, 672-73).

The Sense of the Past contributes to the evolution of the novel of manners by responding to nihilism, which for James means the rejection of established laws and institutions; in short, it responds to the idea that no objective basis for either truth or conduct exists. James's return to this earlier manuscript was a return to his faith in the power of manners, whose amorphous, multidimensional nature made them capable of communicating worlds that were not necessarily better and probably never actually existed, but worlds that through an implied dialogue or the pressure of the unvoiced past still had something to teach.

IV

In a world gone mad, James sought a form that would allow a submerged logic to surface through the interplay of different narratives. He does this historically in *The Sense of the Past* and symbolically in *The Ivory Tower*. *The Ivory Tower* belongs to a group of novels, including Howells's *A Hazard of New Fortunes* (1890) and Theodore Dreiser's *The Financier* (1912), that examine the "poetry" of money (to use Howells's word) and its impact on American culture. In 1913, James wrote Edith Wharton to congratulate her on her "epic Serial" then running in *Scribner's*. *The Custom of the Country* follows the marital fortunes of Undine Spragg and those of her first and fourth husband, the multimillionaire Elmer Moffat. "I hang on the sequences of The Custom," James assured her, "with a beating heart & *such* a sense of your craft, your cunning, your devilish resource in the perpetration of them. . . . But I am sunk in *every* abject incompetence."[46] James's mood soon changed when Charles Scribner commissioned "another great novel to balance *The Golden Bowl*."[47] That novel became *The Ivory Tower*, financed secretly by Wharton's royalties from *The Custom of the Country*.

Worried about James's health and the erosion of his income, Wharton had arranged for Scribner's to divert four thousand dollars from her account to James with the understanding that an equal sum would follow the completion of his manuscript. Even Charles Scribner, who felt "mean and caddish" about the deception, could not deny that it had rejuvenated James.

James set *The Ivory Tower* in his childhood home of Newport, Rhode Island, where he, William, and John LaFarge had spent hours discussing life and art in William Hunt's studio. Revisiting Newport on his tour of the States, he had imagined its palaces and endless lawns and silver air as the scene of "the great American novel" (*American Scene*, 763). The novel's plot picks up where *The Sense of the Past* leaves off; that is, the protagonist, Graham ("Gray") Fielder, comes to America in time to inherit, through the intervention of his childhood friend, Rosanna Gaw, his uncle's fortune. Rather than recapturing the past, Gray enters the future, which James predictably defines in terms of material excess. Challenged to come to terms with the awful legacy of the Gilded Age and its ever-present "chink of money,"[48] Gray falls almost immediately prey to a pair of poor lovers, Cissy Foy and Horton Vint, who envy his wealth.

To a large extent, James's protagonists exist outside, and can therefore critique the fictional social space he associates with the whole of America. Rosanna absents herself from the plot, as Gray embarks on his sentimental education. In an ironic inversion, the symbol of the ivory tower, a gift from Rosanna to Gray, means living in, rather than retiring from, America's social milieu. Newport might as well be Lambert Strether's Paris or Merton Densher's Venice, since it functions as a prelude to self-knowledge. For James, the problem lies in society's inability to separate getting from being. You cannot have anything to do with money, Rosanna explains to Gray, without having to do things "*for* it" (*Ivory Tower*, 136). This partially explains why Gray refuses to act when Horton Vint embezzles his fortune. Gray's belief in a benevolent system of reciprocity allows James to redefine "property" in terms of his protagonist's moral-aesthetic "capacity" (*Ivory Tower*, 197). Understanding something deeply enough makes it count. In this way, *The Ivory Tower* justifies what James's visit to the United States had so undermined: his own process of penetration. And to the extent that *The Ivory Tower* affirms the imagination, it remains a hopeful book.

Contemplating his subject in *The Ivory Tower*, James may well have remembered Nathaniel Hawthorne, whose biography he wrote for the *English Men of Letters* series. In his preface to *The House of the Seven Gables*, Hawthorne hoped without hope that "romance might effectually convince mankind—or, indeed, any one man — of the folly of tumbling down an avalanche of ill-gotten gold, or real estate, on the heads of an unfortunate posterity."[49] James's definition of "romance," articulated in the preface to *The American*, placed less emphasis than Hawthorne's on contrasting historical periods and more on defining atmosphere. "The only *general* attribute of projected romance that I can see," he writes, "is . . . experience liberated, . . . experience disengaged, disembroiled, disencumbered, exempt from the conditions that we usually know to attach to it and, if we wish so to put the matter, drag upon it, and operating in a medium which relieves it, in a particular interest, of the inconvenience of a *related*, a measurable state, a state subject to all our vulgar communities" (*Art of the Novel*, 33). This description sounds curiously like his later description of Newport in *Notes of a Son and Brother* (1914), published the year he reworked the manuscript of *The Ivory Tower*: "Newport imposed itself . . . to so remarkable a degree as the one right residence, in all our great country, for those tainted, under whatever attenuations, with the quality and effect of detachment."[50]

James thought that the most effective romances performed a kind of sleight-of-hand by loosening the moorings of realism. *The Ivory Tower* does this through its setting (the one right place for those aloof from time), its chimeric or heightened prose, and the mythologizing of types. Rosanna is an "urgent Juno"; another Newport hostess hovers like "a bustling goddess in the enveloping cloud of her court" (*Ivory Tower*, 22). These comparisons, at once aggrandizing and satiric, challenge the common assumption that novels of manners derive their authority largely from the accurate representation of specific actualities. James's attenuation of the novel of manners (its appropriation of elements commonly associated with other forms) calls attention to its own construction. Foreshadowing contemporary novelists' self-conscious, often parodic focus on form, *The Ivory Tower* not only allows James to comment on the making of fiction, it subverts notions of a clear trajectory of American fiction from romance to realism.[51]

Oddly for James, the First World War corroborated what it most jeopardized, his own sense of the past. It made him remember the start of another war, fifty-four years earlier, and the hours of tension after the firing upon Fort Sumter. The invasion of Belgium "reproduced with intensity the agitation" caused by President Lincoln's call to arms.[52] The parallel was itself a way of knitting past and present. James wrote his old friend and fellow novelist Rhoda Broughton that the war made him feel sick beyond any cure. They should have been spared the wreck of their belief "that through the long years we had seen civilization grow and the worst become impossible" (Edel, 694). Inconsolable, he found strange comfort in the shock of recognition. Humanity had lived through this bitter, arid, honorless void before.

To James, war was the ultimate expression of barbarism, the opposite of everything that he had always valued about manners themselves — "sympathy, ingenuity, tact, and taste."[53] With others of the time, he felt that the future of civilization hung upon the fate of France, the nation that seemed most to embody these traits. "What happens to France," he explained, "happens to all that part of ourselves which we are most proud, and most finely advised, to enlarge and cultivate and consecrate."[54] James saw monuments like Rheims as sacred symbols, which testified to the collective genius of the human spirit and its will to survive. On receiving news of the bombing of the cathedral, he wrote Wharton: "There it *was* — & now all the tears of rage of the bereft millions & all the crowding curses of all the wondering ages will never bring a stone of it back! . . . it helps me a little to think of how they can be made to *wear* the shame, in the pitiless glare of history, forever & ever."[55] Rheims represented the process he associated with civilization itself, an accretion of history, tradition, and taste that expressed whatever lay inmost in a people. A necessary reminder of the limitations of any single imagination, the medieval church spoke of human yearning and endeavor, of this ephemeral thing James called "culture." "That is my moral," he wrote as though leaving his own epitaph: "I believe in Culture."[56] If the ameliorating effects of manners through the centuries seemed to die from a single Balkan bullet, they also rose from the history of the hour. James looked at a world on the brink of anarchy and found small decencies and heroism in the daily patterns of life. The silent eloquence of manners — the sharing of scant provisions, the honoring of suffering — affirmed humanity itself.

James's complex, sometimes paradoxical thinking about manners reflects their almost limitless capacity for communicating the nuances of human existence. He knew from his expatriation and subsequent visit to America that the attempt to mix them can result in estrangement. He also believed that his father's vision of a "denationalized" humanity, animated by the spirit of fellowship, demanded the effort.[57] Like Howells, James objected to the arbitrariness of manners, their personal and occasional quality. Resisting the knowledge his own novels afforded, he still sought an ideal balance between individual desire and the requirements of society. Manners confirmed what made life worth living, and if he venerated his "own congruous kind,"[58] his definition of who that left in and left out ultimately expanded to include compatriots on both sides of the Atlantic.

CHAPTER THREE

Edith Wharton

A Backward Glance

"The past is the present, isn't it? It's the future too."

EUGENE O'NEILL, *A Long Day's Journey into Night*

"You come among us speaking our language and not knowing what we
mean . . . we're fools enough to imagine that because you copy our ways and
pick up our slang you understand anything about the things that make life
decent and honourable for us!"

EDITH WHARTON, *The Custom of the Country*

I

Edith Wharton (1862–1937) was an avid reader of histories as varied as Steven
Runciman's *Byzantine Civilization*, Pierre Gaxotte's *Siècle de Louis XV*, and Paul
Mariéton's *Une Histoire d'amour*. She loved the "little by-ways of history" so much
that an essay on the court of Piépoudré could make her want to write a poem.[1] On
her spring wanderings through Italy, she felt herself guided by Goethe and Gol-
doni. She remembered playing tag as a child on the Monte Pincio, hunting bits of
colored rock among the statues and stone-pines of the Palatine, and strolling
with her mother across the daisy-strewn lawns of the Villa Doria-Pamphili.
Wharton owed her early years in Europe to the depreciation of American cur-
rency in the depression following the Civil War—a "happy misfortune" that
provided her with a life-long standard of beauty and of "old-established order."
Yet when she finally turned to her own account of eighteenth-century Italy in *The
Valley of Decision* (1902), she could not explain how she had absorbed through
her pores "the gossip of contemporary diarists and travellers" and details about
everything from geography to portraiture.[2]

If Wharton conveniently forgot the lists she kept of popular eighteenth-
century scents (jasmine, musk, and rosemary) and items of personal decoration
such as diamond-hilted swords and curled wigs,[3] she further overlooked her

powers of recall. She possessed — or was possessed by — an uncanny visual memory. From earliest childhood, just the thought of certain places frightened her. She especially hated her Aunt Elizabeth's house, a turreted example of Hudson River Gothic that reflected its owner's "granitic exterior" (*Backward Glance*, 28). Later she realized that her aunt's house signified everything she found wrong with American civilization. "The contrast between the old & the new, between stored beauty & tradition & amenity over there, & the crassness here," she wrote Sara Norton in 1903, made her feel like a one of those "wretched exotics . . . produced in a European glass-house": "*we* are none of us Americans, we don't think or feel as the Americans do."[4]

It might be said that having imbibed European standards of beauty before she lost her first tooth, Wharton never saw the United States from anything save a "foreign" perspective. A kind of American Tocqueville, she settled in Europe "by degrees and stages" until France became her permanent home in 1911. Her friend and historian Gaillard Lapsley explained that

> [w]hen she made her move . . . she was to all appearance standing (in America) between two worlds. . . . The old social organisation was in dissolution, and the society in which she worked, still socially and economically well placed, was in process of being pushed eastward and across the Atlantic; and the time was not yet when anyone could dare to affirm that the old American tradition could maintain, even with notable modifications, its continuous American identity.[5]

Wharton, who was and was not both American and French, wrote about an American past in the context of her European present and about an American present from which she was physically absent. Her particular historical moment, as Lapsley notes, made former contrasts between Europe and the United States increasingly meaningless. No longer could the old world be characterized by wisdom and corruption, the new by ignorance and candor. There was no monolithic civilization called "Europe" but a collection of separate countries impelled, as the events leading up to the First World War demonstrated, by provincial needs and politics. The same was true in a United States divided along ethnic, religious, and regional concerns. To extend Lapsley's point, the notion of a continuous national identity, the settled standards and the slow accretion of history that made one nation this and another that, gave way to fears about anarchy or the ubiquitous spread of mass culture — the underlying focus of much of Wharton's fiction in the 1920s. *The Glimpses of the Moon* (1922), *The Mother's Recompense* (1925), *Twilight Sleep* (1927), and *The Children* (1928) all criticize the banality of modern life.[6] The contrasts that had inspired Henry James's early books or her own letter to Sara Norton simply did not serve.

Whatever their similarities, Wharton was nearly a generation younger than James, and her view of civilization came to differ from his in one crucial instance. James's later fiction is essentially a fiction of exile. It shows, to take *The Ambassadors* (1903) as an example, the impossibility of belonging to either Paris or Woolett. Wharton's Europeanization of America and Americanization of Europe in a novel like *The Custom of the Country* (1913) heralded a different age, one in which the rich formed an international cadre of pleasure seekers with no common stamp except the impress of money. It certainly marked a different understanding of the international novel that in her hands had always grown from the divination of conflicting histories. Now it became cosmopolitan or reflective of civilizations growing indistinct as they responded to the pressure of social changes both at home and abroad. Wharton's late fiction might be called one of concession, no matter how grudging and resistant. It acknowledges, as in *The Age of Innocence* (1920), the gradual conflation of old-world "institutions, traditions, mannerisms, conservatisms" (everything save women's clothes and having to go to church on Sundays), with the "innocence" of the new.[7]

II

Wharton's visual acuity partly determined the way she wrote her "historical" novels, *The Valley of Decision* and *The Age of Innocence*. Places spoke to her in a chorus of past and present voices. Wharton imagined them accruing a kind of logic through time. Where her friend the painter Robert Norton saw blues converging along the coast of the Mediterranean Sea, she saw Xerxes on his throne commanding the Battle of Salamis.[8] It never failed to incense her when Italians seemed unconscious of their surroundings, "& ignorant of the treasures of art & history among which they have grown up." "Better to be an American," she wrote in an atypical burst of patriotism, "& bring to it all a mind & eye unblunted by custom."[9]

Wharton wondered how she could have become a novelist, never having met one. Old New York had tolerated genius in its cooks and wine vendors, not in debutantes with eighteen-inch waists. Nonetheless, its upholstered drawing rooms and antiquities brought home from grand tours fed the imagination of someone whose visceral response to places imbued them with human characteristics. No less than the characters in her novels, they pleaded to have their stories told. Wharton's first story, written around age eleven, already shows her awareness of the social importance of place. It begins, "Oh, how do you do, Mrs. Brown?" said Mrs. Tompkins. "If only I had known you were going to call I should have tidied up the drawing-room." Wharton's subsequent insistence on historical accuracy—knowing the *exact* date that Christine Nilsson sang *Faust* at the Academy of Music, for example—owes something to the reception of this initial effort. Never would she forget the sudden drop of her creative frenzy when her mother returned her story "with the icy comment, 'Drawing-rooms are always tidy' " (*Backward Glance*, 73).

In Wharton's many books of travel, decoration, and fiction, places reflect and shape the people who live in them. "I have sometimes thought," she wrote in her short story "The Fullness of Life," "that a woman's nature is like a great house full of rooms:

> There is the hall, through which everyone passes in going in and out; the drawing room, where one receives formal visits; the sitting room, where the members of the family come and go as they list; but beyond that, far beyond, are other rooms, the handles of whose doors are never turned; no one knows the way to them; no one knows whither they lead; and in the innermost room, the holy of holies, the soul sits alone and waits for a footstep that never comes.[10]

As this passage suggests, Wharton attributed a spatial dimension to manners as well as history. She presents the self as if it were a series of Chinese boxes, each belonging to a particular place. Moving from the publicity of the hall to the solitude of the secreted sanctum, she highlights the tyrannies of time and place (the mandates of the drawing room, for instance, as opposed to the casual solicitations of the sitting room) that would become a central theme in *The Decoration of Houses* (1897), *The Valley of Decision*, and *The Age of Innocence*. These books show the evolution of—sometimes the contradictions in—Wharton's thinking about a veritable Gorgon's knot of topics, from manners and history to civilization and place.

For Wharton, history acquired its meaning from the juxtaposition of events or the assignment of spatial relationships. The reshuffling of events in time, which obviously changes the structure of a narrative, similarly changes its meaning.[11] In Wharton's hands, chronicles of manners read as though they were histories; that is, they tell the story of a particular people or period or civilization. "If we need another past so badly," Van Wyck Brooks once asked, "is it inconceivable that we might discover one, that we might even invent one?"[12] Wharton responded, as

Brooks suggests, by "inventing" or reinventing specific civilizations such as Italy and France, or subcultures of a larger culture, from Nathaniel Hawthorne's New England to, of course, the insular society of her youth. But she did something else, too. She forced her compatriots to think about the concept of "culture," which in Wharton's writing can differ slightly from her use of the term *civilization*. For Wharton, culture meant something greater than Henry James's whole envelope of circumstances; something greater than Lionel Trilling's "hum and buzz of implication."[13] Transmitted from one generation to the next, it comprised what had proved most excellent in manners themselves; whereas civilization (notwithstanding its kinship to culture) is more neutral and includes the full range of practices and credos that make up a given society.

To echo Matthew Arnold, with whom Wharton usually agreed, "the power of social life and manners" acts as "one of the great elements in our humanisation."[14] Changes in manners marked, from Wharton's view, a change in history. They revealed how people have ordered and understood a series of events, how they have seen and represented the self. This last anticipates the other, seemingly contradictory attribute that Wharton imputed to culture — an ahistorical dimension that made it a "land of letters" or a place where compatible people meet across time and cultures. This was the country she appreciated above all others, one where a "common stock of allusions, cross-references, [and] pleasantries" (*Backward Glance*, 192) established a bond of sympathy and exclusivity.

In retrospect, it seems fitting that a "would-be novelist of manners" (*Backward Glance*, 73) began her career with a book that made a historical argument for the importance of place. *The Decoration of Houses* (1897), written with Ogden Codman, an architect whose clients included Cornelius Vanderbilt and John D. Rockefeller Jr., shows Wharton at her most orthodox. Audience and genre naturally affected the tone of this book, as it did that of *Italian Backgrounds* (1905). And so did Wharton's own prejudices about culture. *The Decoration of Houses* is important because it gives Wharton's initial thinking about large topics such as history and civilization that continued to intrigue her over the course of forty years. *The Decoration of Houses* is important for another reason. It gave her the confidence to write her first novel, *The Valley of Decision*, which as a historical novel provided a model for maybe her best-known novel of manners, *The Age of Innocence*.

As a novelist of manners, Wharton has been called a poet of "interior" decoration. Typically, her characters cannot think of themselves apart from their surroundings without "suffering a certain loss of identity."[15] She herself explained that she imagined her subjects "architectonically" like a man and executed them like a woman, sacrificing breadth to focus on the "small incidental effects that make up episodical characterization."[16] In other words, Wharton conceived both her characters and the plots of her novels spatially, continuing or digressing from a series of events that shows the present growing out of the past.

Edmund Wilson once observed that in Wharton's fiction *décors* became "agents of tragedy."[17] In *The Decoration of Houses*, décors possess an equal, arguably less pernicious, power, but one that carries over to her fiction. They project intangible attitudes and behaviors that testify to the cultivation and judgment of their inhabitants' opinions, principles, prejudices, and relations with other people. According to Wharton, human behavior cannot be isolated from the setting, the culture, in which it exists. Neither can it be estranged from what it produces or the responses, the history, it generates. In both her fiction and nonfiction, manners function as cultural indicators or "operating forces" for divining the order and ranking the values by which a people, a community, or individuals live.[18] *The Decoration of Houses* seeks to define class by making assumptions about its ideal reader and codifying patterns of behavior usually associated with the upper classes.[19] Whether by coincidence or design, Wharton fixes the stratification of classes central for historical novels and novels of manners while tracing the customary practices that James thought crucial to fiction.

It should come as no surprise that Wharton framed her history of house decoration in a matrix of European cultures, departing from contemporary architects who advocated a purely "American" style. She thought American designers too bound to English taste, and *The Decoration of Houses* pointedly opens with an epigraph taken from Henri Mayeux's *La Composition Décorative*, followed by a list of books consulted in descending order from France, England, and (coupled together) Germany and Italy. Wharton, who read and (alas) recommended books on evolution and race theory by Joseph-Arthur de Gobineau, George Vacher Laponge, and Vernon Lyman Kellogg, saw English architecture developing from a French model. "In the Anglo-Saxon mind," she explains, "beauty is not spontaneously born of material wants, as it is with the Latin races."[20] Wharton particularly disliked the kind of decorative eclecticism that had little regard for the way people actually lived.

Wharton's second objection to so-called American design concerned its emphasis on openness. The structure of her book—whose individual chapters focus on architectural elements from walls to windows, and, more importantly, on specific rooms—atomizes space. Chapters begin with short histories tracing the evolution of specific spaces such as the ballroom or the morning-room (kitchens do not seem to exist for the readers of *The Decoration of Houses*). The opening chapter, entitled "The Historical Tradition," regrets "the decline of the arts in Italy" and again presents France, specifically Paris, as a model for American designers (*Decoration*, 1).

However conservative Wharton's ideas about culture, they have radical implications that she would probably not have approved and could not entirely ignore. An international aesthetic, for example, blurs national differences. Any globalization of manners approximates and destroys through its democratization her vision of a land of letters composed of a happy few. *The Decoration of Houses*, like other manuals dedicated to manners, ironically undercuts its own conscious elitism by turning the "classes" (to paraphrase William Dean Howells) into the "masses."

Scribner's assumed that they would sell a limited edition of *The Decoration of Houses* to society friends of the authors. Given the popularity of magazines for women and the home, as well as periodicals specializing in furnishings, upholstery, cabinet making, and decor, they surprisingly underestimated the appeal such a manual would have for middle-class householders. Wharton received royalty checks from its sales until she died. Americans had entered a period of new abundance, and their houses, as the economist Simon Nelson Patten noted in *The New Basis of Civilization* (1907), became "crowded with tawdry, unmeaning, and useless objects" that signaled the superiority and success of their possessor.[21] Capitalizing on the middle class's desire for guidance in home decoration, Wharton tried to convince her readers that lace-petticoat lamp-shades, irrelevant bric-a-brac, tufted furniture, and ubiquitous gilt were nothing more than forms of "varnished barbarism" (*Decoration*, 198). Such decoration merely exposed a person's uncertainty about what constitutes "good taste." Though Wharton understood that *The Decoration of Houses* owed its existence to this uncertainty, she did not hesitate to play upon it. The book incorporates a kind of inverse snobbery that denies and then reinforces readers' sense of their own preeminence. A feeling for beauty cannot be bought, she notes, though study can render it "profitable" (*Decoration*, 18). The true aesthete realizes that the " 'tact of omission' " or an artful simplicity characterizes the "master-hand" (*Decoration*, 198), whether it belongs to an interior designer or to a beginning novelist.

The Decoration of Houses can be read as Wharton's response to turn-of-the-century attitudes about the home, consumption, and what Herbert Marcuse calls "the aesthetic dimension." Viewing art in the context of its social relations, Marcuse assigned it a political function that curiously echoes Wharton, perhaps because taste cannot help representing the interests that it would govern.[22] For Wharton, manners contribute to national "progress," but also to the internationalizing of local values. "It is a fact recognized by political economists," she writes, "that changes in manners and customs, no matter under what form of government, usually originate with the wealthy or aristocratic minority, and are thence transmitted to the other classes. Thus the *bourgeois* of one generation lives more like the aristocrat of a previous generation than like his own predecessors" (*Decoration*, 5). Such statements place Wharton's actual reader, who bought her book searching for the very "artistic" hints Wharton scorns, in a tradition stretching back to Louis Quatorze.

The progression of manners and conventions envisioned in *The Decoration of Houses* transforms the average householder into a purveyor of culture. Getting and spending, in this context, indicates cultural ascent, not crass avarice. According to Wharton, the intrinsic beauty of any object "is hardly more valuable" than "its suggestion of a mellower civilization — of days when rich men were patrons of 'the art of elegance,' and when collecting . . . was one of the obligations of a noble leisure" (*Decoration*, 187). This is how Isabella Stewart Gardiner, who filled a Venetian *palazzo* on Boston's Fenway with Renaissance art (selected by Wharton's friend Bernard Berenson), envisioned her role. Despite Wharton's antipathy toward Gardiner, she not only justifies, she ennobles the kind of ardent consumerism Gardiner grandly typified and Thorstein Veblen pilloried in *The Theory of the Leisure Class: An Economic Study of Institutions* (1899).

Wharton's defense of spending seems strange for a writer who went on to criticize the coupling of connoisseurship and consumption in *The House of Mirth* (1905) and *The Custom of the Country* (1913). Although Wharton also wrote dozens of short stories that focus on art, perhaps none so fully articulates her attitude about collecting as "The Daunt Diana" (1909). This story offers a perspective on the performative aspects of assembling and displaying a collection like Mrs. Gardiner's. Wharton had ambivalent feelings about the individual acquisition of priceless objects, as her critique of Berenson's methods of attribution in "The Daunt Diana" make uncomfortably clear. The worth of a collection depends upon the relationship and arrangement of its separate pieces, which have less value individually than commonly. Collecting is itself episodic in the sense that it involves a process of accumulation and divestment. Wharton's protagonist, Humphrey Neave, inherits a collection that he sells at a staggering loss only to have the pleasure of reassembling it: "the discovery, the struggle, the capture, the first divine moment of possession," they had become part of his imagination.[23] For Neave, the act of appropriation, which displays the collector's status and taste, has come to involve agreeable, even sexual associations. Collecting should have its own etiquette and ethics, and Wharton questions a process that can violate the integrity of the objects themselves through Neave's practice of fingering an object until he has secreted its essence ("Daunt Diana," 52) and robbed it of its worth.[24] To some extent, "worth" becomes "relative" (to make an egregious pun), for Neave's uncle amassed the original collection from the sale of women's girdles — a fact that highlights the blurring of commercial and aesthetic values.[25]

In *The Decoration of Houses*, unlike "The Daunt Diana," individual acts of acquisition become a positive force for sociological change. Wharton contends that the law of supply and demand gives control to the consumer, who by buying nothing save the time-honored "best" can impose his or her own aesthetic on producers. Such an insistence on quality affects the design of goods offered to people of all classes, thereby improving the general "manner" of American life (*Decoration*, 27). In an ideal world, there would come a time when people's needs for comfort and beauty had been satiated to the degree that getting and spending would have no appeal. Until that time, civilized people have almost a moral obligation to surround themselves with things of beauty, because they preserve — through their evocation of some ancient "racial power" — what these things meant to "far-off minds of which ours are the . . . reconstituted fragments."[26]

To the derision of her critics, Wharton extended her argument to encompass the education of children, whom she felt were harmed by "daily intercourse with poor pictures, trashy 'ornaments' and . . . namby-pamby prettiness" (*Decoration*, 175, 179, 183). Wharton's belief that a child's sense of beauty will develop in the proper setting was neither revolutionary nor eccentric. It had been part of the standard wisdom imparted by advice books since *The American Woman's Home* (1869), written by Catherine Beecher and Harriet Beecher Stowe, had promoted home decoration as a tool of education. "If art is really a factor in civilization," Wharton wrote in the spirit of John Ruskin, then the formation of a child's aesthetic sense ranks with that of other civic virtues (*Decoration*, 174). She went so far as to put her theories of noblesse oblige into practice by volunteering in the Newport, Rhode Island, schools. Apart from acting as a judge for essay contests, she donated a dozen pictures and selected plaster busts of classical and mythic figures with every expectation that they would make for better conduct.[27] Despite her complaint that "dead and gone predecessors" have a way of exerting a tyrannical influence across the centuries (*Decoration*, 18), she could not resist exerting her own. Thinking education the single most essential factor in the advancement of civilization,[28] Wharton lectured her readers on the transformation of the bedroom, for instance, from a public and therefore more ornate room to a private space. It's pleasant to remember her inconsistency, for Wharton occasionally allowed friends to glimpse her in bed: her head covered with a lace cap, an inkpot precariously balanced on one knee, and "the dog of the moment" curled quietly under her left elbow.[29]

Although Wharton does not mention Oscar Wilde, her argument advances several critical points he made in his 1882 lecture "The Practical Application of the Principles of the Aesthetic Theory to Exterior and Interior House Decoration, with Observations upon Dress and Personal Ornaments." Wherever he went, Wilde found "bad wallpapers horribly designed," horsehair sofas, machine-made furniture, "meaningless chandeliers," and iron stoves "garnished" with funeral urns. To him, no less than Wharton, bad art was "a great deal worse than no art at all." Any piece must be more "valuable" or pleasing than the architectural space its presence modifies. Simplicity, beauty, harmony, and function — these should be the decorator's guiding principles, and they come as the "accumulation of habits of long and delightful observation."[30]

The Decoration of Houses is finally as prescriptive about its readers' behavior as their surroundings. Analogous to a manners manual, it serves as a guide to civilized living. Wharton warns her implicitly female audience that "many houses are deserted by the men of the family for lack of those simple comforts which they find at their clubs" (*Decoration*, 20). Readers should know that a well-appointed room does not in itself constitute good taste. That ultimately rests on the practices of its occupants. Libraries become libraries only when people read in them. Otherwise, they serve as trysting places, as in *The House of Mirth*, or large closets for storing books. A room's definition depends upon its use. Manners must similarly function as an integral part of a person's personality. When they mask a person's nature, they become superfluous — mere window dressing. Wharton's own houses, the Mount, in Lenox, Massachusetts, Pavillon Colombe, in a suburb of Paris, and Ste. Claire, overlooking the Mediterranean in Hyères, had rooms with distinct functions, reflecting the importance Wharton attributed to privacy, decorum, and order. For Edmond de Goncourt, they recalled the world of Balzac, not "some American Babylon of the future."[31]

And this is perhaps why *The Decoration of Houses* continues to interest readers. Wharton, who began by assembling a world that stood in some relationship to her own past, shows how places occupy us as much as we occupy them.[32] Her assignment of manners, hierarchies of culture, and spatial orientation were ways of making sense of the "whole inscrutable mystery" she thought life,[33] that "floundering monster" (*Backward Glance*, 379), which neither cranks nor theorists could wholly master, though "grown-up" writers like Anthony Trollope and Leo Tolstoy came close.[34] Whether Wharton wrote about art or architecture, she presumed enduring truths. She had to. Without them, the world would remain nothing but the welter she believed it to be.

III

Wharton came to think of the past as a "necessary prehistory" of the present.[35] The same might be said of *The Decoration of Houses* in relation to the novels that followed, especially *The Valley of Decision*, which rivals its predecessor's descriptions of material culture. Wharton worried that her "archaeologizing" (*Decoration*, 11) had yielded so many indiscriminate facts — from the breeding of lapdogs to the sexual assignations of rich nuns and the castrati (Lewis, *Edith Wharton: A Biography*, 103) — that they might stick out and bump into the reader. In retrospect, she felt that her historical conscience rather than her developing literary talent had governed *The Valley of Decision*, and as a result she grew to see it as a "romantic chronicle, unrolling its episodes like the frescoed legends on the palace walls which formed its background" (*Backward Glance*, 205). Facts (many of them garnered from books borrowed from her friend Charles Eliot Norton, the fine-arts professor at Harvard, and from the Renaissance scholar Vernon Lee) mattered just so much as they contributed to the story.[36] She finally realized that the weakness of the book lay in its insufficient fusing of facts and atmosphere.[37] Unwittingly, she had draped the novel's architecture with useless ornamentation — what she cautioned her readers not to do in *The Decoration of Houses*. Henry James agreed: a portrayal of history had to be made immediate. Burying his criticism in elaborate praise of "a book so accomplished, pondered, saturated, so exquisitely studied & so brilliant," he admonished her in favor of "the *American Subject*. There it is round you. Don't pass it by — the immediate, the real, the ours, the yours, the novelist's that it waits for. . . . DO NEW YORK![38]

Good advice. Wharton might never have done New York, however, or done it differently, without writing a traditional, historical novel first. That project taught her that manners can communicate the soul of a particular society only when integrally tied to character and place. She had conceived manners too narrowly. Details of speech, dress, and behavior may make the past "visitable," to use James's word,[39] but they do not make it felt. Wharton decided that manners convey history by reflecting a more various reality than the happenings they record. They must go beyond certain social-historical conditions to focus, if not on morals, on how we define ourselves and our society.

Despite every one of her books having been designed to appeal to popular taste, critics and readers have persistently identified Wharton with "high" culture. Like James, Wharton wrote books to make money, and she hoped that *The Valley of Decision* would be a best-seller. The idea was not far-fetched, for among her immediate acquaintance she knew at least two best-selling novelists: her doctor, S. Weir Mitchell, the charismatic inventor of the "rest-cure," who had published *The Adventures of Francois* (1898) just a few years before; and Francis Marion Crawford, the brother of one of her closest friends, whose *The Children of the King* (1893), also used Italy to advantage. The year that Wharton published *The Valley of Decision*, another friend, Owen Wister, achieved instant fame with *The Virginian* (1902),[40] a modern Western whose "primitive" frontier setting parallels that of historical romances.[41] Wharton avoided the nostalgia associated with most historical fiction by focusing on social changes and the historical process itself.[42] "The old forms & traditions of court life were still preserved," she wrote her editor W. C. Brownell, "but the immense intellectual & moral movement of the new regime was at work beneath the surface of things."

The central drama of *The Valley of Decision* concerns "the breaking up" of the small Italian principalities at the end of the eighteenth century.[43] Wharton does not try to reconstruct actual events so much as systems of thought, and these are reflected in her section titles, "The Old Order," "The New Order," "The Choice," and "The Reward." The story, set between 1761 and 1795, portrays the fortunes of perhaps the most unlikely named hero in American literature, the reluctant Duke of Pianura, Odo Valsecca. Inspired by the theories of the French encyclopedists, Odo begins his reign envisioning an ideal state in which the guarantees and obligations of the different classes would be adjusted more evenly; instead, he finds himself subject to the church, the nobility, and — not least of all — to his own people, who prefer royal pageantry to civil rights. "The character of each class, with its special passions, ignorances and prejudices, was the sum total of influences so ingrown . . . that they had become a law of thought."[44] Odo's insight comes to include himself. The reign of terror in France and Napoleon's advance toward Italy ironically realigns him, at the novel's end, with "the beliefs and traditions of his caste" (*Valley*, 652).

The Valley of Decision may be most interesting in a way that Wharton did not intend, for it contains a conundrum that brings the whole historical process, along with Wharton's own sense of "eternal verities," into question. It concerns the historian's (and analogously the novelist's) conceit that the welter of life can indeed be mastered. Wharton draws attention to both history and its making through a series of digressions — on the Roman Catholic Church, for instance, and the practices of the minor nobility — which are encapsulated discourses on manners. "There was nothing unusual in Odo's lot. It was that of many children in the eighteenth century, especially those whose parents were cadets of noble houses . . . [a]ll over Italy. (*Valley*, 7). Wharton's focus on form and process works to undermine the authority of her novel's omniscient voice. As she knew from Howells, fiction and history, by testifying to the sensibility of their interpreter, cannot be impersonal. To the degree that *The Valley of Decision* has duelling narrators, Wharton looks forward to a postmodern world where different versions of history compete.

Part way through her book, Wharton literally suspends her narrative, inserting in its place an "Unpublished Fragment from Mr. Arthur Young's *Diary of his Travels in Italy in the Year 1789.*" Arthur Young *was* a historical figure, an Englishman interested in agriculture, who traveled throughout France and Italy between 1787 and 1789.[45] Wharton designs his impressions to intersect with and diverge from her dominant narrative, "fragmenting," in this way, its historical voice. Young's "Unpublished Fragment," itself a parody of the historical Young's real diary, illustrates how history consists of reconstructed, contested, and fictive fragments. By having Young see only what he has been culturally conditioned to see, Wharton highlights the arbitrariness of any historical account. His unquestioned sense of English superiority, which shifts the scale of the narrative from the world to the provincial stage, underscores the nationalistic impulse that drives so many histories.

Wharton's novel becomes, in a sense, a series of texts with a metatext that self-consciously "historicizes" her story for contemporary readers. Nowhere is this clearer than in the section of Young's fictionalized diary. Engaging in a dialogue of sorts with the dominant narrative, the diary also speaks, through the footnotes of Young and a "Female Friend of the Author," with itself. Young realizes the importance of a backward glance, or how his initial response to Italy does not account for the "late unhappy events in France." In other words, he understands the writing of history to involve an ongoing process of revision. His female friend illustrates the conspiratorial, but also contentious, nature of history when she amends his passage on Odo's mistress, an intellectual named Fulvia Vivaldi: "It has before now been observed that the *free* and *volatile* manners of foreign ladies tend to blind the English traveller to the inferiority of their *physical* charms" (*Valley*, 556). The footnote, which asserts the writer's personal and racial supremacy, ironically joins Fulvia and her unknown rival through their connection to Young, a dyed-in-the-wool sexist who enjoys pontificating about women. The footnote disrupts Young's travel journal by turning it, for the moment, into a courtship narrative of Young and his female friend. Its merging of time and space, of history and manners, anticipates Wharton's focus after the First World War on the internationalizing of culture, as it harks back to *The Decoration of Houses'* presentation of an aestheticized historicism achieved through shared practices.[46]

Structurally, *The Valley of Decision* moves from the broadly historical to the intensely personal, with Odo's abdication, exile, and spiritual awakening. After the assassination of Fulvia, Odo goes back to the place where his story began. There he feels "a prayer, yet not a prayer — a reaching out, obscure and inarticulate . . . a loosening of old founts of pity, a longing to be somehow, somewhere reunited to his old belief in life" (*Valley*, 656). His journey, cyclical only in its chapters, has an immaterial dimension that recalls Wharton's land of letters and, paradoxically, undermines the importance of incidents in time, perhaps of history itself.

To some extent, Wharton shared Henry Adams's bleak view of human evolution and progress. The durable lines of Italian architecture, for example, testify to the evils of feudalism, the passions and ambitions of an entrenched elite. Ideas fail Odo because a gulf of tradition and habit separates him from the people he would serve. In *The Valley of Decision*, human development follows no direct, discernable course, which may explain why Odo never knows the content of the long-contemplated book by his mentor, Fulvia's father, "the Origin of Civilization" (*Valley*, 145). Echoing Darwin's title *The Origin of Species*, Wharton shifts the focus of debates about evolution onto the behavior that makes people human. Where Odo sees a procession of humanity in Tiepolo's portraits of "a fur-clad Laplander, a turbaned figure on a dromedary, a blackamoor and a plumed American Indian" (*Valley*, 392), the reader sees him — an Italian nobleman — as just another passing phase in the cavalcade. If Wharton largely rejects the humanist narrative of progress, she also rejects the notion of "great men" determining history. Instead, she argues, as Virginia Woolf would in *A Room of One's Own* (1929), that many ordinary people have added their lives to the sum of human effort (*Valley*, 370). The novel's simultaneous embrace of contradictory views of history also suggests that history may be nothing more than the "gradual and heterogeneous product of remote social conditions" (*Valley*, 636) — of manners that provide a means of marking, recording, evaluating, and reading the past.

Like most historical novels, *The Valley of Decision* finally tells us less about eighteenth-century Italy than about the United States at the turn of the century, reeling from social unrest, the war in the Philippines, and the 1901 assassination of President McKinley by a self-proclaimed anarchist. Wharton depicts eighteenth-century Italy much as she would the United States in *The Custom of the Country:* a society where manners have no connection to feeling and empty rituals provide a form of social control. Luxurious living, polished manners, "the tacit exclusion of all that is ugly or distressing" — these should be the expression of fine feeling, of an individual's aristocracy. They adorn, however, "a dull and vapid society" (*Valley*, 150) in which decoration obscures the inner texture of life. Wharton responded as she had in *The Decoration of Houses*, by emphasizing what endures: if not the idea of beauty, power, and immortality, then the unending struggle for it (*Valley*, 622–23).

IV

Wharton called *The Age of Innocence* a "historical" novel and considered writing a preface to the second edition that would explain her theory about "the small importance of anachronisms" to the genre of historical fiction.[47] Although sham Buhl tables lend *The Age of Innocence* an old-fashioned charm, Wharton's emphasis is on character — less on that of Newland Archer, his wife, May, and his would-be lover, Ellen Olenska, than on old New York itself, which has a life apart from the people and the things that fill it. Its distillation of ancient voices, like that in Thomas Hardy's Wessex, threatens to engulf the present. The human, almost magical qualities that Wharton attributes to old New York at the beginning of her novel hark back to the time when places seemed incarnations of her inmost fears. With Ellen's defection to Paris and the next generation's irreverence, old New York loses its power to intimidate.

Wharton communicates the ethos of old New York in the way it tries to control Ellen Olenska. Reversing the journey of James's Christopher Newman in *The American*, Ellen comes home to the United States seeking a spiritual harmony between herself and her surroundings. Through Ellen's missteps and discoveries, Wharton explores the complex relationship between manners and history. The wife of a dissolute Polish Count, Ellen has become amorphously European. Now she wants to immerse herself in everything "American," to experience a connection not only to her childhood past but also to rediscover, indeed reinvent, herself as an "American," though what that means remains a mystery.

As Wharton shows, old New Yorkers constitute a separate tribe. They live "in a kind of hieroglyphic world, where the real thing . . . [is] never said or done or even thought . . . only represented by a set of arbitrary signs."[48] Newland Archer, for example, thinks nothing more awful than an offense against " 'Taste,' that far-off divinity of whom 'Form' was the mere visible representative and vicegerent" (*Age*, 1026). Sillerton Jackson, a self-styled genealogist, dines out each evening on stories of old scandals. And Mrs. Mingott, the novel's ruling matriarch, has feasted so long on convention — on the "wastes of error, prejudice and igno-rance" (*Valley*, 260) — that she has grown too fat to leave her own house. Notwith-standing her "liberal" protestations, she sits virtually welded to a place where history has become gossip and manners a substitute for character. Mrs. Mingott's imprisonment foreshadows that of Archer, tethered at the novel's end to similar conventions.

According to Wharton, old New York had always been a kind of makeshift culture. She emphasizes both the theatrical and borrowed nature of its identity by beginning her novel with the Wellands and Archers listening to the German text of a French opera translated into Italian and sung by Swedish artists. Wharton presents a literal stage of manners, a juxtaposition of cultures, that succeeds, if at all, through art. Looking at the progression of Wharton's own books from *The Decoration of Houses* to *The Age of Innocence*, we find a recurring argument for the expansion of civilization through a similar process of amalgamation. Sophy Viner sets off for India at the end of *The Reef* (1912), and Paul Marvel, in the otherwise bleak *Custom of the Country*, will combine the best traits of his three fathers. *The Age of Innocence* suggests that "the only way to enlarge either" the United States or Europe would be "to reach a stage of manners where they would naturally merge" (*Age*, 1098). Wharton pictures manners evolving by degrees or, as New-land Archer thinks of his own small contributions to public life, brick by brick "in a well-built wall" (*Age*, 1291).

Although *The Age of Innocence* has been read as a condemnation of old New York, Wharton both loved and hated what this world represented. "When I was young," she writes in *A Backward Glance*, "it used to seem to me that the group in which I grew up was like an empty vessel into which no new wine would ever again be poured. Now I see that one of its uses lay in preserving a few drops of an old vintage too rare to be savored by a youthful palate" (*Backward Glance*, 5). Her reassessment, while it has something to do with her own age (she was fifty-eight in 1920), also speaks of the age in which she wrote the novel, begun at the end of the First World War. The empty rituals that predetermined the course of her life in old New York kept feeling and knowledge at arm's length. Still, Wharton prized the order and well-bred reticence that produced its surface harmony and general decency. "Anarchy under any form," her close friend Charles Du Bos explains, "was abhorrent to her" (Lubbock, 101), and old New York acquired a retrospective value in a world on the brink of chaos. Families whose names adorn the great cultural institutions of New York City — the Whitneys, Dodges, Morgans, and Delanos — became coupled in her mind with those working to preserve civilization across the Atlantic. In this way, *The Age of Innocence* externalizes, through a dialogue engaging past and present, the autobiographical or semi-autobiographical nature of much modernist writing.

Perhaps the most autobiographical of all Wharton's novels, *The Age of Innocence* is really a tale of two cities. It begins in old New York and concludes in Paris, in the very heart of the Faubourg St. Germain and civilization itself. Returning to the United States, Ellen claims "the inheritances of family and race."[49] As she tells Archer, she has lived in another, more miserable country, where individual pleasure rules and relative values prevail. She craves the refuge of a more determined, less random society than she has known in Europe with her husband's rootless, pleasure-seeking friends. Most, she hopes to abdicate the responsibilities of choice by self sacrifice: "[I]f it's not worth while to have given up, to have missed things, so that others may be saved from disillusionment and misery — then everything I came home for, everything that made my other life seem by contrast so bare and so poor because no one there took account of them — all these things are a sham or a dream" (*Age*, 1208). Ellen seeks "meaning" through self-erasure, an act she accomplishes, at least for the Archers and Wellands, by her exile to Paris after learning of May's pregnancy. As M. Rivière, Count Olenska's secretary, explains to Archer, she has ironically become the kind of American who considers some things morally unthinkable. Perhaps by an odd coincidence, Rivière is also the name of one of the illustrators for Charles Darwin's *Emotions in Man and Animals*, a study that explores the divisions between and within species, one of the major themes of Wharton's novel. Whether Wharton meant the allusion, she advances Ellen as a model for a new kind of cosmopolite, one who experiences no obliteration of nationality but balances multiple allegiances. To Archer, Ellen seems to embody the best all possible cultures, a point that Wharton underscores by pairing her with her "Sicilian" maid, Natasia,[50] and filling her house with belongings from Greece, Italy, and Turkey.

Through her, Wharton imposes a kind of "dynamic cohesion" or "rhetorical unity" (Santayana, 400), on the disparate cultures that she tended to group under the general rubric of civilization.

Wharton argues that civilization grows from the kind of intellectual talk (the "land of letters") old New Yorkers discouraged and Parisians esteemed. For Wharton, "talk had the value and virtues of the very utterance of culture. Everything and everybody was placed by her where it should be placed, related to the never disturbed and never forgotten background of traditional references" (Lubbock, 101). Wharton places Ellen in Paris because it offers this expression of beauty and security, which she and James associated with the best in manners or the most exalted "stage" of culture. Ellen's search for meaning echoes Odo's realization in *The Valley of Decision* that beauty grows from the struggle for its attainment. At the same time, it does not preclude her absence filling a void in Archer's imaginative life—or, for that matter, in the life of a community that retains its identity through the exclusion of parvenus and artists. Her removal from the plot of old New York, which parallels Wharton's own migration to Paris, gives her what one friend thought it gave Wharton: the "room, liberty, [and] encouragement, to be what she was" (Lubbock, 50). "It's worth everything, isn't it," Rivière asks Archer, "to keep one's intellectual liberty, not to enslave one's powers of appreciation, one's critical independence?" (*Age*, 1174). Exile restores Ellen to a place where she can act as if moral conduct still mattered. Through her surrogate daughter and Archer's future daughter-in-law, she helps to shape a new New York.

Certainly Wharton makes old New York take "account" of Ellen Olenska and of itself, though readers have interpreted Archer's decision not to see her after May's death as an affirmation of traditional values: "Say I'm old-fashioned" (*Age*, 1302).[51] As his own experience illustrates, however, "the trenchant divisions between right and wrong, honest and dishonest, respectable and the reverse" (*Age*, 1294) that Archer thinks he chooses have never existed. Unknowingly, he has become like one of the Kentucky cave fish that he pities, creatures who have ceased to develop eyes after centuries of not having to to use them. In contrast, Ellen's choice foreshadows that of the "lost generation," who argued that meaning can be found in process: "What is shaped is the thorough absence of any fulfillment of meaning, but the shaping elevates itself to the rich and rounded fullness of a real totality of life."[52]

If Wharton does make an implied comparison between New York and Paris, Paris remains largely offstage until her closing pages. It exists as a counterpoint to the novel's other illusory places, such as the Patroon's house, associated with illicit love, or Archer's library, "the scene of his solitary musings," "family confabulations" (*Age*, 1289), and his after-dinner talks with the governor of Albany, Theodore Roosevelt. The library is itself a stage where May announces the news of her pregnancy and Dallas takes his first step. Its walls record the family's public history. They also shield Archer from any intimate contact with life. His friendship with Roosevelt, which becomes the supreme justification of his life, mirrors the spiritual union he assumes with Ellen: "He had done little in public life; he would always be by nature a contemplate and a dilettante; but he had high things to contemplate, great things to delight in; and one great man's friendship to be his strength and pride" (*Age*, 1291). When Archer confronts Paris in the novel's closing pages, its incarnation of life defeats him. He walks across the Place de la Concorde and the Tuileries to the Louvre, and comes to the Invalides: "The dome of Mansart floated ethereally above the budding trees and the long grey front of the building; drawing up into itself all the rays of afternoon light, it hung there like the visible symbol of the race's glory." This light foreshadows the light that Gatsby associates with Daisy Buchanan. It becomes, "by some queer process of association," the "pervading illumination" in which Ellen lives, and Archer feels her atmosphere too rich and "stimulating for his lungs" (*Age*, 1300). Unlike New York, Paris is a place where life has continued and gained meaning through its associations with history.

George Santayana, a philosopher whom Wharton admired, may best describe *The Age of Innocence*'s complicated web of history, manners, and memory when he suggests that manners, in becoming history, substantiate a common world. In the end, he argues, history must be viewed as "nothing but assisted and recorded memory" (Santayana, 394, 395) because it grows from a process of referring back to a communally constructed reality. While Wharton never goes this far, she does acknowledge that history may be more an account of humanity's illusions than its facts.

V

The First World War marked a personal as well as a historical apocalypse for Wharton. Bernard Berenson remembers a conversation in which she explained her thoughts about the future of the novel: "Before the war you could write fiction without indicating the period, the present being assumed. The war has put an end to that for a long time, and everything will soon have to be timed with reference to it. In other words, the historical novel with all its vices will be the only possible form of fiction" (Lewis, 423–24). As Wharton indicates, the Great War historicized the present in several ways: it divided history into narrower slices, making the past more past and the present more elusive; and it created a kind of climate, or atmosphere — call it ennui or carpe diem or angst — that changed the values of perception. This may explain why Wharton found it impossible to complete her war novel, *A Son at the Front* (1923), until after she had returned to the bygone world recalled in her consciously historical novel *The Age of Innocence*. Her dilemma and its solution, to put into words "with a new intensity of vision" (*Backward Glance*, 368) what she had felt and seen and lived in Paris, illustrates her theory that postwar novels must respond to recent history.[53]

All of Wharton's so-called war books make their case through manners — from *The Age of Innocence* and *Summer* (1917), set in the Berkshires, to the articles collected in *Fighting France: From Dunkerque to Belfort* (1915) and *French Ways and Their Meaning* (1919). When not critiquing the social machinery (*The Marne* [1918] and *A Son at the Front*) that encouraged boys to go to the trenches, these books tally the human cost of war: "Something veil'd and abstracted" — she quotes Walt Whitman, who nursed sick and dying soldiers during the Civil War — becomes "a part of the manners of these beings."[54]

Wharton's writing from this period presents manners as the last bastion against terror. In *Fighting France*, for example, she juxtaposes the horror of the front's disembowelled corpses with "a hundred signs of intimate and humble tastes."[55] The crash of guns spitting out bullets destroys "the poor frail web of things that had made up the lives of a vanished city-full" (*Fighting France*, 153–54). "Whiskered photographs fade on the morning-glory wall-papers, plaster saints pine under glass bells, [and] antimacassars droop from plush sofas" (*Fighting France*, 153), as though mourning a world gone awry.

Published four years after *Fighting France*, *French Ways and Their Meaning* might be read as a hymn to manners, which, in Wharton's opinion, made it possible for the French to survive four years of desperate resistance. She makes the meaning of those manners accessible by asking readers to imagine France as if it were a neighbor's house: "All the lodgers are on the stairs in *dishabille*. Their doors are swinging wide, and one gets glimpses of their furniture, revelations of their habits, and whiffs of their cooking, that a life-time of ordinary intercourse would not offer."[56] The split second before the house bursts into flame, unsuspected similarities and disagreements declare themselves. Wharton contends that despite the persistence of "race-differences" (*French Ways*, vii) what holds true for individuals also holds true for nations. Manners, gestures toward normality amid chaos, reveal "the deep faiths and principles from which every race draws its enduring life" (*French Ways*, 16). A sense of proportion, scale, and fitness (taste); a wish to preserve communal values (reverence); the fearless examination of one's world (intellectual honesty); a codified system of manners that allows the maintenance of social discipline in the teeth of aggression (continuity) — these signify the cornerstones of civilization. Although she concedes that France would cease to be France or America America without each country having its language or the ministrants of its convictions, these differences do not preclude the two having a shared moral perspective; it is clear, however, where this shared perspective comes from. "Read the history of France," she urges: "Study her art, follow up the current of her ideas; then look about you, and you will see that the whole world is full of her spilt glory" (*French Ways*, 149).

In the wake of monstrous devastation, Wharton came to see all nations as "works in progress, evolving intellectually and artistically in search of themselves." To believe otherwise made the loss too frightening to contemplate. "An idea," she writes in *A Son at the Front:* "that was what France, ever since she had existed, had always been in the story of civilization; a luminous point about which striving visions and purposes could rally" (*Son at the Front*, 366). This thinking, which seems frightening when we consider the rise of fascism in a few short years, also contradicts her earlier argument about the symbiotic nature of human behavior and culture. It harks back to her vision of a land of letters, which in collapsing the anatomy of civilization set forth in *The Decoration of Houses* yearns toward a collective past or internationalism based on discernment. In whatever national guise, "a slowly accumulated past lives in the blood," she writes in *The House of Mirth*, broadening and deepening individual existence by forging "mysterious links of kinship to all the mighty sum of human striving."[57] French habits, manners, and customs may differ from ours even more than those of "more primitive races," her argument goes, but if we dig down deep to those principles "from which every race draws its enduring life," we will find how alike we really are (*French Ways*, 16).

Wharton was a persuasive, though reluctant, propagandizer, never wholly comfortable with her own argument for the erasure of cultural relativism. But in a world where a city like Louvain, Belgium, could be leveled in an act of barbarism, she felt compelled to gather up such bits of threatened life and make them into a memorial. That memorial was *The Book of the Homeless* (*Le Livre des Sans-Foyer*), a 1916 collection of verse, prose, and illustrations reproduced from original paintings and drawings to benefit the American Hostels for Refugees and the Children of Flanders Rescue Committee. A forerunner of fund-raising efforts that bring artists together for political and humanitarian causes, *The Book of the Homeless* includes a musical score from Igor Stravinsky; artwork from Max Beerbohm, Jacques-Émile Blanche, John Singer Sargent, Claude Monet, and Walter Gay; and pieces by William Dean Howells, Henry James, Paul Bourget, John Galsworthy, Joseph Conrad, Rupert Brooke, Paul Claudel, Jean Claudel, Thomas Hardy, and W. B. Yeats.[58] Wharton called her effort a "gallant piece of architecture," and it was. Modeled after *King Albert's Book* (1914) and *The Book of France* (1915), *The Book of the Homeless* was originally conceived as a gift book, its original manuscripts and pictures intended for auction. The title recalls the poem Wharton wrote for *King Albert's Book*, which ends:

> Wherever men are staunch and free,
> There shall she keep her fearless state,
> And, homeless, to great nations be
> The home of all that makes them great.[59]

Like *The Decoration of Houses*, *The Book of the Homeless* packages culture with the express purpose of preserving it for future generations. Although *The Book of the Homeless* endorses a certain manner of being and being in the world that in retrospect may seem elitist or Eurocentric, it also recognizes a responsibility to what it defines in largely artistic terms as "the cause of humanity."[60]

Wharton was practical as well as visionary, and with the help of Elisina Tyler she superintended the American Hostels for Refugees. It included a free clinic, an employment agency, and (recalling her Newport experience) a child-care center, which held classes. This Napoleonic effort provided shelter, food, fuel, clothing, and jobs for thousands of people, including women whom Wharton put to work making lingerie, which her sister-in-law then sold to wealthy patrons in the United States. Facing the destruction of everything she held dear, Wharton put her faith in manners, as though the fact of beautiful garments and useful employment, of meals eaten and rooms appointed, would stay the advance of tanks. She believed that "exteriorizing states of feeling, giving them a face and a language, is a moral as well as artistic asset" (*Fighting France*, 231–32). The formula of manners reminded people not only of their own humanity but also of the dignity and beauty toward which civilization labors. Manners became for her a kind of mantra or her prayer for tomorrow. If this made Wharton seem old-fashioned to Virginia Woolf, so be it. Catastrophe reminds us of history's short memory. Other generations will not likely miss what they have not known. For Wharton's generation, survival seemed tied to the preservation of things that testified to the triumph of the human spirit, as though their continuity insured our own.

In 1919, Wharton published a Whitmanesque tribute to the American soldiers of lowly rank, the privates, who had liberated France:

> Every one of you won the war
> You and you and you . . .
> All of you, all of you, name after name,
> James and Robinson, Smith and Brown,
> You from the piping prairie town,
> You from the Fundy fogs that came,
> You from the city's roaring blocks
> You from the bleak New England rocks . . .
> But you, you Dead, most of all![61]

With this poem, Wharton made her peace with the country she left behind and whose literature she so influenced in the coming years. Writers like F. Scott Fitzgerald and Sinclair Lewis saw themselves in Wharton's debt, even following in her footsteps. Lewis dedicated *Babbitt* to her. Fitzgerald's fatal decision to recount the ordeal of an American couple who mistakenly spent the night in a Paris bordello has passed into literary lore, but less is said about his need for her imprimatur. It might be said that Wharton sent forth her own troop of writers to meet the future. Few things irritated her more than the phrase "the great American novel,"[62] but she did much toward keeping it alive.

CHAPTER FOUR

Willa Cather

"After 1922 or Thereabout"

> Restlessness such as ours, success such as ours, do not make for beauty: good
> cookery, cottages that are homes, not playthings; garden, repose. These are
> first-rate things, and out of first-rate stuff art is made. It is possible that ma-
> chinery has finished us as far as this is concerned. Nobody stays at home any
> more; nobody makes anything beautiful any more.
>
> WILLA CATHER, interview

I

Willa Cather (1873–1947) freely acknowledged her debt to Henry James.
"For me," she remembered, "he was the perfect writer . . . the foremost mind that
ever applied itself to literature in America." "All students imitate," she told an
interviewer, and "I began by imitating Henry James."[1] It did not matter whether
he had anything clever to say about modern society, degeneracy, or the New
Woman. The flawless tone of his sentences delighted her. If, in later years,
Cather disowned *Alexander's Bridge* (1912), written during her self-styled ap-
prenticeship, she never repudiated the master of language himself. His control
and artistry seemed "as correct, as classical, as calm and as subtle as the music
of Mozart."[2]

Cather's work shows the influence of James in both obvious and subtle ways:
her concern with the psychological parameters of self, her use of architectural
metaphors, experiments with point of view, and, above all, her focus on themes of
entrapment and liberation, exile and artistry.[3] After the publication of *O Pioneers!*
(1913), Cather was spared the kind of early comparisons with James that Edith
Wharton found so frustrating.[4] The western locale of *The Song of the Lark* (1915)
and the austerity of *My Ántonia* (1918) made Cather seem an unlikely "heiress" of
James, the moniker Q. D. Leavis applied to Wharton.[5] Cather was neither a
historian of American "Society" nor — at first glance — a chronicler of manners.
Nebraska was, as she said, "distinctly déclassé as a literary background."[6] Its

farming people, its cornfields, pasture lands, and pig yards did not comprise the "proper" subject of novels.

Cather may not have seen Wharton, whose work she admired, as Henry James's heiress, but she thought both in the same tradition of American letters. She developed little patience with writers who imitated their manner without having their skill (*Writing*, 93). Echoing Virginia Woolf in "Mr. Bennett and Mrs. Brown" (1924) and Wharton in *The Decoration of Houses* (1897), she longed to dismiss the novelistic upholsterer. For a long time, the novel "has been over-furnished," she wrote in "The Novel *Démeublé*" (1936). "[T]he importance of material objects"—the things usually representative of manners—"and their vivid presentation" had been excessively stressed, she said:

> There is a popular superstition that "realism" asserts itself in the cataloguing of a great number of material objects, in explaining mechanical processes, the methods of operating manufactories and trades, and in minutely and unsparingly describing physical sensations. But is not realism, more than it is anything else, an attitude of mind on the part of the writer toward his material, a vague indication of the sympathy and candour with which he accepts, rather than chooses, his theme? (*Writing*, 35, 37)

Cather's question about realism has similar import for any discussion of manners. However contradictory or textured, manners communicate the social, often the historical, consciousness at the heart of a novel's "reality." And that consciousness encompasses the writer's attitude toward his or her subject, seen idiosyncratically through an overlay of cultural lenses.

Cather was more an advocate of restraint than an enemy of manners, as her ambivalent attitude toward Honoré de Balzac illustrates. (Wharton saw a direct connection, which Cather may have also felt, between the aims and method of Balzac and James.)[7] Although she thought Balzac second only to Napoleon, Cather faulted him for building Paris brick by brick. Yet almost against her will or reason, she saw him living in every Parisian face and street corner. The city itself seemed "no more real a thing than the great city of thought," which Balzac, that barbarian of letters, had "piled and heaped together and left, a ruin of chaotic magnificence beside the Seine."[8] To her, he made a story of the history of Paris. Perhaps that explains why James called him "the master of us all,"[9] and Cather could not forget how she, at twenty, had read and reread Balzac, living in his world and feeling "Finally, this is life!"

By forty, Cather had grown to prefer the aloofness of Gustave Flaubert's

"peculiar integrity of language and vision."[10] Although she did not want to dis-
card the social facts that Balzac and other realists felt essential to an understanding of personality, she did want the "material investiture of the story" presented
with apparent unconsciousness: a thing not named, an overtone divined but not
heard, a verbal mood or emotional aura emanating from a fact or action (*Writing*,
41–42). She follows William Dean Howells's train of thinking that a people's
most elusive qualities characterize them most fully, and James's wish to render
"the look that conveys . . . meaning, to catch the color, the relief, the expression,
the surface, the substance of the human spectacle."[11] In "On the Art of Fiction"
(1920), an essay that pays tribute to James's "The Art of Fiction" (1884), Cather
wrote that fiction should simplify: the reader must perceive what the writer
suppresses "as if it were type on the page" (*Writing*, 102). Then "literalness,"
ceasing to be literalness, becomes experience (*Writing*, 40). For Cather, manners
disclosed (in the spirit of Emerson) the harmony or dissonance of mind and soul,
private and public selves, character and setting. They were not so much codes for
understanding the world as an atmosphere radiating from the world itself.

Like the historian Francis Parkman, whose narratives of Oregon and New
France she loved, Cather transmits the essence of culture through patterns of
conduct and their biographical import for the writer. To this extent, she herself
becomes a novelist of manners.[12] Her world, always in flux and in the process of
reconstruction, may not provide the stability that many readers see as a precondi-
tion for novels of manners, but, in her own, modernist way, she arrests a moment
in history and tests her characters against accepted standards of conduct. In
novels such as *My Àntonia* (1918), *A Lost Lady* (1923), *The Professor's House*, and
Sapphira and the Slave Girl (1940), history rests in "the persistence of memory . . .
in lost hidden places." According to Eudora Welty, those places "wait to be found
and to be known for what they are. Such history is barely accessible, the shell of it
is only a fraily thing held together . . . [yet] the continuity is *here*."[13]

Cather thought of memory as an inherited "mental complexion, left over from
the past."[14] The continuity in her account of history, illustrated perhaps most by
Shadows on the Rock (1931), comes from her characters' being attuned to "internal
rumors" or to memories, which either corroborate or correct each other.[15] If
Cather's conception of time and being has a greater elasticity than usually found
in novels of manners, her point of view, at once introspective and retrospective,
does not.

Cather's understanding of manners is tied to her brand of "regionalism," and
it presupposes that places can generate certain legacies of thought.[16] American

novelists have consistently been fascinated by indeterminate spaces and historical process. James Fenimore Cooper's wilderness, Mark Twain's Mississippi, and Eudora Welty's Delta remain impenetrable except along those borders where custom breaks down. James envisioned such borders internationally, as hypothetical places where fundamentally separate cultures meet without melding. In Cather's *O Pioneers!* multiethnic generations of immigrants mingle around Alexandra Bergson's kitchen table. Although Cather's name has become almost synonymous with the American West, she was the kind of regional writer Marjorie Kinnan Rawlings called accidental. In other words, she used a specialized locale as a logical or coherent background for commonly shared feelings or beliefs.[17] With the so-called "new regionalists" of the 1930s, especially her friend and fellow westerner Mary Hunter Austin, she hoped to use native imagery to balance fact and mythology.[18] Without being a novelist of manners in a traditional sense, then, Cather helped to revise the way in which manners inform a story. Novelists of manners often feel bound to historical chronology because it seems to imitate a consecutive process of cultural transmission. Cather achieves the same ends by disrupting time through form. Of perhaps all her novels, *The Professor's House* (1925) most conveys the power of manners to impart and comment upon individual and cultural mythologies. Predating more obviously historical books like *Shadows on the Rock* and *Sapphira and the Slave Girl*, it also anticipates her own theory of aesthetics set forth in "The Novel *Démeublé.*"

In *The Professor's House*, Cather experimented with form in several ways: following early French and Spanish novelists, she first inserted a *nouvelle*, or extended story, into her dominant narrative, which she called her *roman;* and second, inspired by an exhibition of paintings she had seen in Paris, she tried to create the feeling of looking at a Dutch interior — that is, a furnished room with a window opening onto a stretch of gray sea or a ship's mast gliding past (*Writing*, 31).[19]

"Démeublé" notwithstanding, Cather literally crams *The Professor's House* with furniture (painted Spanish bedroom sets, chiffonniers, stone closets) to highlight the tension between material culture and its spiritual antithesis.[20] "In my book," she writes, "I tried to make Professor St. Peter's house rather overcrowded and stuffy with new things; American proprieties, clothes, furs, petty ambitions, quivering jealousies — until one got rather stifled. Then I wanted to open the square window and let in the fresh air that blew off the Blue Mesa, and the fine disregard of trivialities which was in Tom Outland's face and in his behaviour" (*Writing*, 31–32). The window throws light on a hidden interior that, in turn, discloses an imaginatively limitless horizon. Intensifying the solid fact of the room, the window offers a view of the reverse side of the looking glass. The other landscape or reality forces an implicit comparison between the two pictures, the detailed outer room and the suggestive inner window. What lies beyond the frames? The viewer — or in Cather's case, the reader — must construct a kind of bridge to join the contrasting frames. The process forces a reconsideration of the objects that fill the room and those that fill or do not fill the window, thereby magnifying, rather than reducing, the social context usually associated with a novel of manners. Cather fixes the reader's gaze through a technique that dynamically extends Henry James's still-lifes — the portrait of Gilbert Osmond sitting in the presence of Madame Merle, for example, or Edith Wharton's *tableau vivant* of Lily Bart impersonating Sir Joshua Reynolds's Mrs. Lloyd in *The House of Mirth* (1905).[21] In other words, Cather's self-conscious emphasis on form, what becomes its repeated breaking up and almost kaleidoscopic reassembling, allowed a novel of manners to survive within the modernist house of fiction.

The dominant narrative of *The Professor's House* concerns a crisis, both spiritual and material, in the life of a middle-aged professor of history, Napoleon Godfrey St. Peter. St. Peter finds himself stranded between two houses or philosophies: the old, dismantled house where he began his marriage, tended his garden, and wrote his eight-volume narrative *Spanish Adventurers in North America;* and the new, with its separate bedrooms and glistening baths for husband and wife. Lacking a history of accumulated memories, the new house reminds him of what he has lost. Never will he be able to recapture joy in his work, love for his family, or the past he shared with the brilliant engineering student named Tom Outland.

The inserted narrative — the *nouvelle* — belongs to Outland, a raw westerner who one day appears as though summoned from the underground. To St. Peter, he seems a younger self recalled, and he brings with him a creative, regenerating magic that transforms ordinary perspective. St. Peter's reading of Tom's diary ushers him outside the confines of his immediate environment into an imagined world that, fictionally at least, transgresses national and generic boundaries. The diary recounts Tom's discovery of an ancient Pueblo village in New Mexico, his failure to rouse the interest of Washington bureaucrats, and the disappearance of his best friend, Rodney Blake, after an argument about ownership of native relics. Through the structure of the novel itself, the past proceeds materially into the present. The diary's interruption of St. Peter's narrative reflects his divided loyalties, while reproducing the intrusion of the First World War, the entropic force that swallows Tom Outland. As Cather writes in *One of Ours* (1922), when the world fell apart in 1922 or thereabout, "the made things" mattered little.[22] The form of *The Professor's House* may account for some of Ernest Hemingway's excessive irritation with Cather. It approximates that of *In Our Time* (1925), his own experiment with literary form and history.

By offering another view of history, Tom's diary undercuts the ideological framework of St. Peter's lifework, in which he conceived marauding Spanish colonialists as adventurers. St. Peter's topic recalls the "monument history" of William Prescott's *Conquest of Mexico* (1843), which covered vast tracts of history told from the perspective of its principal actors. With Parkman and George Bancroft, Prescott saw history as an organic process of conflicting and subsiding forces.[23] St. Peter shares their vision of history as a largely subjective process imagined through the workings of nationalist traits.

The Professor's House encompasses overlapping worlds, each with its own cultural hieroglyphs, or — to use Cather's metaphor — their own sets of furniture: Hamilton, the college town where St. Peter teaches, and Chicago, its nearest commercial center; France, where he lived as a student; the Old Mexico of his conquistadors; the hidden village of the cliff dwellers; the mesa, where Tom and Rodney set up housekeeping; and Washington, D.C., the home of the Smithsonian Institute. As in many novels of manners, *The Professor's House* offers characters who seem a projection of their environments. Evidence of the cliff dwellers comes to Tom "as a sort of message" (*Professor's House*, 216), transforming his sense of the ground he walks. Rodney and Tom establish household routines that make the domestication of the wilderness a male, rather than the traditionally female, enterprise.[24] And not surprisingly, St. Peter, suffering profound ennui, finds himself in a near empty house that — to return to James's *The Portrait of a Lady* (1881) — may or may not express him.[25] Shorn of furniture save a table and a cane-backed chair, it seems perilously close to a nightmarish extension of the novel *démeublé:* a structure as devoid of meaning as his own life.

Also in the spirit of James, the protagonist's sensibilities, at once finer and more acute, come into conflict with the standards of his age. Waking from his dream of old Mexico, St. Peter discovers that the current of domestic life has left him stranded on a foreign shore. His wife, Lillian, appears more sensible and less intelligent than he remembers her; Rosamond, the young girl who had once been engaged to Tom Outland, has become the socially conscious Mrs. Louis Marsellus; and Kathleen, his other daughter, so envies her sister that she seems a

stranger. As St. Peter has divested himself of material and emotional considerations, his family has grown increasingly acquisitive. He thinks it distasteful that
Rosamond and her husband have become wealthy from an Outland patent. He
cannot countenance the thought that their home, Outland — the Marselluses'
version of a Norwegian manor house — converts Tom's "very bones into a personal asset."[26]

Despite his implicit collusion in what he dislikes in his colleagues and family,
St. Peter, like Newland Archer in *The Age of Innocence*, gets much of his moral
authority from his standing above the passions and familial or class interests that
blind the other characters.[27] Cather uses objects to position her characters in
relationship to one another. Louie, for example, "pounces upon" an old Spanish
blanket that Rodney gave Tom and drapes it across his chest like one of the
professor's conquistadors: "And a very proper dressing-gown it would make for
Louie?" (*Professor's House*, 199). The seizure of the blanket and its ensuing transformation underscore Louie's confiscation of Tom's life and the adulteration of
his values. Similarly, the glass-door-knobbed house of St. Peter's younger daughter represents her middlebrow tastes; and the books that Rodney and Tom read
in their mesa cabin, *Robinson Crusoe* and *Gulliver's Travels*, gloss Tom's own naive
understanding of the cliff dwellers and his problematic return to contemporary
society.

Cather recognizes that any code of behavior or organizing principle of society
represents vested interests, no matter how altruistic. St. Peter's wife asks, "Just
when did it begin, Godfrey, in the history of manners — that convention that if a
man were pleased with his wife or his house or his success, he shouldn't say so,
frankly?" (*Professor's House*, 125). Cather dismisses outright the external sem-
blances of etiquette — as, for example, "the football-playing farmer boy" who
thinks a new suit or an elegant turn of phrase a short cut to culture (*Professor's
House*, 130) or Tom's eating mashed potatoes with his knife. Rather, she divides
manners into two distinct categories: those that follow the laws of society and are
based on property; and those that encompass "the fine, the almost imaginary
obligations" (*Professor's House*, 134). If the first category permits Rosamond the
use of Outland's inheritance, the second obligates her, at least in her father's eyes,
to share some of it with Tom's mentor, Dr. Crane. "I don't think you help people
by making their conduct of no importance," St. Peter lectures — "you impoverish
them" (*Professor's House*, 137). He willfully chooses not to see that Kathleen, too,
loved Tom, that Lillian turns to her sons-in-law following her husband's with-
drawal, or that Rosamond carries the macabre burden of being Tom's "virtual

widow" (*Professor's House*, 123). Wanting manners to embody moral forces, he mistakes the greenish tint of one daughter's skin, the sensuous furs of another, as signs of their natures. The relationship is far more complicated, for manners may disguise or protect as much as they reflect. In Cather's world, signs mirror the shifting and idiosyncratic social realities they suggest. Most importantly for the novel of manners, their absence can sometimes have greater significance than their presence. Where, for example, is the turquoise, set in a dull silver bracelet, that Tom gave Rosamond? The reader never finds out. Cather uses that ignorance to grant Rosamond a more complex interior life, to highlight how little we know those closest to us — or, for that matter, how little we know or can trust ourselves.

The Professor's House may be Cather's most pessimistic book. The corruption she associates with materialism in this novel is as inescapable as moral collapse. St. Peter lives by a simple formula that any increase in material wealth inversely decreases his creative power — the history that earns him the Oxford prize for history, for example, costing him his love of life. Although he prides himself on never "profiting" from his relationship with Tom, his plan to edit Tom's diary for publication shows how closely Cather sees the economies of friendship and finance to be allied.

For Cather, personal needs drive cultural enterprises. Tom's diary, begun in an account book, underscores this point — and something more. It asks readers to take into "account" not only Cather's characters but also the way in which she tells their story. As she herself writes of "the haunting interiors" of Leo Tolstoy's old Moscow, "[they] are always so much a part of the emotions of the people that they are perfectly synthesized; they seem to exist, not so much in the author's mind, as in the emotional penumbra of the characters themselves. When it is fused like this, literalness ceases to be literalness — it is part of the experience" (*Writing*, 39–40). Tom's diary creates this effect. It contains minutely detailed descriptions of the furnishings of the pueblo, every tool, every piece of cloth and shard of pottery. Greater than a catalog of things, it reveals the values, customs, and manners of a people who "lived for something more than food and shelter" (*Professor's House*, 233). Tom's story makes them part of a human family that extends, through him and the first section of the novel entitled "The Family," to St. Peter himself.

Cather suggests that the most valid histories must be personal histories. The diary's autobiographical content and outspoken politicism — so very different in design from St. Peter's panoramic *Adventurers* — makes a tacit argument for different kinds of histories that late-twentieth-century historians have valued. The publication of Tom's diary would mark a departure for St. Peter from the "monument history" of William Prescott by aligning him with the anthropological approach of John Fiske.[28] And, in fact, St. Peter has Fiske—whose *Myths and Myth-Makers* (1872) was dedicated to William Dean Howells—proposed to him as a future model (*Professor's House*, 116). Like many historians, St. Peter wants to reconstruct a past moral life that will illustrate his own ideals, including his beatification of Tom. As St. Peter envisions them, the Tom Outlands of this world belong to more innocent times. What, he wonders, would have happened to Tom had he lived? "What change would have come in his blue eye, in his fine long hand . . . which had never handled things that were not the symbols of ideas? A hand like that . . . must have been put to other uses. His fellow scientists, his wife, the town and State, would have required many duties of it. It would have had to write thousands of useless letters, frame thousands of false excuses" (*Professor's House*, 257). Cather indicates that the young man whose invention revolutionized aviation may well have turned into another Louis Marsellus or, like the father in Arthur Miller's *All My Sons* (1947), learned to tally costs in dollars rather than lives lost.

Contrary to St. Peter's idealization of Tom, Cather uses him to demonstrate the limitations of rigid codes of behavior, no matter how honorably meant. Less innocent and more complicated than St. Peter would have him, Tom has his own areas of moral blindness. When Rodney Blake, hoping to finance his friend's education, sells artifacts to a German collector, Tom renounces him:

> I admitted I'd hoped we'd be paid for our work, and maybe get a bonus of some kind, for our discovery. "But I never thought of selling them, because they weren't mine to sell—nor yours! They belonged to this country, to the State, and to all the people. They belonged to boys like you and me, that have no other ancestors to inherit from. You've gone and sold them to a country that's got plenty of relics of its own. You've gone and sold your country's secrets, like Dreyfus" (*Professor's House*, 247)

For Cather, any civilization carries within it ambivalences in need of compromise. Tom's investment has not been, as he admits, wholly disinterested. Rodney feels betrayed because he thought that they stood equal partners. Their quarrel forces him to see himself as "a hired man" who sold the boss's property (*Professor's House*, 249) when he was away. Rodney has a point. Tom did assume possession of the relics, both imaginatively and physically, never questioning, for example, his right to retain items of pottery or to dispose of them as gifts. His original plan of turning the site over to the Smithsonian is also compromising. To preserve the artifacts, archaeologists would have to profane the Pueblos' sacred site. Any appropriation violates their integrity because it places them in another cultural context even as it houses them in a larger history.

While critics have sometimes read Cather's censure of materialism as anti-modern,[29] Cather uses Tom's diary, which allows St. Peter a momentary suspension or turning back of time, to undermine any nostalgia for earlier periods of history or "primitive" peoples. In Cather's view of history, the present has the ability, whether or not the resolve, to learn from the past. What catastrophe, Tom wonders, could have annihilated a people not only advanced for their time and place but also possessing the fortitude to build high above the mesa? The answer lies in the things they left behind: water jars, yucca mats, grinding stones, corn cobs, strings of pumpkin seeds, and the preserved body of a woman nicknamed Mother Eve. According to the local priest, Father Duchene, evidence points to her murder: "There was a great wound in her side, the ribs stuck out through the dried flesh. Her mouth was open as if she were screaming, and her face, through all those years, had kept a look of terrible agony" (*Professor's House*, 229). Tom and Father Duchene conclude that her "tragedy" was personal: "In primitive society the husband is allowed to punish an unfaithful wife with death" (*Professor's House*, 235). Her murder seems to have no bearing on the greater tragedy of her tribe, perhaps exterminated by a horde of roving Indians "without culture or domestic virtues . . . [who] killed and went their way" (*Professor's House*, 234). St. Peter accepts such assumptions as fact. Cather's juxtaposition of domestic violence and genocide suggests something different, however — that individual acts of brutality can lead to sweeping atrocities. Both find expression centuries later not only in domestic conflicts of the St. Peters family or the disappearance of Rodney Blake but in the wholesale conflagration of the Great War.

The effects of cultural imperialism permeate every strata of the lives of Cather's characters. St. Peter's foster brother dies in the Boxer Rebellion, which Chinese traditionalists hoped would stop European control. St. Peter poses his sons-in-law dressed as Richard Plantagenet and the Saladin for a historical tableau, and he disapproves of a colleague who teaches American history with a painstakingly acquired British accent. Cather equates Tom's pueblo pottery with pieces from Greece and Crete and presents the mesa as a western Garden of Babylon. Such comparisons unite cultures; no less, they remind us that many people found their land conquered by royal decree before it had even been discovered.[30] Outland and his friends inevitably misread the civilization of the cliff dwellers because they understand it in the context of their own codes, which preclude other possible readings. Their backward reading of history illustrates Cather's point, taken from Emerson, that "all history becomes subjective." According to Emerson, "there is properly no history, only biography. Every mind must know the whole lesson for itself — must go over the whole ground. . . . [W]hat it does not live, it will not know."[31] Cather could not agree more. After Mother Eve topples into the bottom of Black Canyon, no one can own her. The fall highlights multiple treasons (or past skeletons) from Eve's original sin to Tom's mistrust of Rodney's motives to the betrayal of national histories and the awful waste of war. Through analogy, various times — past and present, social and private, mythological and (what Heidegger called) "public time" — coalesce.

Cather finally locates meaning in form, the rituals of everyday life or art itself. Her character wakes to a similar conclusion. Acquiescent about living or dying, St. Peter still derives comfort from certain utilitarian "forms" that belong to his wife's dressmaker, a devout German Catholic named Augusta. He refuses to relinquish these archaic mannequins: one, an armless, headless torso nicknamed "the bust," for its obvious development in that area; and the other, a legless "full-length female figure in a smart wire skirt with a trim metal waist line" (*Professor's House*, 107). Their parodic nature aside, these forms seem to offer the hope of order, security, and continuity. It seems fitting that Augusta, a deeply religious, unthinkingly conventional woman (a latter-day Mother Eve) should rescue St. Peter from his gas-filled study, in yet another reminder of the Great War. In the interlude between death and waking, St. Peter realizes that he has let something go, and gained something, too: the knowledge that he can accommodate change and live without desire.

The Professor's House ends with many questions unanswered. Apart from the mystery of Rosamond's bracelet, we do not know Rodney's fate, whether St. Peter publishes Tom's diary, nor whether desire can return. Perhaps finally the answers are unimportant in a novel where material details illumine the immaterial "facts" of life. No matter how Cather yearned to clean house, *The Professor's House* shows that familiar things put to new uses can serve another season.

II

We do not often think of Cather apart from the southwestern setting of her best-known novels, but the concerns that drew her to an American past also drew her to the wilderness of Quebec. *Shadows on the Rock* attests to Cather's continued interest in social boundaries, this time from a spiritual perspective. Set in seventeenth-century Quebec (or New France), the novel chronicles the daily rituals that comprise the life of a young girl named Cécile Auclair. Cather uses Cécile to tell parallel stories; one belongs to Cécile herself, the other to an emerging nation. Perhaps the most obviously historical of her many historical novels, *Shadows on the Rock* explores the evolution of Canadian nationality in the years Quebec gradually separates itself, philosophically, economically, and emotionally, from France.

Cather's account of early Quebec comes close to equating spirituality with patriotism. Cécile's crèche, for example, holds a Holy Family who resemble French peasants, "a little *cabine* of branches, like the first missionaries built down by Notre Dame des Anges," and a handcarved beaver, Canada's "special animal."[32] Over the course of the novel, Cather obscures the past from the present by layering shadows upon shadows — that is, analogous practices upon one another. In France, for example, apothecaries, like Cécile Auclair's widowed father M. Auclair, display a jar filled with pulverized human skulls. In New France, the Hurons eat their enemies, and Mother Catherine de Saint-Augustin seasons gruel with a pinch of ground martyr's skull in hopes of winning a convert. France may be, as the citizens of Quebec believe, the most civilized nation in Europe, but Cather argues that its king is no less culpable of pointless torture than the so-called "savages" who have their own conceptions of duty, honor, and courage.

Manners play a crucial role in linking the Old World and the New. Like Wharton, Cather envied the French their values, their aims, their point of view, their wisdom acquired "from enduring verities" (O'Brien, 248) because she thought that only a long chain of cause and effect produced a nation's cultural eminence. In *Shadows on the Rock*, the perspective that makes one generation "French" and another "Canadian" has much to do with the accident of place, the feeling, born of early association and familiarity, that identifies one spot as "home" and another not. Moving through three generations, Cather relays a sense of the vast social and political changes that will determine Quebec's future. M. Auclair and his generation live as vassals to Count Frontenac and the church. Their children barely recall France, and their children's children will live to see (in 1759) the transfer of Canada from the French to the British Crown.

If Cather communicates the ethos of another time, she does so atypically. In a colony where great events can be worthless and trifles dear as the heart's blood, time moves forward in daily increments, while it also stands suspended between eight-month installments from France. Waiting for letters from "home," colonists remain in perpetual doubt whether a parent has died or recovered, a marriage been made or lost. The discrepancy between fact and its mirror, between act and response, which can make the actual news surreal, contributes to the colonists' growing awareness of France as a foreign country.

Cather's appreciation of immanence makes time and even identity seem fluid, part of a process that exceeds any of its individual elements. The type of realism (accumulation of historical and material detail) usually associated with historical novels and novels of manners opens onto another reality in which no space exists entirely isolated from others. Dead sinners and saints ask favors of the living. Despite Auclair's wish to keep his house aloof from that of the local prostitute, he adopts her son, Jacques, and Cécile teaches him the stories she has learned from her birth mother and from Mother Juschereau, an Ursuline superior. In a similar manner, the domestic services that Cécile performs in her mother's memory create an oasis of French civilization in the Canadian wilderness. Before she dies, Cécile's mother instructs her how to care for her father's physical and spiritual health. It is the small things, like his evening meal, that make him "a civilized man and a Frenchman" (*Shadows*, 474): "You will see that your father's whole happiness depends on order and regularity, and you will come to feel a pride in it. Without order our lives would be disgusting, like those of the poor savages. At home, in France, we have learned to do all these things in the best way . . . and that is why we are called the most civilized people in Europe and other nations envy us" (*Shadows*, 479).

Cécile's mother entrusts to her a "feeling about life" that has come down through the centuries. She wants to think that when she dies life will go on almost unchanged, that each object will keep its proper place, that amenities will be observed. The individual character of the Auclairs's house lies in the "moral qualities" (*Shadows*, 480) of mother and daughter, which seem to infuse every object in their house. With coppers, brooms, clouts, and brushes "one made, not shoes or cabinet-work, but life itself. One made a climate within a climate; one made the days, — the complexion, the special flavor, the special happiness of each day as it passed; one made life" (*Shadows*, 589).

For Cather, the traditions, glimpsed in Cécile's living room, sustain the community no less than her father's medicines or the priest's prayers. Cécile possesses an almost "mystical concern" with "the supernal virtues of *things*,"[33] because they are the secular tools of God.[34] The routines originally established in honor of her mother have become necessary for her own being. By analogy, the novel itself might be read as a tribute to the novelist Sarah Orne Jewett. Although Cather dedicated *O Pioneers!* (1913) to the memory of her friend, *Shadows on the Rock* more obviously recalls the elegiac tone of Jewett's *The Country of the Pointed Firs* (1896).

According to Cather, manners can confer a kind of grace, with Cécile standing for its secular fulfillment. Intuiting the connection between the demands of the body and the soul, Cécile continues her mother's practice of giving an indigent laborer named Blinker his evening bowl of soup. Blinker is a paradigmatic Roman Catholic figure. The Auclairs' kindness prompts him to confess that he had earned his living in France as a king's torturer and that he feels as if he had ingested the faces, voices, words of those he persecuted. Listening to Blinker's confession, M. Auclair sees him change from the "ugly piece of furniture" he has always imagined him to be to one of those "terrible weather-worn stone faces on the churches at home, — figures of the tormented in scenes of the Last Judgment." Ill and in bed, Cécile catches the misery in Blinker's voice. "Our poor wood-carrier is like Queen Dido" (*Shadows*, 568), her father tells her that night: the puppet of gods and kings, he has known misery and now pities the miserable. The next morning, Auclair's daughter rises from her sickbed, as if cured by soup and sympathy. In a wilderness colony, the renewal or loss of any one soul can affect the welfare, even the survival, of the entire community.

The thematic structure of *Shadows on the Rock* suggests a parallel between eucharistic rituals and historical transformations. Cather presents Cécile, born in France and brought to Quebec before her fifth birthday, as a transitional figure linking the past with the future. On his deathbed, Count Frontenac wills her two gifts, which commemorate the transubstantiative practices at the heart of this community. The first is a crystal bowl of exotic glass fruit, a present from a Turkish prisoner whose life the count has spared. The second gift is linens. Together they represent the aesthetic and pragmatic necessities of life. Both will pass from generation to generation, an action that mirrors their passing from country to country. The linens will wear thin marking marriages and births until they are cut into napkins or rags and distributed among the far reaches of Cécile's family; and the fruit will grow plump with meaning as its story is told and retold. To his Canadian progeny, the count transmits a respect for domesticity, beauty, and imagination — the ingredients Cather thought essential to civilization.

In this novel, objects function like Cather's "window" in *The Professor's House* by focusing inward and outward. Jacques, for example, refuses to drink from Cécile's christening cup, as if one sip would rob her of her identity. He sees in its polished surface the fleeting nature of individual existence, as if the mutability of the world testifies to its divine creation.[35] Objects contain an ability to convey history and myth, to make the familiar miraculous and the miraculous familiar. Cather draws attention to this process by including in her novel several footnotes that create an implicit argument for the preservation of historic sites. Summoning us to the present, these footnotes have the effect of making *Shadows on the Rock* sound like a work of history. When Cather steps out of her fictional voice, she restores us to the more prosaic world of traditional histories. The social practices of New France herald the democratic principles of the 1789 Revolution, nearly a century hence. In the cobbler's shop, for example, the models of each citizen's foot represent the body politic. The wooden lasts of the governor are indistinguishable from those of his subjects, except for the initials scratched on their soles. Cécile's future husband, a trader named Pierre Charron, speaks for successive generations of Canadians when he says that the smell of Versailles sickens him. Recalling Tom Outland's diary, Cather's novel focuses on the subjects and the people historians usually omit. It, too, leaves much out, only hinting at the point of view of native inhabitants. What is the significance of a young girl's experience? A true pioneer, she enjoys "the idea of things more than the things themselves."[36]

At the beginning of the twenty-first century, we read Cather's characters against or cradled in our knowledge of a Canada still divided by language, religion, and ancestry. *Shadows on the Rock* illustrates how a novel of manners need not be set in or against a fixed society. In it, manners permeate barriers to recreate a texture of life that is at once modernist in its fragmentation and antimodernist in its spiritual wholeness. They demonstrate how little history, civilization, or memory itself remains static, yet how individuals, as well as nations, can remain faithful to an ideal; how "the history of every country begins in the heart of a man or a woman" (*O Pioneers!* 65).

III

Although *Shadows on the Rock* seems as though it should have been Cather's last novel — in the same way that readers might wish that Mark Twain's later work was less pessimistic — that distinction belongs to *Sapphira and the Slave Girl.* Cather's bleaker, more circumscribed view of history in this book might be related to her choice of subject, the ante-bellum South. Few people consider Cather a southern writer,[37] though in fact she was born near Winchester, Virginia, the setting of *Sapphira and the Slave Girl.* It was not until she turned ten that she moved with her family to Red Cloud, Nebraska. As a westerner, Cather witnessed the gradual gentrification of the prairie and the absorption of people who resembled her own Àntonia. And as a southerner, she inherited the burden of tragic remembrance and guilt that southern writers such as Ellen Glasgow and William Faulkner associated with the Civil War.

When Cather approached a subject like slavery, she brought with her an essentially western outlook. One could always head west, where the inheritances of race or class or social obligations retained little meaning, and the "West" now stretched beyond the borders of the United States. Not surprisingly, *Sapphira and the Slave Girl* has characteristics of both a southern and a western novel. Like much of southern fiction, it recognizes the human capacity for evil, while finding solace in history and the familiarity of place. At the same time, it acknowledges, like much of western writing, a need for elbow room (to use Wallace Stegner's definition) both in the way people think and in the way they write. This leads us to the *novel démeublé* and Cather's affinity for pillaged provinces.

Sapphira and the Slave Girl chronicles Sapphira Colbert's futile struggle for power: her jealous torment of the slave girl Nancy; her battle for dominance over her husband; and her fight against paralysis and death. Aided by Sapphira's daughter, Nancy escapes to freedom in Canada, where she marries and raises a family. The novel's last chapter—narrated by an "I," who seems to be Cather herself—describes Nancy's return to Virginia twenty-five years later. The shift from limited third-person omniscient to first-person narration parallels a histori-cal shift, in which the dueling perspectives of Cather's characters give way to a comforting, collective voice that the years following Reconstruction will prove false. Cather asks readers to finish her narrative, to reread the past of her novel in light of succeeding events.[38]

The form of Cather's novel is "historical" in the way that William Dean Howells defined it—"a certain passage in the real life of the race." Where her novel differs from a novel like *An Imperative Duty* (1891), which asks related questions, is in approach. If Howells defines race by class and other social con-structs, Cather focuses her attention on systems of government and power itself. The novel looks back at a specific period in history when people like Sapphira assumed they were superior to people like Till and Nancy. The structure of the novel reinforces a sense of disintegration as it moves from "Sapphira and Her Household" (book 1) to its individual components, including "Nancy and Till" (book 2) and "Sapphira's Daughter" (book 4). Although obvious, Sapphira *is* the main character, and Cather's critique of southern history probes the psychology of slaveholders more than their victims, with whom she assumes a shared humanity. In one way, Cather relegates issues of racial inequality to the past by proceeding as if they no longer existed. In another, the implied dialectic of any historical novel asks its readers to make a comparison between then and now, which in *Sapphira and the Slave Girl* reframes race almost entirely from the perspective of economic and cultural control.

It might be said that in *Sapphira and the Slave Girl*, Cather uses manners, which maintain the hierarchies they collapse in *Shadows on the Rock*, to highlight regional and racial difference. Nothing separates Sapphira and her husband more from their neighbors than their owning slaves, a practice that goes against "the custom of the country." Their property, with its working mill, functions like a feudal manor. Its survival depends on a system of fine distinctions. Sapphira, for example, discriminates between selling any of "her people" and "obliging" faraway friends in need of domestic help. Similar "delicacies" characterize the relationship between master and slave. Whatever leaves the kitchen in a gourd vessel, whether meat, or lard, or gravy, will not be questioned: "The gourd vessels were invisible to good manners."[39] In return, "self-respecting negroes never complained of harsh treatment" (*Sapphira*, 788). Fixed ways, Sapphira thinks, satisfy folks. And this is exactly contrary to Cather's point that fixed ways benefit those in power.

A set of observances common to the relation of master and slave allows Sapphira to rule from her crude invalid's chair "as if it were a seat of privilege" (*Sapphira*, 786). The system works to the extent that her slaves have internalized her values. Virginians born and raised, they feel superior to their African counterparts. Taught long ago by an English housekeeper to value her place, Nancy's mother, Till, assumes that her first duty belongs to her mistress, rather than her child. In the ante-bellum South of Cather's novel, behavior will never erase the "fact" of color. Till may conduct herself like a middle-class Englishwoman; she is and will remain, in Sapphira's mind, a slave and, therefore, property. While Cather shows the inequalities inherent in an implied contract between master and slave, indeed that their relative positions prohibit such a contract, she makes clear that sentiment helps to keep an exploitive system in place. The novel raises an interesting question about the relationship of manners and systems of oppression. To be sure, manners work to keep people in their place. In *Sapphira and the Slave Girl*, they also function oppositionally. They dignify the immorality of slavery, and they make the better-mannered Nancy Sapphira's superior.

Cather undermines myths of southern womanhood and of the ante-bellum South by giving a female face to slaveowners. In the 1850s, people like Sapphira debated how to care for their slaves most advantageously. Sapphira's views of her responsibilities reflect the general consensus in the four decades preceding the Civil War. Southerners routinely aired their philosophies of slave management in the agricultural press, which carried reports, prize and commissioned essays, articles, and letters aimed at an audience intent on larger profits. The correspondents, usually men but an occasional woman, considered themselves Christians and thought of their slaves as they would animals: "Surely there is no subject," a Mississippian wrote in 1851, "which demands of the planter more careful consideration than the proper treatment of slaves, by whose labor he lives and for whose conduct and happiness he is responsible in the eyes of God."[40] Rarely circulating outside the South, farm journals carried advice on principles of slave management and plantation order, not to mention practical matters concerning food, clothing, shelter, health, and religious education. Owners believed that slaves were particularly susceptible to diseases such as "drapetomania," the affliction of running away, and "dysaesthesia aethiopica," an "obtuse sensibility of body" popularly called "rascality" (Breeden, 172, 174). Authors listed rules for the government of slaves reminiscent of Adam Nehemiah's *The Masters' Complete Guide to Dealing with Slave and Other Dependents* in Sherley Ann Williams's *Dessa Rose* (1986). One advice column reads:

> Rule 1st. Never punish a negro when in a passion. No one is capable of properly regulating the punishment for an offence when angry.
>
> 2nd. Never require . . . what is unreasonable. But when you give an order be sure to enforce it with firmness, yet mildly.
>
> .   .   .   .
>
> 5th. In giving an order, be sure you are understood, and let the negro always know that he can ask for an explanation if he does not understand you. (Breeden, 9–10)

According to the "etiquette" of slave management, the slave owes the master obedience and service; the master owes the slave "fair" treatment and ample provision for physical and moral well being. *Sapphira and the Slave Girl* addresses the inherent inequality of such a system of exchange in its very title, which names Sapphira and types Nancy. Three years before Cather published her novel, a book was published under the title *The Etiquette of Race Relations in the South: A Study in Social Control* (1937) — words that suggest how little basic premises about blacks and whites had changed. Etiquette, the book's author Bertram Wilbur Doyle explains, has traditionally functioned to define and maintain social distances.[41]

Cather measures those distances in *Sapphira and the Slave Girl* through her characterization of Sapphira, a woman literally crippled by her own racism. She also explores, however, ways by which manners lessen the distance between master and slave. Whether those times serve to undermine or perpetuate existing injustices depends upon the individuals involved and circumstance. Till, for example, has raised Nancy to have her "own good manners" and something more — "a natural delicacy of feeling" (*Sapphira*, 803). Nancy's manners infuriate Sapphira because they make her husband, Henry Colbert, forget his — and by extension her — place: "Whatever he was pressing upon that girl, he was not speaking as master to servant; there was nothing to suggest that special sort of kindliness permissible under such circumstances. . . . It was personal" (*Sapphira*, 839). Henry Colbert genuinely appreciates Nancy's "quiet ways and respectful manner," (*Sapphira*, 815) which remind him of Mercy in the Bible. But in Sapphira's mind, Nancy has no claim to social standing, no right to privacy, no identity; she is a set of "hands," to sweep or dust. Sapphira hates Nancy because she realizes their positions appear analogous. Nancy presides over the mill as Sapphira does the big house. Nancy threatens Sapphira's image of herself, her rule, and her last vestiges of sexuality. When Sapphira arranges for her nephew Martin Colbert to visit, she is deliberately arranging a surrogate rape — an act that will finally show Nancy her place. The magnitude of Sapphira's moral violation leads her daughter and husband to help Nancy escape to Canada. It claims in implied expiation the life of Sapphira's granddaughter Betty. And it estranges mothers and daughters (Sapphira and Rachel and Till and Nancy). When Nancy returns twenty-five years later, her silk dress, gold watch, and fur coat indicate the distance she has traveled. She bears no resemblance to the Nancy of song and legend: "Down by de cane-brake, close by de mill / Dar lived a yaller girl, her name was Nancy Till" (*Sapphira*, 931).

The new Nancy has entered the era of Howells's *An Imperative Duty*, in which race becomes more a matter of class than color. Having adopted a different country and history, she has a social identity commensurate with her material rank, and Sapphira's daughter and the narrator's mother entertain her as a social equal. Nancy's pronunciation of each syllable in the word *history*, as opposed to the southern pronunciation, *his'try*, signals both her expanded heritage and her altered legal status. That status necessitates a rethinking of social mores that have previously governed the conduct of blacks and whites in relationship to one another, and in fact Nancy's children, of Scots, Indian, and African-American ancestry, illustrate the melting-pot theory of racial histories. The intervening quarter-century between Nancy's flight and her return recalls the division of *The Professor's House* into sections before and after the First World War. Those years mark, at least fictionally for Cather, a dramatic reconstitution of American society to include those of African descent.

Despite Cather's ending, *Sapphira and the Slave Girl* offers a more conservative or stratified view of history and human nature than an earlier book such as *Death Comes for the Archbishop* (1926), in which she breaks down cultural hierarchies. The novel "reconstructs" a regional literature to make it more inclusive, while safely removing Nancy from the plot, perhaps from American history itself. In the South, as Cather herself knew, Nancy would still have had no public social identity. Virginia newspapers well into the twentieth century tended to refer to black citizens by racial designation rather than name (Doyle, 144). Ironically, Till becomes the keeper of the old order, treasuring its last symbol, a brooch that holds Mr. Henry's black hair and Miss Sapphy's brown. And here Cather shows how traditions can be perpetuated by the people they have most harmed. When Till takes the young narrator to the family graveside, her stories of Sapphira and her husband seem to inspirit their memories. These stories continue to grow in the narrator's mind until they herald a gathering of ghosts — until they belie for Cather's readers the last line of her novel: "Nobody [here] was anybody much" (*Sapphira*, 931). At the same time, they allow history to slip into the realm of myth, in this case myths of the Old South.

For many, the hope that Cather offers takes shape in her story's gaps. At their worst, these gaps serve to erase or appropriate whole peoples from history, to give a false homogeneity to human experience. At their best, they replicate the nature of the historical process itself by inviting readers to become writers, possibly even pioneers, as they creatively reimagine both the past and the present.

Like Henry James, Cather remains a curiously amorphous writer, whose straddling of periods and approaches makes easy categorization impossible. When James wrote "The Art of Fiction," he could not have predicted that a young Nebraskan would take his advice as a mantra:

> It goes without saying [he advised] that you will not write a good novel unless you possess the sense of reality; but it will be difficult to give you a recipe for calling that sense into being. Humanity is immense, and reality has a myriad forms; the most one can affirm is that some of the flowers of fiction have the odour of it, and others have not. . . .

. . . All life solicits . . . and to "render" the simplest surface, to produce the most momentary illusion, is a very complicated business. (52, 53)

In her novels of manners and history, Cather learned and extended the lesson of the master, and with that lesson in mind she helped to transform American fiction itself.

CHAPTER FIVE

Ellen Glasgow

A Social History of America

"Manners for me, and morals for those that like them."
MARIA EDGEWORTH, Belinda

I meant by a social history the customs, habits, manners, and general outer
envelope human nature had assumed in a special place and period. My place
happened to be Virginia, and my period covered the years from 1850 to the
present time. But the inner substance of my work has been universal human
nature — or so I have always believed — and if the great Balzac had not been
ahead of me, I should have called [my] books the Human Comedy.
LETTER OF ELLEN GLASGOW TO JAMES BRANCH CABELL

I

Ellen Glasgow (1873–1945), a self-proclaimed historian of manners, spent
her entire life trying to unravel the mystery of a single state, her native Virginia.
Her achievement — a novelistic meditation on Virginia from the decade before
the Confederacy to the Second World War — is perhaps unparalleled in American literature.[1] Yet Glasgow saw herself as much more than a "Southern" writer.
"The significance of my work would not have varied," she wrote Allen Tate, "if I
had been born anywhere else." For her, the codes of Virginia encompassed the
conventions not only of the South or even the United States but of "the world we
call civilized."[2]

In retrospect, it seems astounding that Glasgow imagined herself as a kind of
southern Balzac. She started writing in the 1890s, when no "well-brought-up
Southern girl" would have admitted to knowing what a "bastard is"[3] and when
historical romances sold in the hundreds of thousands. If Glasgow showed her
independence by making a bastard the protagonist of her first novel, *The Descendant* (1897), she also looked to literary realism as an antidote to romance. "I could
remember," she writes of her childhood, "that when I wanted a doll with 'real

hair,' I was told I could not have it because we had 'lost everything in the war.' A war in which one had lost everything, even the right to own a doll with real hair, was not precisely my idea of a romance" (*Certain Measure*, 12). Glasgow's working title for *The Descendant*, "Sharp Realities," captures her feeling that most fiction remained false to experience (*Certain Measure*, 8). She had only scorn for the "plantation school" of local-color writing popularized by a fellow Virginian, Thomas Nelson Page. Books such as Page's *In Old Virginia* (1887) and *The Old South* (1892), which nostalgically depict happy slaves and kind masters idling in Eden, read like revisionist histories. To a contemporary writer such as Grace King, they proved that southerners now had a chance at "literature."[4] To Glasgow, such books hardly deserved the title. "Life never was and never will be like this,"[5] she decided. The public may expect novelists, especially those who present themselves also as historians, to please and instruct, not to "interrogate" (*Certain Measure*, 131), but it is precisely Glasgow's skepticism that gives her social history its moral dimension.

Glasgow said that she had no interest in recording "spectacular events or dramatic moments." The few she does record — the Civil War, in *The Battle-Ground* (1902), for example — show the impact of those events through the lives of ordinary people. Her main purpose was to study "the prolonged effects" of social transition upon ordinary lives in an "intransigent democracy" (*Certain Measure*, 29). As Glasgow herself states, her grand subject was change, her approach sociological. Although she thought people products of heredity and environment, and their behavior shaped by social and economic pressures, she objected to the "barbaric fallacy" (*Certain Measure*, 58) behind literary naturalism. Similarly, she had few kind words for the "school of refined realism" she saw flourishing under William Dean Howells's directorship, though on the occasion of his eightieth birthday she (and dozens of other writers) thanked him for showing "that great fiction is great truth telling."[6] Having rebelled against the South's sentimentalism, Glasgow had no intention of falling victim to the North's gentility. The epigraph taken from Henrik Ibsen to book 4 of *The Descendent* suggests her mood and situation: "It is not only what we have inherited from our fathers and mothers that walks in us. It is all sorts of dead ideals and lifeless old beliefs. They have no vitality, but they cling to us all the same, and we can't get rid of them."[7]

Writing the prefaces to her social history, something few American writers had attempted apart from Henry James, Glasgow could not remember whether Howells had praised or blamed her first novel. There could, however, be no doubt about the response of Hamlin Garland, a protégé of Howells's known for his pessimistic stories of Midwestern farm life. After reading the novel in a single sitting, Garland declared *The Descendant* "one of the most remarkable first books produced within the last ten years." Positive that Glasgow would never "dodge, or pander to weak readers," he echoed Emerson's welcome to Whitman and extended her a "cordial greeting."[8] Garland's confidence was not misplaced. Glasgow become the first southern writer to present a "wholly genuine picture of the people who make up and always have made up the body of the South."[9] As her publishers loved to announce: with her debut, realism finally crossed the Potomac. And they were right.

Glasgow's early novels, *The Voice of the People* (1900) and *The Deliverance* (1904), illustrate her major theme, "the rise of the middle class as the dominant force in Southern democracy." But it is not the whole truth about someone whose career spanned nearly fifty years and insisted that she had never been "a pure realist" nor a "pure" anything (she even objected to James Branch Cabell thinking her a virgin).[10] The "whole truth," to her mind, had to embrace more than "external appearances"; it had to illumine an "interior world" (*Certain Measure*, 28). If any word could communicate her method, she decided, it might be "veritism," the word that Garland coined to describe the extension of realism beyond the transcription of grim facts to some realm of inner truths.

Glasgow's understanding of "realism" grew largely from a strange mix of sources: the Presbyterianism of her Scots-Irish father; her reading in political economy, the natural sciences, particularly Charles Darwin's theories of evolution; and her immersion in Eastern philosophy. As we might expect, the thirteen novels that she officially included in her social history reflect to differing degrees these various influences — *The Descendent* incorporating, for example, her studies of social Darwinism; *The Wheel of Life* (1906) the teachings of the Bhagavad Gita; and *Vein of Iron* (1935) the Calvinism of her youth from an adult feminist perspective.

Looking back at her career in 1943, Glasgow maintained that she had been a "modern" before the term had been invented:

> Since, even in the year 1897, I was, in the present sense of that abused word, a modern, it is natural that I should have welcomed with interest the whole modern movement in letters. For the modern process, as I take it, means a breaking up on the surface of facts, and a fearless exploration into the secret labyrinths of the mind and heart. . . . it is the interior world that contains the deeper verities and the sounder realities. (*Certain Measure*, 113–14)

Glasgow could make that claim — as she indeed does — not on the experimental form of her early novels but on her vision of history and manners as part of the unremitting, unstable process she called "life."

As a historian of manners, Glasgow concluded that "the only permanent law in the social order, as in art," remains "the law of change."[11] She differed from previous novelists of manners in the degree to which she made and announced "process" her subject. She never relied, as other writers did, on worlds in static opposition (a scientific impossibility); nor did she concentrate on a particular moment of social dissolution or disruption except in the broadest sense. She gives, for example, rough dates for the periods covered in each of the volumes of her social history, from *The Battle-Ground* (1850–65) to *In This Our Life* (1938–39), yet she subverts this organization by grouping them thematically: "novels of the Commonwealth at Large," "of the country," and "of the city." For Glasgow, the real drama lay in the natural instability of personal consciousness and historical mechanisms, in a world brimming with "fermenting processes, of mutability and of development, of decay and of disintegration" (*Certain Measure*, 60). Glasgow's attempt to account for these processes may be what most makes her fiction "fundamentally American" and original in conception (*Certain Measure*, 67). It is certainly what makes her important in any history of the evolution of the novel of manners.

Glasgow's explanation of her own social history is nothing if not controversial. It may never be clear whether she planned (as she asserted) her series from the beginning or later imposed (as Cabell claimed) a design on the books she had written.[12] The structure of her history does not coincide with the sequence of the books' composition — the setting of her fourth novel, *The Battle-Ground* (1850–65), for instance, predating that of her third, *The Voice of the People* (1878–90). Chronology may have more to do with a writer's imagination than intent, however. Glasgow published *The Battle-Ground* the same year Edith Wharton published her historical novel *The Valley of Decision* (1902). Like many writers at the beginning of a new and unknowable century, they turned to the lessons of history and the historical form of the novel. Glasgow explained the order in which she wrote her social history by saying that she needed time for ideas to geminate. Those who agree with Cabell's statement that she invented it in retrospect might cite the books she does not include: *The Descendant, Phases of an Inferior Planet* (1898), *The Wheel of Life* (1906), *The Ancient Law* (1908), *The Builders* (1919), and *One Man in His Time* (1923) — books either set in New York City or generally considered her least successful. Here again, who can say that a writer should be limited to a particular locale or deny that few literary reputations survive on more than a handful of books, sometimes even a single book? Not Glasgow, who invited reviewers—and also prominent members of the Modern Language Association—to her home. (She had wanted to invite every academician attending the 1936 MLA conference until told she would be deluged with bewhiskered Chaucerians and specialists in Old Gothic and High German, French, and Spanish.)

When Glasgow thought about her own development as a writer, she saw her novels divided into those that preceded and those that followed *Barren Ground* (1925). "I wrote *Barren Ground*," she recalled, "and immediately I knew I had found myself . . . I was at last free" (*Woman Within*, 243–44). Glasgow was fifty-two and *Barren Ground* her fourteenth novel. *Barren Ground* is, arguably, Ellen Glasgow's own story told from the point of view of Dorinda Oakley, a woman who survives every adversity life hurls at her: her lover's desertion, the loss of her unborn baby, the death of her parents, and the whims of nature. The facts of Glasgow's life only casually coincide with Dorinda's. Glasgow was never a farmer, for example; and though she may have felt deserted by her fiancé when he went to run the Red Cross relief effort in Romania and fell under the spell of that country's beautiful Queen Marie, they remained friends up to her death. Whatever the invented "facts" of Dorinda's life, Glasgow felt connected to her by "a living nerve." She knew "the open country of her mind and the secret labyrinth of her heart" (*Certain Measure*, 163). For Glasgow, the significance of her achievement in *Barren Ground* came from its "double" fidelity to life, or its simultaneous illumination of external "realities" and internal truths, a "Reality" that can only be grasped by intuition and sympathy. Glasgow knew Dorinda because Dorinda expressed everything she had learned about living without joy. *Barren Ground* "freed" Glasgow, for she now understood, in some profound sense, the autobiographical nature of writing. It brought home to her what Henry James had called "a very obvious truth": "that the deepest quality of a work of art will always be the quality of the mind of the producer."[13]

In terms of her history of manners, the significance of *Barren Ground* comes from Glasgow's experimentation with a form that could evoke both "Time and Space." Glasgow imagined Dorinda against a background of unlimited space, "'where the flatness created an illusion of immensity'" and of "the unconquerable vastness in which nothing is everything" (*Certain Measure*, 158–59). Time she saw flowing from the theme of the story, with her characters reflecting the "slow rhythm and pause of the seasons" (*Certain Measure*, 159). Glasgow hoped to upset the usual barriers that time and space interpose between reader and character by not allowing the reader any knowledge beyond Dorinda's own. *Barren Ground* marked, in this way, Glasgow's liberation from the more traditional form of her earlier novels, which tend to have the length, span, and multiple climaxes of Victorian triple deckers. To her mind, she had found a prose style that could "bend without breaking" (*Woman Within*, 123), one that would convey, through a kind of prose rhythm, realized most fully in *Vein of Iron* and *The Sheltered Life* (1932), her sense of life's unremitting process.[14]

James Branch Cabell was one of the few people to recognize the musical nature of her prose, and she included a passage he scanned in *A Certain Measure*.[15] It shows the matriarch of *Vein of Iron*, a woman called Grandmother Fincastle, drifting in and out of sleep:

> Wéaving ín and óut of her bódy and sóul, and
> knítting her ínto the pást as she knítted lífe iñtŏ
> stóckings, móved the famíliar rhýthms and páuses —
> nów — of the hóuse; and móved as a cásual wáve, as
> bárely a mínutes ébbing and flów, in the tímeless
> súrge of predéstinátion. (*Certain Measure*, 182)

Without a trace of false modesty, Glasgow claimed that "only a mature art could have dared" what she had done in *Vein of Iron*.[16]

While critics have followed Glasgow's lead, focusing on her novels written in the 1920s and 1930s, the merits of her earlier books should not be overlooked. Glasgow defined many of the elements now commonly attributed to southern literature: a tragic sense of life, a deep-rooted pessimism, an awareness of humanity's capacity for evil, and the imperatives of history and place. Her recognition of the individual and integrated histories of white and black southerners led the way for the next generation of southern writers, including William Faulkner, who ungenerously claimed not to give a "damn" for either Glasgow or her books. So be it. Marjorie Kinnan Rawlings, Allen Tate, Caroline Gordon, Stark Young, Sarah Haardt Mencken, Douglas Southall Freeman, and Margaret Mitchell did.

Faulkner notwithstanding, the strength of Glasgow's social history comes largely from its complex, rather than polemical, vision of human experience — a vision that examines the overthrow of the aristocratic tradition, the transfer of hereditary power to a rural underclass, the continued disenfranchisement of African Americans, and the evolving status of women. This ambitious design fell nothing short of redefining both the scope of the novel of manners and southern fiction itself.

To give just three examples, in order of chronology not composition, *The Battle-Ground*, set before and immediately after the Civil War, shows how the tone and movement of an age could gain immediacy through the narratives of individual families, the Amblers and the Lightfoots. Historical novels naturally become simultaneous meditations on the past and commentaries on the present, and Glasgow realized that any "past" continues to be reformulated into new forms, which respond, in turn, to the various needs of the immediate world.[17] In this context, *The Battle-Ground* obliquely comments on the changing role of women,[18] minorities, and the underclass in turn-of-the-century America. The novel similarly establishes an implicit critique of conventional histories, which Glasgow supports through her characterization of Aunt Aisley, an old conjurer who dominates *The Battle-Ground*'s first chapter. Aunt Aisley represents a different kind of historical tradition than the one that *The Battle-Ground* ostensibly details, and Glasgow designates it older than either God or the Devil. Aunt Aisley's world, her stoicism and unacknowledged humanity, frame that of the southern aristocracy, and the anthropological analogy that Glasgow establishes works to the disadvantage of the culture traditionally assumed to be more "civilized." Aunt Aisley's history is oral and therefore unrecorded; it continues through memory. History becomes, to this degree, a record of the dreams and stories that people deem necessary to existence.

Glasgow's third novel, *The Voice of the People* (1900), begins five years after *The Battle-Ground* ends in 1865. It follows Nicholas Burr's rise from the son of a poor peanut farmer to governor of the state and ends with his sacrificial murder by a mob intent on lynching a black man. Glasgow's analysis of post-Reconstructionist politics focuses on the alliance between former masters and slaves against the rising middle class, represented by Nicholas himself.[19] The voice of the people dies with Nicholas, assassinated by the very people he represents. Freedom of speech becomes a sign of oppression, granted to servants or wives who have exchanged the "devotion of their lives . . . in extenuation of the freedom of their tongues."[20]

In *Virginia* (1913), the title of which refers both to its heroine and setting, Glasgow underscores the intersection of personal and cultural histories from ten years after the end of Reconstruction to the eve of the First World War. Ill-educated, sentimental, and submissive, Virginia sacrifices youth and beauty in the service of a husband and children who are helpless not to outgrow her. Once the feminine ideal, Virginia gives way to the new woman, represented not only by her husband's lover, a woman of burning vitality and intellect, but by her own daughters, Lucy, a pre-flapper, and Jennifer, a young Jane Addams and possibly a lesbian.[21] Because Glasgow envisioned "the Problem of the South" as one of race as well as gender,[22] she has little sympathy for the young Virginia, who can gaze nonchalantly past a man beating a mule toward the site of the old slave market. Virginia does not have the imagination to feel the horror of people having been sold there. Glasgow called this kind of self-satisfied moral blindness or code of polite behavior that serves the status quo "evasive idealism."[23] In her opinion it had almost single-handedly determined the historical status of women, the plights of black southerners, and the state (or state of mind) of Virginia.

As *The Battle-Ground, The Voice of the People*, and *Virginia* suggest, Glasgow had, in fact, experienced a series of breakthroughs that made the writing of *Barren Ground* possible. If the earlier novels relied, as Glasgow herself thought, too much on "fact" or frameworks borrowed from other thinkers such as Darwin, Herbert Spencer, and John Fiske, they were nevertheless unlike anything else being published in America. First, she realized that the South was made up of many Souths: the country poor in *The Miller of Old Church*, working women in *Life and Gabriella*, and families whom even the paltry gleanings of the breadline seldom reached in *Vein of Iron*. Second, she realized that these stories could best be told through manners or "the living character of a race," defined across class and racial boundaries. She does this covertly in *The Descendant*, with its "dark," socially ostracized protagonist Michael Akershem; overtly in *The Voice of the People*'s exposé of the widespread practice of lynching.[24] (Just two years after Glasgow published *The Voice of the People*, Thomas Dixon published *The Leopard's Spots: A Romance of the White Man's Burden — 1865–1900* [1902], a pro–Klu Klux Klan novel that triumphantly ends with the lynching of a black man.) Other novels, notably *Virginia* and *The Sheltered Life*, stress social commerce between the races (customarily the exploitation of black women) or the ambiguities of identity so tragically enacted through the degradation of an innocent young black man in her last novel, *In This Our Life* (1941).

As Glasgow's publishers announced, she took the South out of the South and gave it "a touch of the universal." Van Wyck Brooks wrote that "Ellen Glasgow was a part of the world movement of her time — just as her Virginian scene was, in fact, a wider scene, the all-American scene of two generations. For characters especially of her later novels, while Southern recognizably, were also Americans of all the other regions, type for type, that is, and group for group."[25] This might seem impossible to believe about someone whose books so obviously have a provincial focus. Nonetheless, the scale and range of those books, and their emphasis on the amorphous and often idiosyncratic qualities of life, redefined her contemporaries' sense of what constituted "regional" literature and southern modernism. Julius Rowan Raper defines that movement proceeding from Glasgow's representation of unconscious forces and other dimensions of being.[26]

Such critical observations lead us to the central paradox of Glasgow's social history. Glasgow's attempt to get beyond historical or sociological motifs to Reality with a capital *R* oddly challenges the project's own social-historical construction. Her definition of her work as a "social history" began to make her feel trapped. In 1932, the year she published *The Sheltered Life*, for example, she asked her editor, "Will anyone suspect . . . that I am writing again, not of Southern nature, but of human nature, not of Southern characteristics (whatever that may mean!), but of the springs of human conduct and the common heritage of mankind! [*sic*]. Will anyone even begin to suspect that always, whether I wrote social history or fiction, I was treating the South as part of the world?"[27] When, the preceding year, she addressed the first Southern Writers Conference, Glasgow looked around the room at people such as Irita Van Doren and Isa Glenn, who lived in New York City, and Sherwood Anderson, who jokingly declared himself a southerner by virtue of his Italian blood; then she observed how "elastic" and, in truth, how meaningless the epithet "Southern" writer had become.

An almost singular case in American letters, Glasgow began writing early and wrote until her death, improving along the way. Only *Virginia* of the novels that Glasgow thought her best — the others being *Barren Ground* (1925), *The Romantic Comedians* (1926), *They Stooped to Folly* (1929), *The Sheltered Life* (1932), and *Vein of Iron* (1935) — was written before the First World War. The novels written after *Barren Ground* respond to contemporary social issues and literary movements, through Glasgow's experiments with stream of consciousness (or "reverie," as she called it). *Vein of Iron*, for example, chronicles the fortunes of the Fincastle family during the Great Depression, which serves as a metaphor for contemporary spiritual malaise, while *In This Our Life* explores the parameters of sexual and racial identity. Addressing the relationship between "manners" and "race," the protagonist of *In This Our Life* (1941) thinks:

> How little we actually know of the Negro race. Our servants know all about us, while we know nothing of them. They are bound up in our daily lives; they are present in every intimate crisis; they are aware of, or suspect, our secret motives. Yet we are complete strangers to the way they live, to what they really think or feel

about us, or about anything else. And the less colored they are, the more inscrutable they become, until, when they have so nearly crossed the borderline [into whiteness] . . . they seem almost to speak another language, and to belong to another species than ours.[28]

The passage ironically suggests that the more we perceive people to be like us, the less we can ever know them — or, it seems, ourselves.

This leads to another apparent paradox, for Glasgow sees history as fixed and changing, and manners as both fundamental and inconsequential. They are fundamental, in the Calvinist sense that character determines fate, and inconsequential because behavior forms "only the outer envelope of personality" (*Certain Measure*, 28). Glasgow never reconciles these contradictory assumptions. She believed that human nature cannot be corrected, though history proves that behavior can.[29] Manners permit a conspiracy of civility that keeps our own beasts at bay. At the same time, they sanction the most heinous crimes, conspicuously in times of war, for the highest possible ideals.

The singularity of Glasgow's social history comes both from the quality of its individual volumes but also from the resonance of their combination. Take any given topic — race, class, gender, manners — and a dialogue ensues between books, historical periods, particular locales, and characters representing different interests and beliefs. This dialogue makes almost any statement about Glasgow and manners sound reductive. She resented being identified with a "provincial" class or code affiliated solely with Virginia (*Certain Measure*, 67) — deploring, for example, the trend of "patriotic ethnology" (*Certain Measure*, 68) in books such as Cather's *O Pioneers!* (1913) that arbitrarily elevated the experience of Swedish immigrants to Nebraska. Not to be outdone by Faulkner, nothing drew her scorn more than the revival of the grotesque, for which she held him and Erskine Caldwell chiefly responsible. She claimed to have passed through her own "peasant stage" at the beginning of her career, at a time when those in fashion read Henry James, Oscar Wilde, and "even Edith Wharton."[30] "One may admit that the Southern States have more than an equal share of degeneracy and deterioration," she conceded. Nonetheless, "the multitude of half-wits, and whole idiots, and nymphomaniacs, and paranoiacs, and rakehells in general, that populate the modern literary South could flourish nowhere" except in "the weird pages of melodrama" (*Certain Measure*, 69).

As Glasgow's comments suggest, she felt anxious about the reception of her own work and its ultimate place in literary history. She deeply resented the fact that New York publishers and reviewers regarded the South "as a lost province, to be governed, in a literary sense at least, by superior powers."[31] Accustomed if not reconciled "to the national apotheosis of the average,"[32] she decided that reviewers calculated literary merit on some inverse scale of pedigree: the more ill-bred the author, the better the book.[33] Sinclair Lewis was not — as Carl Van Doren pronounced — "America writing."[34] Neither did the chief intellectual and moral resources of America lie in Appalachia.[35] Glasgow was only slightly more outspoken than writers such as Wharton and Tate, who thought that propagandists, midwesterners, and men with ragged sleeves and dinner pails had outstripped them. Glasgow hoped that her own fiction would benefit from the continued popularity of the historical novel, which she attributed to several sources: readers revolting against the monotony and sordidness of modern fiction and the genre's reaffirmation of America's origin. Still, she did everything in her power to insure her reputation, from enlisting friendly reviewers to imploring that her books not be remaindered. In the end, she was only partly successful. As Cabell explained, subsequent shifts in literary fashions after the Second World War tended to hide her history's "real merits as a work of art" (*Reviews*, 355).

Three years before her death, Glasgow received the Pulitzer Prize for *In This Our Life*. The award — given to Wharton for *The Age of Innocence* (1920) and to Glasgow's chagrin to Cather for *One of Ours* (1922) — was bittersweet. She had hoped to win with *Barren Ground* and then again with *The Sheltered Life*. "Too little too late,"[36] she told Margaret Mitchell, as she urged her publisher to print and sell another fifty thousand copies. (If nothing else, the prize had to be "excellent for advertising purposes.")[37]

When Glasgow died, the *Saturday Review of Literature* praised her "contribution to the manners and mores of the country."[38] The *Lynchburg News* declared Virginia "better for her having been born in it, having lived in it, and especially for having written about it."[39] In other words, her fiction not only helped to explain Virginians to themselves, it challenged them to do or to be "better" — something Glasgow herself had given up hoping. The conundrum Glasgow raises may be impossible to resolve. How do we separate being from the behavior that defines it? For Glasgow, the question had comic as well as tragic overtones.

II

Glasgow bore witness to a rich and complex past. Nowhere is this perhaps more evident than in the comedies of manners she called her "Queenborough" trilogy, set in her fictional equivalent of Richmond: *The Romantic Comedians, They*

Stooped to Folly, and *The Sheltered Life*. In some ways, these books form an unlikely trilogy. The first two books are obviously comedies of manners that spoof myths about the sexes, but *The Sheltered Life* is something very different—a comedy only in the ironic sense that Balzac called the total of his many, varied novels the *comédie humaine*.

Glasgow's novels combine, as do Balzac's, minute observation with something that exceeds it, a kind of "central vision" or "inmost light" (*Certain Measure*, 210), an imaginative quality that makes their worlds seem both real and more than real. For Glasgow, this quality comes in part from an unlikely source, her own hearing loss. The onset of Glasgow's deafness coincided with her mother's sudden death in 1893 from typhoid fever. (Bouts of violent crying exacerbated a hereditary condition affecting her eustachian tubes, already damaged from influenza.) For most of her adult life, Glasgow carried a cumbersome hearing aid, a box with a loudspeaker that indiscriminately amplified every sound. "I know it is silly to be sensitive about such a thing," she told a friend, "but I can't help wincing when anyone speaks of my deafness."[40] She avoided going into shops unaccompanied or seeing callers alone. Her whole life became a struggle not to be helped, and deafness was "a wound in soul" from which there could be "no escape until death" (*Woman Within*, 113).[41] Not surprisingly, Glasgow's deafness, which turned her further and further inward, had a profound effect on a social history that became more consciously "autobiographical" after *Barren Ground*. The novels that form the Queenborough trilogy, for example, revolve around the central metaphor of deafness as a condition of modern life.

The immediate setting of these novels falls between 1910 and 1924, but the trilogy stretches back, through the character of *The Sheltered Life*'s General Archbald, to the Civil War. Although the First World War takes place significantly offstage, they might be called Glasgow's "war novels." Glasgow did write two novels that deal more directly with the First World War, *The Builders* (1919), which calls for the United States (and particularly the South) to shed its provincialism and serve the cause of international peace, and *One Man in His Time* (1922), which is, among other things, the story of a young man and a region suffering from shell shock. Glasgow declined to include either of these novels in her social history, feeling *The Builders* too jingoistic (more representative of the politics of her then-fiancé Henry Anderson than her own), and *One Man and His Time* severely flawed, having been written at the height of her own war with Anderson, which climaxed with Glasgow's taking an overdose of sleeping pills only to find herself the next morning still alive.

Glasgow found a more effective way of approaching war in the Queenborough trilogy, because she located the cause of human suffering in human nature rather than in specific historical events. War becomes both specific, the backdrop of the novels' action, and also panoramic, a sweep of history that comments on the abiding war, as Glasgow conceived it, between "human beings" and "human nature" (*Woman Within*, 225). Seen in sequence, the novels build in strength, severity, and scope: *The Romantic Comedians* focuses on divisions between the pre- and postwar generations, *They Stooped to Folly* on the world of sensation, and *The Sheltered Life* on the tragedy of the civilized mind "in a world where even the civilizations we make are uncivilized."[42]

Glasgow originally conceived *The Romantic Comedians* as a stage comedy in which listening or not listening has droll consequences. Knowing that her own talents lay elsewhere, she still pushed herself to advance the plot through dialogue, successfully replicating the slangy speech of the postwar young — "all the little things," as one friend phrased it, that "you don't say to a deaf person."[43] Dealing with miscommunication between the generations, *The Romantic Comedians* falls into two parts. The first positions the newly widowed Honeywell (based on Anderson, Glasgow's erstwhile fiancé) between two women — the twenty-three-year-old Annabel Upchurch and Amanda Lightfoot, a woman who has waited for him longer than Annabel has lived. (By the 1920s, Anderson had acquired a reputation for flirting with young flappers and dancing to dawn at "the Hot [Springs].") The second part chronicles the exhausting year of Honeywell's marriage to Annabel and his nervous collapse after she leaves him for a man her own age. The novel ends as it began, with Honeywell's recrudescence at the sight of his nurse — "younger than his memory of his mother, younger even than Annabel." "There," he thinks," is the woman I ought to have married!"[44] An unrepentant happiness-hunter, Judge Gamaliel Honeywell, may have prompted James Branch Cabell's observation that Glasgow wrote "salty reams about chivalry," whereas he (the author of *Jurgen*, a book banned by the New York Society for the Suppression of Vice) sprinkled "sugar upon the same topic."[45] Those who recognized Anderson in Glasgow's elderly Don Juan thought it Glasgow's most brilliant, and most cruel, book.[46]

Much of the book's comedy comes from characters not understanding or willfully not remembering what they have heard. Annabel turns "a deaf ear" to the platitudes that her husband learned from his first wife, Cordelia, and which he himself ignores: do not nurse disappointment, accept things as they are. He stubbornly refuses to hear the women in his life, especially his much-married but commonsensical twin sister Edmonia Bredalbane:

"Why, Gamaliel! Are you pretending that you don't know Amanda has stayed single all these years on your account?"

. . . "I can only reply that your assumption is unwarranted. . . ."

"My dear brother, she was over head and ears in love with you, and she has been always. . . ." (*Romantic Comedians*, 25–26)

Honeywell cannot acknowledge Annabel's claim without acknowledging his prejudice against elderly women with gray hair who remind him of his own mortality. His refusal to discuss the matter, to hear the other side, frees him to make a fool of himself. It also nearly kills him. Glasgow gives deafness an omnipresent quality, as it spreads through Queenborough, atomizing its citizens and disrupting any shared notions of reality. The beauty of deafness lies in the freedom it grants from social responsibility, the menace, in its portent of anarchy.

For Glasgow, manners act as an index of social morality (*Certain Measure*, 199). How can people like Honeywell reconcile individual desire with the general good? Glasgow comes to much the same conclusion as Sigmund Freud in *Civilization and Its Discontents* (1930). They cannot. Although Glasgow had mixed feelings about Freud, she agreed with his basically cynical view that civilization helps people to adjust their relations by protecting them from their own natures.[47] Because people have little power to affect their world, they have no choice except to follow its rules.

The Romantic Comedians evaluates the role that manners play in this "civilizing" process of consent and resistance. According to Judge Honeywell, manners are those rules of conduct that reflect "everlasting principles of morality" (*Romantic Comedians*, 60) and the divine rights of men. His sister, Edmonia, could not disagree more. As she explains to Honeywell, "Behavior as much as beauty is a question of geography, and . . . my respectability increases with every mile of the distance I travel from Queenborough. In France, my reputation is above reproach; by the time I reach Vienna, I have become a bit of a prude; and contrasted with the Balkan temperament, I am little more than a tombstone to female virtue" (*Romantic Comedians*, 215). Despite Glasgow's fun at Queen Marie's expense, her real target remains the discrepancy between morals and manners, tradition and "truth." In Glasgow's opinion, manners finally offer little defense against "the unalterable laws of biology" (*Romantic Comedians*, 7). The human propensity, she concedes, will always sway toward the prohibited, the unhealthy, and the immoral (*Romantic Comedians*, 30).

As the name of her trilogy suggests, Glasgow holds women largely responsible for their own exploitation. Without their dissembling, the myths that feed male vanity would die. The cost can be read in Honeywell's long-suffering ideal, Amanda Lightfoot: "The women of her generation had known how to suffer in silence [Honeywell thinks]. What an inestimable blessing was this knowledge, especially when it had passed into tradition! What suavity, what harmony, it infused into human relations! What protection, what safety, it afforded the chivalrous impulses!" (*Romantic Comedians*, 40–41). Glasgow's criticism of the tradition centers on its corruption of human relations. Honeywell has license to act the cad and call himself a gallant, while Amanda's suffering only makes her a cliché. Her ability to look simultaneously pleased and pained indicates a larger cultural schizophrenia that Glasgow associates with sentimental pretense.

Glasgow contrasts the "evasive idealism" of Amanda's generation with the ruthless egotism of Annabel's. After the First World War, manners have little power to stay a woman's tongue or inhibit her libido. Not a stereotypical flapper, Annabel nevertheless represents the riot usually associated with that vogue. To her husband, she seems devoid of moral principles, though cognizant of a "crude" kind of justice that recognizes the "universal rights" (*Romantic Comedians*, 122) of poor people and animals—concerns close to Glasgow's heart. Nothing, she insists, is anybody's fault. "You were all afraid of life," she tells her mother, "and you called your fear virtue" (*Romantic Comedians*, 205). In Annabel's cosmology, manners keep people enchained. They prevent the pursuit of beauty and joy, the things that make life meaningful and that she ironically embodies for Honeywell. Annabel is more ignorant than innocent, however. When she consents to marry her cousin Cordelia's widower for his money, she shows herself to be her mother's daughter. Queenborough sanctions this "incestuous" union because it seems a fair exchange for youth—"this instinct of fatherhood [as Honeywell calls it], which, bursting suddenly from a seed of sympathy, had shot up like the fairy beanstalk in his mind" (*Romantic Comedians*, 48). Glasgow's language leaves little doubt about Honeywell's motives or Queenborough's collusion in the debauchery of children. The relative power of men and women makes the sacrifice of one generation to the next as inevitable as war itself.

Between Annabel and Amanda, Glasgow positions Bella Upchurch, Annabel's widowed mother. Bella is an author of sorts, or at least one who knows how to create fictions soothing to the male ego. To her, manners simply designate epochs. Behavior becomes good or bad, moral or immoral, in the context of particular circumstances. A natural skeptic, she nevertheless craves (not unlike Glasgow herself) something ultimate, abstract, or permanent (*Romantic Comedians*, 207). Applauding youth's need for privacy and its hatred of hypocrisy, she still wonders where its lack of shame will lead: "Religion, yes, but even more than religion, she craved the efficacious belief in reticence, in refinement, in perfect behaviour. If the world continued to grow away from, not only from God, but from good breeding as well, what, she wondered despondently, could be trusted to keep wives contented and the working classes in order?" (*Romantic Comedians*, 135). Glasgow refuses to condense experience into any formula, sentimental or otherwise. Her burlesque of manners suggests that only by groping "beyond creeds, beyond forms and self, can we grasp the spirit of life" (*Romantic Comedians*, 229) or the genuine meaning of civilization, defined in this novel as small kindnesses. The comedy lies in the circular nature of the journey. Like figures on a Grecian urn, her characters chase something just barely outside their grasp. Glasgow directs her irony less at individuals than at the human condition itself. The tragedy of one generation or sex will forever continue as the low comedy of another. What makes *The Romantic Comedians* poignant is Glasgow's recognition of the amoral will to life and happiness. Beginning as a satire, it becomes, if not a tragedy, a poignant tale of human fallibility and yearning.

III

The Romantic Comedians sold more than 100,000 copies in the first months following its publication. Three years later, Glasgow hoped to repeat her triumph with the second book of her Queenborough trilogy, *They Stooped to Folly*. *They Stooped to Folly* partly grew from Glasgow's literary flirtation with James Branch Cabell. In 1927, he dedicated his novel *Something about Eve: A Comedy of Fig-Leaves* to "Ellen Glasgow — very naturally — this book which commemorates the intelligence of women." Set in Lichfield, Cabell's equivalent of Queenborough, and Poictesme, its twin world of randy shadows, *Something about Eve* parodies an ageless etiquette of adultery. Glasgow returned Cabell's compliment with *They Stooped to Folly*, a book that honors — or debunks — the chivalry of men. Her dedication reads:

To James Branch Cabell
. . . In Acknowledgment of Something
About Eve . . .
This Book Commemorates the
Chivalry of Men.

Glasgow's subtitle "A Comedy of Morals" obliquely recalls that of Cabell's *Jurgen* (1919), "A Comedy of Justice," whose suppression made Cabell temporarily famous — as he liked to joke, "through accident."[48]

Like *Jurgen* and *Something about Eve*, *They Stooped to Folly* analyzes what Henry Mencken called "the Southern attitude toward fornication" (*Reviews*, 31). Realizing that novelists had "an inexhaustible [and profitable] subject in Women,"[49] Glasgow decided to exploit the myth about those who had fallen to show that morals have their own seasons, like bloomers or fashions in fiction. When women were busy with life, she explains in the book's preface, men had time to create myths about their nature. These falsehoods, which paint women either as muses or impediments, have fed writers from Samuel Richardson to John Galsworthy. The first myth dominated the English novel until Arnold Bennett; then the modern school of drab gave birth to the second. Even the book that tells us something about Eve, she chided Cabell, tells us more about Adam (*Certain Measure*, 233).

In *They Stooped to Folly*, Glasgow recounts the fate of three generations of ruined women: Aunt Agatha, whose pregnancy in the 1880s made her the subject of sermons; Mrs. Dalrymple, a divorcee reclaimed by war work in (where else?) the Balkans; and Milly Burden, the unrepentant heroine of a seduced-and-abandoned story. The novel's epigraph comes from Oliver Goldsmith: "When lovely woman stoops to folly, / And finds too late that men betray, / What charm can soothe her melancholy? / What art can wash her guilt away?" For Glasgow, the answer to Goldsmith's question is simple: time. In Aunt Agatha's day, the "unwritten etiquette of seduction" demanded that a woman refuse to name her seducer.[50] By Milly's time, she thinks nothing of shouting it from every rooftop. Now that the war has made the scarlet letter a badge of courage, Glasgow writes, women can finally abdicate their responsibility for men's morality. Although the war has ended at the beginning of this novel, it comes to stand for the chaos of unchecked desire masquerading as altruism. Mary Victoria, the daughter of the Littlepages, sent to find Milly's fiancé, rescues and then marries him. Their positions mark a cultural shift after the Great War: the demobilization of men from centers of power and eventually from the heart of American life.

Showing that myths about women harm the men whose vanity they feed, Glasgow begins and ends her novel in the consciousness of its male protagonist, Mary Victoria's father, Virginius Littlepage. As always in a Glasgow novel, names have importance, Virginius's underscoring a diminishment in human nature from the days of the Roman empire to the present—not to mention the innocence and inconsequence of southern, and analogously American, provincialism before the Great War. Virginius's point of view literally envelops—or at least encases—that of his wife, Victoria, who speaks for herself in the second of the novel's three sections. Shifting the novel's central consciousness, Glasgow refigures reality while insisting that myths about a mother's love and male chivalry never die. Neither does evasive idealism. The Littlepages pride themselves on making their spouses perfectly happy. Victoria refuses to acknowledge that Virginius lusts after Mrs. Dalrymple; and he has no understanding of the inner life she most fully shares with her childhood companion Louisa Goddard.

Glasgow argues that prevailing attitudes about psychology and sex are no more permanent than mutton sleeves and wasp waists. It was fortunate, Victoria thinks, that her friendship with Louisa "had come to flower before the serpent of Freudian psychology had poisoned" its "sinless Eden" (*Folly*, 185). The happiness of the Littlepage marriage rests on habit and a shared myopia. A "perfect" marriage like the Littlepages may be perfect because it leaves the secret core of both partners undisturbed, if unsatisfied. Its focus on the largely socioeconomic mechanics of living, works as a form of self-protection, a way of retaining what one most desires to conceal.

This paradox of yearning and aversion unites the three volumes of the Queenborough trilogy. Most people, to Glasgow's mind, lead double, frequently quadruple, lives. Virginius suffers the painful process of becoming Victoria's ideal. She dreams of a more primitive man who would make her forget her duty. Worn out with the strain of being a good "influence," Victoria dies, significantly, of heart trouble; and Virginius, discovering her silent suffering, inconsolably mourns the woman who, for the last thirty-five years, had had the privilege of almost boring him to death. Hypocrisy reigns as the one art that has "reached its peak in America" (*Folly*, 81). Yet where would America have been without it? Glasgow suggests that without certain myths or cultural prohibitions, no one could be persuaded to marry or—as the end of Mary Victoria's marriage illustrates—stay married. Her husband joins the ranks of other American Rip van Winkles, as he escapes to the margins of the book and the consequences of his social being. In this way, he mimics the position of many later-nineteenth- and twentieth-century heroines such as Ellen Olenska, whose unconventional plots must be imagined.[51] His escape comically signals the transfer of cultural authority from men to women like Mary Victoria—her name ironically bringing to mind the Virgin and the nineteenth century's queen of propriety. That Mary Victoria has already shown herself to be neither virgin nor proper is of little importance; she is as bossy, narcissistic, and misguided as any male in the novel.

They Stooped to Folly turns on Glasgow's conflation of manners and morals.

Human relationships necessitate the constant clarification of societal precepts: You can take "genteel conduct for granted," she writes, but not the heart's "fatal indulgence" (*Folly*, 37). People like Virginius want a magic formula against strong feeling, whereas more vagrant souls such as Milly or Virginius's brother, an artist named Marmaduke, would sacrifice anything — position, wealth, security, honor — for freedom. Glasgow implies that too often manners serve the status quo. In the New South, she makes clear, they have become so aligned with capitalism that "the men who saved our country would receive scant applause in the presence of men who were selling it" (*Folly*, 150). Manners — and here Glasgow parts from contemporaries such as Willa Cather in *Shadows on the Rock* — do not necessarily represent any discernible sign of spiritual grace, assumed or genuine. They have come to perform a purely social function.

Glasgow's response to life's vagaries can be read in her most conventional character, Virginius's wife, Victoria. In the months preceding her death, Victoria tries to resist the advancing cavalcade of the New South. Like Glasgow, she suffers from an ailment called tinnitus — a ringing in the ears that signals her incipient deafness and the intolerable din of modern life. Yet it also brings a strange relief, for the voices of Victoria's family grow fainter and fainter as the tinnitus escalates. "It is the loudest kind of confusion," she tells Louisa. "I have at moments a ridiculous feeling that the tumult is all in some other dimension, that something beyond time and space is trying to reach me" (*Folly*, 144–45). This "rustling vacancy" (*Folly*, 190), this din, drowns out every moral problem, including the most pressing one of wayward women, and leaves Victoria on the shore of a new world, where the whole century appears merely a "ripple in the current of being" (*Folly*, 164). Victoria comes to see her deafness as a function of her "imagination" (*Folly*, 145). It separates her from everything and everyone she holds dear, but it also brings an unexpected gift. When Victoria sheds the onerous burden of self, she also wakens to something greater than herself.

After reading *They Stooped to Folly*, Allen Tate told Glasgow that it showed her to be almost a new writer, "with immense gains in style, form, and dramatic power" — changes that she brought to near perfection in the last of her Queenborough trilogy, *The Sheltered Life*.[52] Notwithstanding that Tate responded to the heightened irony of Glasgow's tone and the terser economy of her prose, its power may indeed come — as Glasgow wrote of *Barren Ground* — from the translation of lived experience into art. "I have always wanted to put my best into my books," she told Tate, "to make them compensate, in a way, for the kind of life I have had. Strangely enough, I have a feeling that my best work is ahead."[53]

Glasgow's genius lay in her acceptance of the paradox of mutability and perma-
nence. In her history of manners, manners offer an appraisal of contemporary
culture against "enduring" standards, the timeless, ahistorical standards that she
and Tate thought art communicated. Glasgow's views about art do not mean that
she wanted to retreat from the present. "We need insight; we need integrity and
audacity," she wrote, but we also "need really to live in the modern world we
inhabit" (*Reasonable Doubts*, 172). She merely refused to be reconciled to its
imperfections.

IV

Despite Tate's compliment that Glasgow had become a "new" writer, she
represented for him a particular period in American literature mostly of his own
imagining. Reading her early books, Tate had thought her "an incredible old
snob" and "one of the worst novelists in the world."[54] (His grievance included
that her books sold by the hundred thousands.) After making her acquaintance at
the Southern Writers Conference (which she helped to organize in 1931), he
decided that the more he considered her the more he fell in love with her: she
"has one of those fine impeccable consciences that live entirely alone; that's what
I feel about her—she has something deep and indestructible in her character
which was possible to her generation but not mine."[55] Partly nostalgic, partly
self-serving, Tate's comment unconsciously, and perhaps more accurately, recalls Joseph Conrad's observation about Henry James. Although a very different
writer than James, Glasgow was, if not a "historian of fine consciences," then one
of multiple consciences.

Like Tate, many of Glasgow's contemporaries considered *The Sheltered Life*
her crowning achievement, or in the words of another friend, the book that—
"Well, damn it!"—should have won the Pulitzer.[56] What was it that made this
novel stand out among her many novels? According to Tate, *The Sheltered Life*
went "beyond the province of manners into the tragic vision." Tate thought that
Glasgow's conception of character in terms of "manners" had actually marred her
first books because manners themselves had little to say about the transcendent
power of the creative imagination. "There is the late nineteenth-century liberal-
ism," he told her, "that gives one the notion that all these people, their defects
and virtues, even their sufferings, might be altered or improved if only the Code
were different."[57] Responding to the Darwinistic thrust of books like *The Deliverance*, Tate rightly acknowledges her more organic vision of human experience

in books such as *Virginia* and *The Sheltered Life*, which exceeds the boundaries of a strictly regional history.

Glasgow's own intent was far more ambitious. By "the sheltered life," she wanted to imply "the whole civilization man has built to protect himself from reality."[58] She set her novel on the eve of America's entry into the First World War, but she wrote it at a time when people, having shown an unwillingness to learn from history, predicted a second and even greater catastrophe. Through the imagination of her elderly protagonist General Archbald, she links (as did Henry James) the First World War to the War between the States. In an interview, entitled "Miss Glasgow Talks of War and Literature," she recounts her indignation at a man who declared that America needed the First World War. "America might need it," she retorted, "but the South didn't; it had had its war already." Glasgow meant that the Civil War divided history for southerners as the Great War divided generations abroad and at home. In her opinion, Reconstruction had further segregated the South from the rest of the nation, leaving it doubly defeated. The South's legacy of suffering and its cult of mourning had imbued the region with a heightened spiritual consciousness, which, in turn, made its suffering — at least in retrospect — bearable.

The First World War merely corroborated Glasgow's pessimistic vision of human nature, which she articulated in a little known story called "Dare's Gift." A partial template for *The Sheltered Life*, it recounts the history of Lucy Dare, who, like all the inhabitants of her family's house, committed acts of betrayal. The first Dare betrayed his leader in Bacon's Rebellion, and Lucy Dare surrendered her Northern lover to Confederate soldiers. The recovery of Lucy's story, which "failed to arrest the imagination of her time,"[59] acts as a contemporary warning about the nature of manners, for Antigone lurks beneath the belle's demure exterior. "There are many such women among us," a character cautions. They move "in obscurity — reserved, passive, commonplace — and we never suspect the spark of fire in their natures until it flares up at the touch of the unexpected" (*Collected Short Stories*, 108). Glasgow ends "Dare's Gift" with a chilling example of the cost of preserving illusions. A latter-day Madame LeFarge, the elderly Lucy spends her days knitting mufflers for the Allies.

In *The Sheltered Life*, violence also lurks beneath the "enamelled surface of beautiful behaviour" (*Folly*, 331). Glasgow structures her novel around analogous systems of manners that belie myths about chivalric manhood, romantic love, and young girls' innocence. More importantly for the evolution of her social history, they reflect the social organization of Queenborough complicated by issues, in an arguably descending order, of gender, race, age, and class. Like *They Stooped to Folly*, the novel follows the representatives of three generations: General Archbald, who fought in a war he could not support and married a woman he could not love; Eva Birdsong, the town's reigning belle, who has a mulatta proxy named Memoria; and the general's granddaughter, Jenny Blair Archbald. Glasgow links the women, who represent sociosexual models of conduct, through their connection to Eva's philandering husband, George. When nine-year-old Jenny Blair finds George in Memoria's house, she thinks: "Nothing was important except this queer sense of his belonging here, of his being at home in Canal Street, in Memoria's house. For he stood there, in the centre of what Jenny Blair thought of vaguely, as "a coloured room," with an unchanged air of physical exuberance, of vital well-being, of sanguine expectancy."[60] The room seems "coloured" to Jenny Blair because the customary hierarchies of her society have momentarily collapsed: the cavalier tradition associated with her courtly grandfather, the tenets of "true womanhood" embodied in Eva Birdsong, and the received history of Queenborough and the South, which Memoria's relationship to George contradicts. In truth, Jenny wakes to womanhood — realized years later through her own affair with George.[61]

Glasgow commemorates the history of black women through the character of Memoria, who testifies to the impossibility of separating her history from that of Jenny Blair and the other women of Queenborough. In her depiction of Memoria, who embodies (as her name suggests) memory itself, Glasgow intertwines social history and private lives. By conflating the lives of Memoria and Eva, specifically through their sexual relationships with George Birdsong, she reveals the arbitrary and despotic character of racial division. White women, who have typically derived power from motherhood and femininity, continue sentimental traditions that rob them of autonomy and individuality, and black women like Memoria have little choice except to collude in their community's larger conspiracy of silence.[62] If Jenny Blair chose, she could read the South's forgotten and forbidden history in Memoria's white features as well as in those of her apparently fatherless son. Instead, she agrees to keep George's secret, ironically trapping herself in the childlike world of make-believe.

The Sheltered Life explores the tyranny of tradition that similarly inflamed Edith Wharton. "People who have tradition are oppressed by tradition," Glasgow writes, "and people who are without it are oppressed by the lack of it — or by whatever else they have put in its place" (*Sheltered Life*, 217). Glasgow illustrates this process through her book's divisions: "The Age of Make-Believe" begins in

Jenny Blair's nine-year-old consciousness, "The Deep Past," in General Archbald's, and "Illusion" knits them — the impossible — together. The first section focuses on myths that self-perpetuate, the second on a reality that eludes analysis, and the third comes full circle. Book by book, Glasgow pushes her trilogy toward disaster, from Jenny Blair's discovery to her own predestined passion, to Eva's "awakening" and George's death and to the Great War itself.

The book's humor, however grim, comes from the characters' failure to hear and heed. "Do you want me?" George asks Jenny. She thinks, "Did she want him?" (*Sheltered Life*, 287). "Do you want me?" he repeats. She ignores the question. "If you cared — " she prompts, and his arms go around her, then drop. "George, I want you" (*Sheltered Life*, 289), Eva calls to the husband she has just shot. There's a kind of poetic justice in George's death — especially if the reader knows that the author also happened to have been the president of Richmond's SPCA and scornful of the "anthropomorphic fallacy" that people deserve consideration before animals. The day of his death, George comes home with twenty-five ducks, having shot and discarded three times as many. Before depositing his bounty in the library, he takes it upstairs to show his wife. The carcasses cover every inch of the couch and chairs, and she has "to stop his putting them on the bed" (*Sheltered Life*, 285): "Nobody ever seems to think of what is really important [she tells Jenny]. Though, I suppose . . . ducks are more important to themselves than anything else. Do you imagine they would consider it an honour to be sent round to one's acquaintances with visiting cards tied to their necks?" (286). "[W]ith clots of blood . . . on some of the noble breasts," they seem "decorated as if for a wedding feast, with bits of green ribbon" (287). Symbolizing the end of the Birdsongs' marriage, Eva's dreams, and George himself, the ducks also link these supposedly small and inconsequential murders to the slaughter in Europe. "I can never understand," says Eva unwittingly of herself, "why men enjoy killing, especially killing beautiful wild things" (*Sheltered Life*, 285).

Eva teaches that pretense kills, yet the novel ends with a series of lies, ironically restoring the obsolete order: "It was an accident"; Jenny Blair *is* innocent. "Oh, Grandfather," she cries, "I didn't mean anything . . . I didn't mean anything in the world" (*Sheltered Life*, 292). The cipher of Jenny Blair serves as Glasgow's critique of modernism. As she reads history, all ages call their own cruelties "civilization" (*Romantic Comedians*, 85). For civilization to go forward, Glasgow writes, it "must recoil from individualism and seek some fairer design" (*Sheltered Life*, 279). Not surprisingly, she articulates that design through her central character, General Archbald. "Into his lonely spirit," she wrote, "I have put much of my ultimate feeling about life" (*Certain Measure*, 204).

Archbald's meditation on the past, which signifies so much of Glasgow's own feeling, is really a meditation on manners told through three separate yet related memories. To some extent, they undercut Glasgow's statements about her protagonist by exposing the limits of his self-knowledge. At the same time, they highlight the larger point that history, like fiction, is both an act of memory and creation. It reflects human beings' changing views of themselves and the universe, or what Glasgow liked to label the "accommodating processes of evolution" (*Certain Measure*, 23). Archbald illustrates what she herself believed: that no matter how much we imagine ourselves freed from time or place or history, these factors have nevertheless determined the nature of our rebellion, the scope of our emancipation.

Archbald's reverie illustrates how the past continues into a present it has shaped. His first memory, the ritual killing of a deer, exposes the deforming power of tradition:

> With blood on his hands and a savage joy inflaming his face, his grandfather strode over to smear stains on a milksop. "If you don't like the taste of blood better than milk, you'll have to be blooded. Hold still, sir, I say, and be blooded." Then, as the blood touched him, the boy retched with sickness, and vomited over the anointing hand and the outstretched arm. . . . "I don't love people!" he sobbed passionately. "I don't love people!" Was it fair to blame him because he had been born different? (*Sheltered Life*, 104–5)

The memory, which begins with the killing of a defenseless creature and ends with Archbald's own estrangement, if not outright misanthropy, provides a sketch of the process that turns a boy into a soldier. Glasgow sees little difference between the process that makes Archbald a man and the one that makes his granddaughter a lady. Both extinguish some inner light. The tragedy of a civilized man in an uncivilized society (as Glasgow describes Archbald's situation) is that he can and almost certainly will be trained to evil.

Archbald's second memory, which recounts the help he gave an escaping slave, provides a measure of the man he became against the boy he had been. As in Willa Cather's *The Professor's House*, the man fairs poorer: "For the second time in his young life he was defying the established order, he was in conflict with the moral notions of men. Is it true, he asked himself now, that man's pity and man's morality are for ever in conflict? Is it true that pity is by nature an outlaw? Well, he liked to think that he had not hesitated; no, not for an instant" (*Sheltered Life*, 110). Archbald brings the unnamed slave clothes, food, and a paper that declares him Abram Jones, property of Gideon Archbald going to visit his wife in Spottsylvania. Significantly, Archbald never learns the fate of the runaway, whose history, like Memoria's, has been lost or whose rights he ultimately denounced as a general in the Confederate army: "His soul, it is true, had been a rebel; but he had given lip-homage, like other men all over the world, to creeds that were husks" (*Sheltered Life*, 109). Ironically, Archbald's youthful "defiance" ends with his own liberation. When his father learns that he has "defied not only the moral notions of his age and his place, but the law and the Constitution and the highest court in the land" (*Sheltered Life*, 111), he sends him to Europe. There he meets the subject of his third memory, a married woman, who kills herself after their failed elopement.

Archbald's repeated capitulation to appearances reveal his character as much as his social milieu: "He had been a good citizen, a successful lawyer, a faithful husband, an indulgent father; he had been, indeed everything but himself. Always he had fallen into the right pattern; but the centre of the pattern was missing. Once again, the old heartbreaking question returned. Why and what is human personality?" (*Sheltered Life*, 120). How do we know when the formulas of being *become* being? he asks. Manners, as Archbald's life illustrates, tyrannize as much as they liberate. Their grace — and their pathos — resides in the protective camouflage they grant.

In "The Deep Past" section of *The Sheltered Life*, Glasgow tests the parameters of the realistic novel of manners. She does this in several ways. First, she experiments (as she would in her next novel, *Vein of Iron*) with sentence length and rhythm to recreate the stream of Archbald's consciousness. Second, she disrupts the chronology of the narrative much as Virginia Woolf does in *To the Lighthouse* (1921). And third, she addresses the topic of time directly. "Time was stranger than memory," Archbald thinks. "What was time itself but the bloom, the sheath enfolding experiences? Within time, and within time alone, there was life — the gleam, the quiver, the heart-beat, the immeasurable joy and anguish of being. . . ." (*Sheltered Life*, 109). Glasgow's titles "The Age of Make-Believe" and "The Illusion" underscore the fictive nature of time, history, and memory as she challenges the "realities" recorded in the sections that proceed and follow "The Deep Past."

As her social history testifies, Glasgow never made her peace with the South she loved. How could she? She never made her peace with life. Instead, she claimed to have reached a kind of stasis, what she thought of as an "accord without surrender" (*Woman Within*, 296). There was not an age in history, she wrote, "when I should not have felt myself to be both an exile and a stranger." If her quarrel was "less with the world than with the scheme of things in general" (*Woman Within*, 279), she never lost her interest in the parade of human nature. In her mind, humanity was measureless and reality various,[63] and her social history, which illustrates, volume by volume, the form's response to current literary trends, shows how the novel of manners can be both particular and general, true to the realities and the Reality that Glasgow valued more.

Glasgow realized that every writer's work "must sooner or later become 'dated.'" Nevertheless, she took some comfort in the fact "that, provided the reversed view is long enough, all dates come at last to look alike in the indifferent pages of history" (*Certain Measure*, 7). This certainly proved true for Glasgow, whose reputation fell faster than a Confederate dollar after her death, to rise again in the ensuing decades (*Reviews*, 355). Today the books that she considered her best have been reprinted. No matter that Glasgow anticipated the time when her social history might become another "unhappy anachronism" (*Certain Measure*, 7). With William Faulkner's Yoknapatawpha saga — or, closer to Glasgow's own heart, Thomas Hardy's Wessex novels — it continues to deserve consideration not only for its design but for its comprehensive and compassionate wisdom.

CHAPTER SIX

Jessie Fauset

The Etiquette of Passing

> No matter how much a person desires to write he cannot write unless he has practice, and he cannot practice without models. . . . Do our colored pupils read the great writers and stylists? Are they ever shown the prose of Shaw, Galsworthy, Mrs. Wharton, Du Bois or Conrad, or that old master of exquisite phrase and imaginative incident — Walter Pater?
>
> JESSIE FAUSET, "The Prize Story Competition"

> Sometimes it seems to me that I have never really been a Negro, that I have been only a privileged spectator of their inner life; at other times I feel that I have been a coward, a deserter, and I am possessed by a strange longing for my mother's people.
>
> JAMES WELDON JOHNSON, *Autobiography of an Ex-Colored Man*

I

Langston Hughes called Jessie Fauset (1882–1961), along with Charles S. Johnson and Alain Locke, one of the "midwives" of the Harlem Renaissance.[1] In the 1920s, most people knew Fauset primarily as the literary editor of *The Crisis*, the magazine founded by her mentor W. E. B. Du Bois.[2] Fauset used her position to recover forgotten black heroes and history and to promote the careers of many now famous writers, including not only Hughes but also Countee Cullen, Claude McKay, Jean Toomer, Nella Larsen, Arna Bontemps, and Zora Neale Hurston.[3] She also edited for its short life (1920–21) *The Brownies' Book*, a magazine designed in part to give black children "a code of honor and action in their relations with white children."[4] Always a teacher, Fauset hoped to shape the tastes and politics of her readers, young and old.[5]

The Crisis's political agenda distinguished it from other purely literary magazines. The editors denounced racial prejudice, celebrated black accomplishment, and promised to serve "the rights of all men irrespective of color or race, for the highest ideals of American democracy" and "human brotherhood" (Wall, 45).

The Crisis, which took its name from James Russell Lowell's antislavery poem "The Present Crisis" (1844), reflects Du Bois's interest in sociology and Jamesian pragmatism — as he understood it from William James himself: before testing the workable logic of any hypothesis, its truth should be assumed.[6] The founding of the NAACP in 1909, followed by the publication of *The Crisis*, its official magazine, in 1910 gave legitimacy and, in time, prestige to the cultural principles that Fauset and Du Bois identified as the strength of the black community: originality, endurance, loyalty, and faith.

From Du Bois, Fauset learned the impossibility of scientifically categorizing the races. In *The Negro* (1915), he presented race as a dynamic concept, "the typical races . . . continually changing and developing, amalgamating and differentiating."[7] Racism continued from a confusion of the people who were enslaved with the practice of slavery itself. Professing to be more puzzled by the origin of whites than blacks,[8] Du Bois claimed that African culture, which predated and influenced that of white America, produced "the first, the ur-American."[9] Fauset wanted "to teach our colored men and women *race* pride, *self*-pride, self sufficiency (the right kind) and the necessity of living our lives as nearly as possible, *absolutely*, instead of comparing them always with white standards." She thought that blacks should adopt standards of Anglo-Saxon behavior only when they were "the *best*," not because they were white.[10] This belief in the "best" expressly aligns her with Edith Wharton as well as with the "New Negro writers," who advocated standards of "excellence" unaffected by considerations of race.

For the readers of *The Crisis*, Fauset defined the "best" in a cross-cultural context of racial equality and pride. She saw African-American literature belonging to a larger tradition of American, European, and Caribbean writing, the relationship more reciprocal than contentious. (The title of *The Brownies' Book*, like that of *The Crisis*, extends another tradition, in this instance, Palmer Cox's immensely popular "Brownies" series about a race of good-natured elves.) Her name belongs alongside other influential editors such as James Russell Lowell, William Dean Howells, and Walter Hines Page who envisioned themselves changing the entire tenor of American life, making it more democratic in practice and more international in perspective. Fauset deeply believed, as Lowell had written seventy-five years before, that "new occasions teach new duties," and she wanted to steer a community in the making. If the readers of *The Atlantic* and *Harper's* sought confirmation of their intellectual superiority, readers of *The Crisis* found a chorus of competing voices affirming their identity as "Negroes" and citizens of the United States.

Although Fauset became the first Harlem Renaissance writer famous enough to autograph books at Macy's department store (Lewis, 274), her literary ascendancy was short. By the 1930s, she had fallen out of "vogue" (to use Hughes's word) with the rising wave of young proletarians. Her imposing manner, Sorbonne education, and old Philadelphia background, as restrictive as any found in old New York, made her appear hopelessly middle-class.[11] No matter that Fauset criticized the pretensions of that class, she heard herself dismissed as too "genteel," the label that has plagued novelists of manners from Howells to the present day.

Unlike Edith Wharton, who satirized the new wave of midwestern writers in *Hudson River Bracketed* (1929) and *The Gods Arrive* (1932) and Ellen Glasgow, who publicly resented William Faulkner and Erskine Caldwell's "Raw-Head-and-Bloody Bones" approach, Fauset chided her critics in private. When Alain Lock, in a 1934 issue of *Opportunity*, disparaged her novelistic style as mid-Victorian, she forgot "ladylike" proprieties and fired off a blistering letter accusing him of bad taste, personal prejudice, pedantry, and, worse, sycophancy toward whites.[12] After her rebuttal to Locke, Fauset published no more novels. Yet those written between 1924 and 1933 — *There Is Confusion* (1924), *Plum Bun* (1929), *The Chinaberry Tree: An American Novel* (1931), and *Comedy: American Style* (1933) — provide, in the spirit of Glasgow, a "social history" of the United States. By focusing on interracial and intraracial relationships, Fauset not only helped to bring the black, urban, middle class into the mainstream of American and continental literature,[13] she further politicized the novel of manners by focusing on the theme of passing, or the exchanging of one race for another. Her characters of mixed blood who pass as white eventually pass for other blacks, in the sense that they take a stand against injustice.[14]

II

"To be a Negro in America," Fauset wrote in her introduction to *The Chinaberry Tree*, "posits a dramatic situation."[15] It could hardly be otherwise for a nation obsessed with questions of color. As a novelist, Fauset wanted to show how little — and how much — color mattered. She insisted, for example, that black characters resembled their white counterparts in everything except the color of their skin. It bothered her that publishers considered stories about educated blacks uninteresting and that fiction taught whites to see blacks as foolish or criminal. Why, she asked, should black artists be any more constrained by stereotypes than whites? "People suffer, not because they are black," she writes, "but because of the construction which a dominant white world has put on that color."[16] Fauset suggests that identity exists apart from, yet responsive to, social circumstances. The tension in her fiction comes from opposing definitions of the self at once stable and unstable, socially constructed and inherent.

For Fauset, the problem of racial definition had much to do with the white world, but it also had something to do with blacks themselves. Her cast of characters in *Comedy: American Style*, for example, includes Olivia Blanchard Cary, a mother who asks her dark-skinned son to play her Filipino butler; Olivia's daughter, Teresa, who would have her fiancé pass as Mexican; Phebe Grant, a girl too black for one suitor and too white for another; and so-called "race people" hungry for lighter-skinned grandchildren. Fauset had the courage to expose what others wanted to deny — that color did indeed affect one's mobility and status in the black community.[17] The characters in her first novel, *There Is Confusion*, describe this overemphasis on color as a "complex" that affects every aspect of black life, from education to marriage and the rearing of children. Fauset's definition of color — "some slight deformity" (*Confusion*, 19) — recalls William Dean Howells's depiction of race in *An Imperative Duty* as a form of cultural neurasthenia. "Either you concern yourself with it violently as the Southerner does and so let slip by all the other important issues of life," Fauset writes; "or you are indifferent and callous like the average Northerner and grow hardened to all sorts of atrocities; or you steep yourself in it like the sentimentalist . . . and find yourself paralyzed by the vastness of the problem."[18] Following Howells and Du Bois, Fauset attributes the color "complex" to a system of social conventions rooted in the old regime of slavery.

The subject of Fauset's fiction also determined her historical perspective. Wharton thought that the First World War would make the historical form of the novel the only possible form because the present could no longer be assumed. But Fauset agreed more with a southerner like Glasgow who declared that the South did not need the First World War to know suffering. It had had its war already. For Fauset, as for Glasgow, the "great war" could be none other than the Civil War, with whose legacies she and other African Americans continued to contend. Du Bois tried to articulate the historical forces giving rise to black expression in a 1926 essay entitled "Criteria of Negro Art": "There has come to us . . . a realization of that past, of which for long years we have been ashamed, for which we have apologized. We thought nothing could come out of that past which we wanted to remember; which we wanted to hand down to our children. Suddenly, this same past is taking on form, color, reality, and in a half shame-faced way we are beginning to be proud of it."[19] Fauset's *The Chinaberry Tree*, which honors the love between Aunt Sal and her former master "the Colonel," might have been written to this prescription. Although such a plot seems in danger of also bowing to the formula of plantation romances, Fauset's real target is the black community's conspiracy to suppress history. In *The Chinaberry Tree*, this denial of the past almost results in an intraracial marriage between siblings, a half-brother and a half-sister ignorant of their true relationship.

As a writer, Fauset often found herself in an impossible position. Whatever difficulties she had because of her sex were not only compounded by race but also by class and perhaps most by questions of audience. In the September 1926 edition of *The Crisis*, she wondered whether "the situation of the educated Negro in America with its pathos, humiliation and tragedy [might not] call for artistic treatment at least as sincere and sympathetic as 'Porgy' received." Her first respondent, the literary and social historian Benjamin Brawley, replied with one word: "Certainly."[20]

No matter how well meant, Brawley's response did not get at the heart of Fauset's desire to write for a general, rather than a racially segregated, audience. Nor did it address the problem of serving the warring gods of art and politics or her own ambivalent, sometimes contradictory feelings about the relationship between race and identity. Fauset's social agenda, which further complicated choices about representation, aligns her less with Brawley than an unlikely, turn-of-the-century predecessor named E. M. Woods. As the author of *The Negro in Etiquette: A Novelty* (1899), Woods faced many of the same difficulties that would confront Fauset almost three decades later. His book is interesting because it highlights the encumbrances that any single narrative strategy carries.

Like other African-American proponents of good manners, Woods argued that the practice of polite behavior would lead to better relationships with whites. Even Du Bois noted that middle-class blacks answered those disbelievers who questioned the ability of his race "to assimilate American culture."[21] The Palmer Memorial Institute, opened by Charlotte Hawkins Brown in 1902 and continuing into the next decades, owed its success to a curriculum that stressed a combination of social graces and liberal arts.[22] "Acquire manners," Brown wrote as late as 1940, "and the rest will come."[23] Although etiquette columns formed a staple of black newspapers such as the *New York Age* and *Half Century Magazine*,[24] their publication, usually in the women's section, did not preclude blacks reading the same etiquette books as whites. In fact, a member of Philadelphia's old black society who stumbled across a copy of Woods's book, with its chapters on sidewalk etiquette, dancing the "rag," the cake walk, and too much freedom in kissing—rather than debutante balls or the intricacies of correspondence—would probably have found it useless and probably insulting.

The Negro in Etiquette speaks to the same questions of morality, status, and conformity that interested Fauset. By providing a kind of "social history," it also shows, through Woods's use of fictionalized anecdotes, dialect, and cartoon-like illustrations, an almost unavoidable confusion about audience. Questions of audience cannot be wholly separated from those of tone, and Woods, like Fauset, seeks to contain and legitimize certain notions of race, class, and color. Not surprisingly, Fauset's novels and Woods's advice book revolve around a series of buried questions that evoke the structure of slave narratives. What defines the races? Should blacks and whites marry?

What occurs subtly in Fauset's novels—a rhetoric working against itself—occurs dramatically in *The Negro in Etiquette*. Dedicating his manual to his "sainted mother," Woods reinscribes a Victorian ideal that ignored black women, while the curious subtitle of the book, "A Novelty," captures his own ambivalence. Woods winds up contradicting himself because he tries to address the divergent needs of his readers, whose expectations collide with his express or tacit purpose. Many blacks may have, as Woods asserts, far better breeding than whites (23); still, they need to know their "place": "Colored men, don't you know that white men don't like too much gallantry from negro men around their women any more than negro men like too much of it from white men around theirs?" In a chapter entitled "White Neighbors," he writes that it must "be distinctly understood and everlastingly remembered that people of refinement don't go where they are not wanted."[25]

Woods wants to rid his readers of the "bad habits" associated with the minstrel, from the "shuffling, awkward walk" (29) to "nigger" expressions such as "Thank you, Boss" (83), to the "color worship" at its core (43) by replacing one kind of minstrel based on passing (black performers in black face, men playing women) with another.[26] Yet the illustrations accompanying Woods's text, which contain dark-skinned figures with exaggerated racially coded facial features, sabotage his stated intent of fighting prejudice and injustice. Under the picture of a black man wearing a bowler, a suit, and carrying a cane stands the caption "Sidewalk is as Free for Me as it is for You." Although the caption appears obviously political, the picture designates a certain type of behavior—"swaggering down the broadway . . . brushing against ladies and colliding with gentlemen" (103)—with physiognomy. If Woods begins to sound like an apologist for inequality in his idealization of "the old darky's politeness" (100), he also argues that black men can become the equal of white men by practicing "a virtuous manhood"[27] — that is, never appearing to be a "lick-spittle" (60) or arrogant. Women's "social, mental, and moral strength" (62), by comparison, resides in their chastity. In this way, Woods tries to set a standard of polite behavior comparable to that of the white community without denying the social, historical legacies of his readers. His solution foreshadows Fauset's portrayal in *Plum Bun* of the forces bearing on female sexuality and the relationships between black men and women in a white world.

Woods's manual, like Fauset's novel, is ultimately about passing. In this, it does not deviate, in the most general sense, from standard etiquette books such as *At Home and Abroad* (1853), *Never: A Handbook for the Uninitiated and Inexperienced Aspirants to Refined Society's Giddy Heights and Glittering Attainments* (1883), or *The Gentle Art of Pleasing* (1898), which train readers to pass for sophisticates or ladies and gentlemen. Nonetheless, Woods's bifocal emphasis on class and race makes his manual unique. Unable to talk about class without addressing race, Woods advocates a standard of behavior usually associated with the white middle-class. He supports, in this implicit "manner," a theory of race history based on passing and gradual assimilation that makes his book more radical than many novels of passing, including Pauline Hopkins's *Of One Blood Or, the Hidden Self* (1902–3), Nella Larsen's *Passing* (1929), and Fauset's *Plum Bun*, all of which end with the protagonist's return to the black community. The restoration of social divisions in these novels honors history while bolstering the black community's sense of a continuous identity. More pessimistically, such endings give the public what W. D. Howells thought it required: a tragedy with a happy ending.[28]

As we might expect, the dynamic of passing affects blacks and whites differently. Whites feel anxious about the notion of passing because they perceive that they have the most to lose. The practice not only exposes the inherently racist structure of society but also the tenuous nature of identity itself—a point that Kate Chopin's short story "Désirée's Baby" (1893) illustrates. Chopin's heroine is an orphan whose husband rejects her when their baby appears to have mixed blood. Heartbroken and frantic, she drowns herself and the baby. Later the husband discovers that his mother had been his father's slave; that he belongs to the race "cursed with the brand of slavery."[29] The revelation turns his world, his very self, inside out. Such sensational reconsiderations of self may partly explain the popularity of stories about passing, which, despite their didacticism, grant the dual thrill of peril and license. The trope, to different effect, can be seen in Francis Harper's *Iola Leroy, or Shadows Uplifted* (1892), the story of a woman who discovers her slave status and its sexual consequences at her white father's death, and Mark Twain's *Puddn'head Wilson* (1894), a more ambivalent tale of two babies, one white, one black, switched at birth.

Passing can seem for blacks, no less than whites, a traitorous act. The denial or rejection of one's past, family, or race acknowledges prejudice and perhaps reflects its internalization. People who "pass" go over to the other side. They metaphorically die, yet their spirit lingers as it does in the pictures that the African-American photographer James VanDerZee took of survivors embraced by shadows of the departed.[30] At the same time, they ask those they have disavowed to collude in their masquerade. Passing becomes to this extent a communal act. When, on the street, relative "passes" relative without greeting, as the Murray sisters do in *Plum Bun*, they share knowledge and pain denied to others. The deception makes them in effect nonpersons divorced from any agreed-upon social context. Passing carries within it the kernel of exile, the titillation associated with the freedom of belonging or not belonging at will. The possessor of a secret self has a sense of power and authority over those duped. To echo Ralph Ellison, passing makes one a spy in enemy territory. A constant gamble, it protests, apart from sociopolitical conditions, the distillation of a hundred selves into one self defined solely by color.

Because passing necessitates the suppression, if not the obliteration, of the past, it becomes, as the First World War approaches, a kind of cultural metaphor for the increased atomization and relativity of American life. What is truth when we cannot define the self? — when we cannot trust our own perceptions? Allegories of passing ironically reaffirm the notion of an immutable identity, "an unchangeable hold of at least one origin and 'community,' "[31] even as they speak to concerns about a transient and rapidly changing society. In response, definitions of the self and its relationship to society often become more rigid — hence the perennial popularity of manners books as guides through indefinite territory.

Although passing usually refers to a conversion from black to white, the opposite also holds true. Maybe no novel illustrates the toll of indeterminate racial identity and multiple passings more than William Faulkner's *Light in August* (1932). Joe Christmas, ignorant of his exact racial heritage, nevertheless feels his "white" blood warring with his "black":

> it was the black blood which snatched up the pistol and the white blood which
> would not let him fire it. . . . It was the black blood which swept him by his own
> desire beyond the aid of any man, swept him up into ecstasy out of a black jungle

where life has already ceased before the heart stops and death is desire and fulfillment. And then the black blood failed him again, as it must have in crises all his
life. . . . He crouched behind the overturned table and let them shoot him to death,
with that loaded and unfired pistol in his hand.[32]

Faulkner retells the tale of Dr. Jekyll and Mr. Hyde from a peculiarly American
perspective. The contending definitions of black and white, which the narrator
presents as innate, are in fact social. Although the passage seems to reinforce
certain stereotypes of "black" and "white," those definitions become muddled,
even inverted, within the passage itself. Christmas dies because his "black" blood
acts "white" and his "white" blood "black." Singly and together, they find fulfillment and desire in violence.

Just as a social commentator like Woods defined passing chiefly in terms of
class, Fauset defined it almost wholly in terms of color. If Fauset's fascination
with the topic of passing did not lessen over the course of her career, her attitude
to it did, as illustrated by several stories she published in *The Crisis* published
between 1912 and 1923. An early story, entitled "Emmy" (December 1912 and
January 1913), revolves around the same question that underlies *Plum Bun*: Is the
light-skinned protagonist obligated to tell people he is black? He decides he
must or lose everything of value, including Emmy, his darker-skinned fiancée.
"Emmy" differs from Fauset's later work most in its uncritical response to white
patronage. When he reveals his race, the protagonist loses his job with a pres-
tigious engineering firm, but the owner's son restores it. Fauset implies that
racism dissipates with each successive generation, yet the fairy-tale ending supports what Zora Neale Hurston would describe as the "pet Negro system," in
which the entitlement of one person at the expense of all others allows the patron
an easy conscience.[33]

The "Sleeper Wakes" (1920) reverses the conclusion of "Emmy" by presenting race as more assumed than given. Published in three installments, "The
Sleeper Wakes" (1920) follows the career of Amy, a beautiful young girl who does
not know her antecedents.[34] Raised by a black foster family, she runs away to New
York, where she passes for white and marries a wealthy southerner, whose prejudices about women and blacks foreshadow those of *Plum Bun*'s Roger Fielding.
Amy decides that the world holds two categories of people: whites who desire
power and have enormous pride; and blacks who are unthinkingly loyal and too
inclined to trust. Fauset leaves the mystery of Amy's birth unsolved for her
readers, if not for Amy herself. When you have the choice to declare for one race

or the other, decency demands — as Virginia Murray of *Plum Bun* tells her sister Angela — that you "put yourself, even in the face of appearances, on the side of black blood and say: 'Look here, this is what a mixture of black and white really means!'" (*Plum Bun*, 80). When Amy chooses to be "colored," she consciously decides to conduct herself according to certain ethical principles. As Fauset suggests, the subject of race involves a comprehensive philosophy for living.

In the novels written after these stories, Fauset considers color to be a mask, and, transposing Paul Laurence Dunbar's metaphor, she associates that mask with being or appearing white. The mask of "whiteness" and its corollary of passing carries the threat of racial extinction and the transformation of existing social orders. In *There Is Confusion*, for example, the dark-skinned heroine wears a mask when dancing as the symbol of "America." At the end of her performance, the audience demands: "Let's see your face, America. Pull off your mask!" (*Confusion*, 232). Its removal pushes the history of black Americans to center stage, forcing a reconsideration of everything "American." Fauset uses the same trope when representing the colonization of Africa in an article entitled "Dark Algiers the White" (1925). The white garments that the women wear hide their misshapen bodies, broken by neglect, abuse, and childbearing.[35] The French call this country of white sun "Alger la blanche!" but, as Fauset shows, its white veil conceals another reality and the major theme of all her novels: the psychological cost of being black.

For African-American writers like Fauset and Woods, no matter how different their genres, any discussion about race seemed to form part of a larger discussion about social and economic uplift. They could not ignore sociopolitical realities. As late as 1926, *The Crisis* stated that a lynching — what one writer called a "regrettable" form of "entertainment" — still occurred every twenty-three days,[36] and, only six years before, Du Bois had warned, in a column entitled "A Matter of Manners," that "bumptiousness or excessive egotism on the part of a young colored boy is risky enough to lead to murder, riot, and social upheaval."[37] Ida B. Wells, a journalist who stressed the economic, rather than the social, impetus behind lynching, held that "a Winchester rifle should have a place of honor in every black home" (Gaines, 86).

The philosophy of racial uplift, which made prosperous blacks responsible for those less fortunate, exacerbated intraracial class tensions at both the turn of the twentieth century and after the First World War. Members of the middle class sought to educate or provide a standard for the masses, who sometimes thought them traitors to the race. No one would have called Fauset a traitor, but from the beginning she was accused of elitism. More to the point, her commitment to racial uplift turned her into the kind of propagandist Edith Wharton made herself into for France.

Fauset never felt wholly comfortable as an advocate for black artists, though Du Bois asserted that all art was propaganda, and Claude McKay unfairly accused her of practicing, as literary editor of *The Crisis*, a kind of censorship that checked "contact with real life."[38] She was more inclined to side with her brother, Arthur Huff Fauset, who thought it suicidal to believe that once "a sufficiently large number of persons" had "properly qualified themselves in the arts," social and economic recognition would inevitably follow.[39] Fauset herself asserted that art knew no color line, as she paradoxically tried to define "Negro Art" for the readers of *The Crisis*. Soliciting opinions about the nature of black literature from both black and white writers, she hoped to accomplish varied ends: to mediate between white and black artists; to create a larger audience for black writers; and to free them from formulaic "primitivism," which she considered a latter-day version of minstrel, or what Howells called in *A Hazard of New Fortunes* (1890) "low-down show business," associated with the banjo, "end-men . . . blackened faces and grotesque shirt-collars."[40]

One of the first white writers to respond to Fauset was Sherwood Anderson. He suggested that a group of artists — Du Bois, Jim Johnson, Walter White, Countee Cullen, Carl Van Vechten, Roland Hayes, and Joel Springarn — meet to discuss whether "American Negroes [should] write as Americans or Negroes."

> Should they follow the pattern of an Edna Ferber who is quite as likely to write about Wisconsin Nordics as about her fellow Jews [Anderson asked]; or that of Zangwill, who is of the slightest importance only when he is writing about Jews? Should there be a Negro publishing house so that the Negro author can tell all of the ordinary publishing houses to go to the devil? Should there be a club — a comfortable small hotel in Paris to which the American Negroes can go and be more than welcome?[41]

For his part, Anderson thought the current emphasis on "the economic and social problems of the colored race" misguided. Because this emphasis generated a limited number of topics, it tended to make black authors seem identical. "Why not quit thinking of negro art?" he urged. "If the individual creating the art happens to be a negro and someone wants to call it negro art let them."[42] As a writer, Fauset wanted to agree with Anderson; in her capacity as editor of *The Crisis*, she rejected his advice as socially irresponsible.

Fauset was neither born nor inclined, as Anderson counseled, to let things be. The United States had an unwritten law that white artists such as Carl Van Vechten, the author of the controversial novel *Nigger Heaven* (1926), or Julia Peterkin, who won a Pulitzer Prize for her depiction of South Carolina's Gullah blacks in *Scarlet Sister Mary* (1928), could imitate black artists without allowing the opposite: "In other words, grease-paint may be used to darken . . . never to lighten."[43] Fauset had heard her own success cited as proof of equality in the arts. "Keep quiet! Don't complain! Work! All will be well!" — Du Bois (who was inducted into the National Institute of Arts and Letters at the same time as special awards were presented to Willa Cather, Theodore Dreiser, and Paul Robeson) called this chorus a conspiracy designed to stop black agitation for equality.[44] Fauset did her best to negotiate the color line by keeping a white audience in mind without granting it final judgment on her novels or the content of *The Crisis.*

Writers in the 1920s had to contend with white readers' ideas about African-American identity and sexuality, and with the black middle-class's call for inspiring stereotypes. As Alain Locke writes, "for generations in the mind of America, the Negro has been more of a formula than a human being — a something to be argued about, condemned or defended, to be 'kept down,' or 'in his place,' " or 'helped up,' " to be worried with or worried over, harassed or patronized, a social bogey or a social burden."[45] In her novels, Fauset turns racial clichés on their head by making irresponsibility, irresoluteness, and ingratitude predominant markers of white blood, and a mixture of bloods — African, West Indian, and Anglo-European, for example — the heritage of the new cosmopolites. She shows the ways in which someone concerned with questions of civilization, history, and racial identity combines different novelistic traditions to write a quintessentially American story of passing.

III

Jessie Fauset subtitled *Plum Bun* "A Novel without a Moral," and in one very real sense this is true. Its heroine, a young woman named Angela Murray, is a kind of black Lily Bart, a high-stakes gambler with artistic inclinations and a love of luxury who decides to pass for white. Cutting all ties with her sister, Virginia, and changing her name to Angèle Mory, she moves to New York City, where she studies art and becomes the mistress of a rich white bigot, Roger Fielding. Her story differs most from Bart's in Fauset's refusal to punish her heroine for her sexuality. Fauset plays with the conventions of the sentimental novel to subvert myths about women's nature, but also to explore the historical exploitation of black women by white men like Fielding. If Angela nearly succumbs to the nineteenth-century plot of the "tragic mulatta," seduced, abandoned, and not long for this world, Fauset balks at making her "tragically colored."[46] Instead, she ends *Plum Bun* with two marriages, doubling the old convention by restoring Virginia and Angela to their true mates and to each other. Of course, any novel that claims not to have a moral must have one, and *Plum Bun* has several. Above all, it suggests that the "American Dream" excluded black citizens at great cost, which is to say that "If you're black in America, you have to renounce" (*Confusion*, 284). In *Plum Bun*, however, the net loss works out to be a gain, for the moral riches of the African-American community exceed any Angela finds when passing.

As this summary might imply, *Plum Bun* can also be read as its author's claim to multiple traditions. A baggy, splay-footed monster, the novel moves in assorted directions, conforming or deviating from traditions associated with romantic fiction and novels of manners, whose protagonists consider themselves superior to or at odds with their environment. Angela is a "marginalized insider," envied or romanticized in the same spirit as James's cosmopolites, Wharton's old New Yorkers, or Glasgow's Virginians, who find that privilege comes with its own price of self-abnegation: the public "obliteration of the personal, the intimate, the hidden, [and] the passionate."[47] Fauset pays ironic tribute to fairy-tale endings by using lines from the childhood nursery rhyme "To Market, to Market,"[48] while warning that, in a world where appearances mislead and identity becomes a performance, we cannot trust our own perceptions of reality, even our own concepts of self.

After the publication of *Plum Bun*, Fauset gave an interview in which she claimed that more than twenty thousand blacks, fed up with second-class status, were passing as whites in New York City. "They want to be white," she explained, "to get away from the disabilities which are the heritage of the Negro."[49] For Fauset, that heritage had everything to do with the artistic traditions open or not open to black artists, who felt themselves pulled in sundry directions by the often conflicting demands of white publishers, white and black intellectuals, and general readers of both races. Fauset urged her readers to vote with their pocketbooks. Zora Neale Hurston claimed to be amazed by the Anglo-Saxons' lack of curiosity about the lives of anyone who was non-Anglo-Saxon or above the class of skilled labor. And Dorothy West, who had consciously never mentioned the word *black* in her fiction, cried when she saw the illustrations for one of her first stories and the characters were obviously colored.[50] It seems almost unavoidable that Fauset's novel, which is also part *Kunstlerroman* — or the story of a would-be artist who fails and becomes, paradoxically, a better human being — should explore the consequences of declaring or not declaring for one's race, as it asks readers to reconsider divisions between so-called American and African-American literature.

Fauset uses the parable of passing to explore forbidden spaces, which are sexual and artistic as well as inter- and intraracial. While Angela literally passes for white, her passing captures the position of the woman artist who exists both inside and outside society. When identity becomes a largely social performance, some integral essence of self is lost or commodified, as Angela's talent in portraiture and her assumption of the stage name Angèle Mory suggest.

Like other women writers, including Wharton in *The House of Mirth*, Fauset presents femininity as a kind of command performance or (to use the term that Joan Rivière popularized in the 1920s) a "masquerade."[51] In this context, manners become props that can have their own amoral protocols. Angela first learns to pass from her mother, Mattie, who thinks it a Saturday diversion, a game granting her entry to popular department stores and hotels that would ordinarily deny her service. The light-skinned Angela accompanies her mother on these days, while rosy-bronze Virginia goes with Junius, their black-skinned father. Junius does not mind his wife's passing as long as it remains strictly a game; that is, divorced from principle and unrelated to envy. Yet it has terrible consequences for his children, who grow up playing their own game of passing. "Pardon me, is this Mrs. Henrietta Jones?" says Virginia; to which Angela haughtily responds: "You have the advantage of me." " 'Oh pardon!' says Virginia. 'I thought you were Mrs. Jones and I had heard my friend Mrs. Smith speak of you so often and since you were in the neighborhood and *passing*, I was going to ask you in to have some ice-cream' " (*Plum Bun*, 35; emphasis mine). The game, which acknowledges the hedonistic basis of human exchanges, is, however, no game when Virginia greets Angela as Mrs. Jones in Roger's presence, and Angela literally passes her.

In Fauset's American tragedy "color or rather the lack of it" comes to be "the one absolute prerequisite" for happiness (*Plum Bun*, 13). And sadly enough, in *Plum Bun* color means as much if not more to blacks than whites, for it represents a double caste system. Fauset wants, as one of her characters says, to show *us* (blacks) to the (white) world (*Confusion*, 76); she also wants to show blacks to blacks. Junius's deep-black color makes him undesirable to "lots of coloured girls" (*Plum Bun*, 31); Mattie, however, whose whiteness seems an affront to blacks and whites alike and an invitation to rape, loves Junius's color because it makes her feel (despite her penchant for passing) safe. Her feeling of safety comes in large part from having a home within the African-American community.

From her mother, Angela understands only that those who can pass will, and she adopts the "soft-speaking . . . conformity and sheer opportunism," which James Weldon Johnson thought historically necessary for survival.[52] "If you're light," goes the common rhyme, "you're all right. / If you're brown, stick around. / But if you're black, get back" (Graham, 378). Angela thinks that happiness belongs to anyone free, white, and twenty-one, and "power, greatness, [and] authority" (*Plum Bun*, 88) to anyone free, white, twenty-one, and male. If passing can grant her the characteristics she thinks a male birthright, her color separates her from schoolmates who consciously isolate her, as though her light skin testifies to some ancestral shame. In truth, her whiteness makes it possible for them to enact their general anger at society and an entrenched color hierarchy, which normally favors light-skinned blacks like Mattie and Angela.

Fauset's parable has a historical dimension, for her characterization of Angela allows her to undermine popular notions about mulattoes, thought in the late-nineteenth and early-twentieth centuries to be hybrids whose presence in the black community perverted the whole social system of stratification (Gatewood, 152). The word *mulatto* originally referred to people having one white and one black parent. Soon identified by degrees of color, rather than by formulas of blood, the mulatto seemed to be both an intermediate race and an intermediate class. (The well-known journalist T. Thomas Fortune urged the adoption of the word *Afro-American* in 1890, because terms such as *mulatto* and *Negro* seemed exclusive.) Fauset was certainly aware of Du Bois's critics who argued that the "upper tens"—a corruption of Du Bois's Talented Tenth—valued color above education and culture. They suffered, as one antagonist said, from "colorphobia as badly as the white folks have Negrophobia" (Gatewood, 154). Many blacks simultaneously envied and resented mulattoes, possibly because many whites considered them the most intelligent members of their race. In *Plum Bun*, a caste system based on gradations of color victimizes Angela more than it privileges her. It also undermines a sense of community, as the antagonism directed at Angela from other blacks nudges her toward permanent passing, or what some people called "crossing over."

For Fauset, the figure of the mulatto captured the dual loyalties that comprise a black birthright, whatever one's place of origin. If many blacks mythologized the motherland as "Africa," the presence of the mulatto highlighted the increasingly tenuous nature of that relationship to a people who came from across the globe. After Fauset attended the Second Pan-African Conference in 1921,[53] she concluded that: "We have got to learn everything—facts about Africa, the difference between her colonial governments, one foreign language at least (French or Spanish), new points of view, generosity of ideal and of act. All the possibilities of all black men are needed to weld together the black men of the world against the day when black and white meet to do battle."[54] Fauset's apocalyptic view of the future, which seems to deny the "mulatto" a place, underscores the necessity of choosing sides. In her subsequent fiction, the mulatto becomes a reminder of forfeiture, someone who belongs neither here nor there, and whose light skin brings neither social nor economic advancement.

Like Howells, Fauset associates the mulatto with the neurasthenic, not because Angela represents the weakening of blood lines but because she does not know her own mind. She thinks that she can assume and shed her color as if it were a "badge" to be pinned on or taken off. To her, color functions reductively in opposite ways: positively, "like the colours on the escutcheon of a powerful house" (*Plum Bun*, 88), and negatively, like a stain on one's reputation—"a blot," as the old adage goes, "on one's escutcheon." Fauset's metaphor suggests both the ornamental and protective aspects of color. Although Angela associates her color with European gentility and dreams of having a salon along the lines of the famous Parisian hostess the Countess Rosa de Fitz-James, Fauset ironically comments on Europe's colonial history and the interracial lineage it sees as a "stain." Angela forgets the "salon" at her father's home in Opal Street, with men talking of rents and lynching, the women of childbearing and sacrifice. If Angela represents a special "type" (*Plum Bun*, 89), for whom passing can be either active or acquiescent, she also highlights its fundamental problem. The denial of past influences and affections—not to mention the discrepancy between life and its representation—disavows everything that has made Angela who she is. The silence that should bring her "happiness" ironically makes her a tacit racist, someone who allows the eviction of a black couple from a public restaurant and who patronizes a fellow art student, a black woman named Miss Powell.

While *Plum Bun* obviously differs from a novel like *The House of Mirth* in its bifocal look at race in the United States, it, nonetheless, advances its own equivalent of Lawrence Selden's "land of letters" or of a society based on shared interests. To Fauset, "society" had nothing to do with white values or a black equivalent of the Astor Four Hundred. Society grows from the relationship between moral and intellectual equals. Fauset's view foreshadows that of Zora Neale Hurston and recalls the novelist and editor Pauline Hopkins, who defined her social equal as someone "whose society affords the greatest pleasure, whose tastes are congenial . . . be he white or black, bond or free, rich or poor."[55] Two decades separated Fauset from Hopkins, but whether one decade or ten, the greatest impediment to social equality remained "the problem of the color line" — *the* problem, as Du Bois wrote, of the twentieth century.[56] Fauset criticizes a social system that demands that all blacks, to some degree, pass. In one painful example, Junius cannot retrieve his wife from a white hospital unless he plays her chauffeur. Fauset suggests through the subsequent deaths of Junius and Mattie the physical and psychic costs of such charades. *Plum Bun* may part company most with *The House of Mirth* in its final support, even idealization, of black society epitomized by Virginia's ability to forgive.

At the beginning of the novel, Angela thinks of her passing as "stolen" time, and, in the sense that it removes her from friends and family, it is. The illicit nature of her position communicates itself to Roger, who intuits her attraction to risk. She has a "foreign" (*Plum Bun*, 123) quality, partly because she dares what other women would not, partly because she is passing. It does not occur to her that Roger would never consider marrying someone without wealth or position. Eligibility in her mind rests entirely on race. Angela thinks that she can win Roger by following the age-old wisdom of advice books for girls: make him like you more than you like him, and never succumb to sexual advances. "If we give too much," a women friend tells Angela, "we lose ourselves" (*Plum Bun*, 145). Angela, driven by loneliness and passion, forgets that men have their own rules for female conduct, and that "no woman with an ounce of pride" (*Plum Bun*, 230) would call a man at all hours. Passing has taught her that manners do not necessarily reflect being. For Roger, however, her insensitivity to social niceties that protect him become a sign of, or at least an excuse for, her unsuitability.

According to Fauset, the rites of courtship and passing involve similarly large doses of duplicity, and in refusing to let Angela be tragically colored, she makes her tragically female. Angela's "white" lie becomes a form of masochism, when she knowingly becomes the mistress of a man who hates blacks. Her plan to sponsor black artists hardly ennobles what some might call prostitution. Virginia attributes Angela's obtuseness to an extra infusion of white blood that allowed ante-bellum southerners to mistreat their mulatto relatives; it also comes, as Fauset describes it, from a long, learned tradition of black self-loathing. Relationships without "visible bonds" (*Plum Bun*, 192) serve the powers that be. Roger's complete "absorption" (*Plum Bun*, 203) of Angela may be read as a parable about theories of racial assimilation. Subjugating herself to Roger's needs, she forgets her own ideals and ambitions — and worse, the hereditary rights of a next generation. Traditions have their place, she comes to realize, to the degree that they promote "fundamental facts," "the laws of civilization" (*Plum Bun*, 228, 232), and human decency.

Fauset's social history, which addresses the practices that have kept black men and women subjugated from decade to decade, recounts civilization's "progression" through three versions of the tragic mulatta plot. Two versions belong to the generation preceding Angela. The first involves Junius saving Mattie from the clutches of a would-be seducer. The second concerns the parents of Angela's future husband, Anthony Cross. The product of a Brazilian mother and an African-American father, Anthony passes for a Spaniard originally named Cruz — perhaps another pun on passing ("cruising"). Anthony's father inherits a prosperous farm in Georgia, where the townspeople, already envious of his wealth, become outraged by his marriage to an apparently white wife. When Anthony's mother slaps a white man for accosting her, a mob feels justified in burning the family out. Anthony's father dies defending his home, and the mob mutilates his body in a way that recalls the terrible fate of Nat Turner. Anthony and his mother escape physically, though not emotionally, for she develops a pathological fear of blacks. They must be cursed, she reasons, to be so abused and hounded, and several years later she marries a German, leaving Anthony essentially orphaned. In an odd twist of the plot, he becomes engaged to Angela's sister, Virginia, thinking that he can never love anyone, let alone a white woman like Angela.

Fauset has the stories of the preceding generation provide a context for Angela's. Seduced, abandoned, and in love with her sister's fiancé, she nonetheless refuses to be ruined. As Mattie taught her daughters, the first duty belongs to life. Fauset accomplishes several ends by allowing Angela and Anthony their own histories. She claims for women the knowledge and experience usually accorded males, and she dismisses the importance of a white perspective on black identity or history.

Plum Bun ends, as do most novels of passing, with Angela's declaring for those connected to her in suffering (*Plum Bun*, 340–41) perhaps even more than in "blood." She no longer chooses to remain silent when the American Committee rescinds Miss Powell's scholarship on the grounds of race. Angela's decision comes down to the central point of etiquette that Woods addressed in his manual:

Should blacks go where they are not welcome? "You imply that she's not wanted because she's coloured," Angela explains to reporters. "Well, I'm coloured too." Fauset's climax differs from other novels of passing in one crucial instance, for Angela insists on her dual heritage. The world will never be divided (as Fauset presented it in her coverage of the Second Pan-African Conference) simply into white and black. The paradox of passing lies in the movement of life itself. "You cannot fight and create at the same time" (*Plum Bun*, 354), Angela tells her sister as she leaves for Paris, her sentiments commenting obliquely on Fauset's own position. Social exigencies give the novel a happy resolution, though one that is qualified. Virginia is reunited with her childhood sweetheart and, Angela gets her year in Paris and her young man. Still, *Plum Bun* remains a "tragedy." Angela, so desirous of freedom, finds no real respite from the tyranny of color consciousness. At the beginning of the novel, she asks: "Doesn't anyone think that we have a right to be happy?" (*Plum Bun*, 54). The answer appears to be no. Her plan to announce her biracial heritage and accept its consequences puts her future almost entirely in other people's hands.

Fauset did not see the artist as the sole or the most powerful agent of social change. She believed that any man or woman who served as an example to the race would "live on and on in their own people, in the world" ("Looking Backward," 126). The sacrifice of Angela's career to future generations places race above art, altruism above narcissism. This conclusion, which echoes so many turn-of-the-century stories — from Elizabeth Stuart's Phelps's domestication of her artist-protagonist in *The Story of Avis* (1877) to Kate Chopin's *The Awakening* (1900) — makes Fauset appear strangely old-fashioned, at once more conservative and practical than someone like Du Bois, who insisted that women should have education, economic independence, and the right to control their own bodies.[57]

For Fauset, the problem of color knows no boundaries. Harlem may have, as Charles Chesnutt notes, "a population in all shades from ivory to ebony, of all degrees of culture, from doctors of philosophy to the lowest degree of illiteracy," of various origins and morals, "ranging from the highest to the most debased."[58] But Fauset sees it as a limited mecca, where people dwell in "dark and serried tents" (*Plum Bun*, 98). France, which so inspired writers like Wharton and Willa Cather, seems more a figment of black yearning to Fauset than a real place. In *Plum Bun*, France offers only a respite, a half-developed promise, a place where Anthony and Angela can prepare for their return to the United States. In *Comedy: American Style*, Fauset's last novel, France becomes the permanent home of the desperately lonely Olivia Cary, who finds the French much like her white son-in-law: indifferent, miserly, pitilessly logical, and racist. Fauset understands that every society has its bans and taboos, its particular intolerances and condescensions. In her mind, Olivia is a tragic mulatta because she lives as though she has no race, belongs nowhere and to no one.

Fauset argues, like Woods and Du Bois before her, that blacks may not be separated from the rest of humanity by an absolute physical line, but they are separated socially. On this fact, she builds her social history, challenging conventional notions of a common heritage and history that Du Bois and many of his followers wanted to posit in Africa. Further, her valuation of community denies the centrality of the individual in American mythology. The fulfillment of Fauset's dream lay all in the morrow, in a creative revisioning of the American novel and American identity.

It might be said that Jessie Fauset passed for many things: teacher, translator, poet, journalist, novelist, activist — the list seems almost endless. Perhaps this accounts for the difficulty people have had trying to place her. To Claude McKay, her novels seemed an imitation of white life and she herself as imperious as Edith Wharton — "prim and dainty as a primrose," with "no time to waste on a non-influential and down-and-out fellow-writer!"[59] Yet to Langston Hughes, the slightly plump, tan-brown woman, with gentle eyes and a fine smile, seemed to epitomize graciousness itself (*Big Sea*, 94). Fauset felt caught like one of her own characters in a net of others' making. As with Wharton, she lived to see herself dismissed as the advocate of a "closed decorous circle." To McKay, this group seemed composed of proud people who imitated the better class of conventional whites as well as they could on much less money.[60] McKay's criticism aside, Fauset was one of the first writers to make this group the subject of fiction, to present the diversity of African Americans and protest their narrow portrayal in fiction. Without her, it is hard to imagine James Baldwin living in Switzerland and writing "Stranger in the Village" or Dorothy West portraying the lives of upper-class blacks in Boston. As an editor and a novelist, Fauset helped to shape the ways in which we have come to think about American literature, its absences and parameters, its complexities, and above all its colorations.

Excursives

It is on manners, customs, usages, habits, forms, upon all these things matured and established, that a novelist lives, they are the very stuff his work is made of. **LETTER OF HENRY JAMES TO W. D. HOWELLS**

I feel that to your generation, which has taken such a flying leap into the future, I must represent the literary equivalent of tufted furniture and gas chandeliers.
LETTER OF EDITH WHARTON TO F. SCOTT FITZGERALD

I come back to my earlier statement that the novel of manners was a dominant form, perhaps *the* dominant form, in American fiction at the end of the nineteenth century and the beginning of the twentieth. From James Fenimore Cooper's *Leatherstocking Tales* and Washington Irving's fictionalized history of New York to Herman Melville's *Omoo* and Nathaniel Hawthorne's *The Scarlet Letter*, there has been a recurring, a determined focus on the twin questions of civilization and manners. However much writers like Henry James and Willa Cather envisioned themselves belonging to an international community of past and present writers, whatever their protestations to the contrary, they also looked closer to home. Edith Wharton, who thought it immature of many modern writers to dread doing something that had been done before, did turn to Henry James, and James to Hawthorne and Howells. Ellen Glasgow could not approach the Confederacy without thinking about the novels of Thomas Nelson Page, so beloved by Richmonders that they commemorated his death by flying the capitol flag at half-mast. And while Cather freely acknowledged her debt to Sarah Orne Jewett and James, and Fauset hers to Wharton, they had any number of predecessors in American fiction.

It may well be a truism that American novelists feel pressured to assert their originality by demonstrating how their work proceeds or departs from that of previous novelists, and the writers I study were no exception. James and Glasgow wrote books of prefaces that were in part arguments for their own narrative innovations, and Wharton published a collection of essays under the title *The Writing of Fiction* (1925) that ends with a tribute to Marcel Proust. As editors, Howells and Fauset might have had the grandest goal, each wanting nothing less than to redirect the course of American letters. But here, too, they were not alone. Like Howells's columns for *Harper's*, James's book reviews and Glasgow's opening address to the Southern Writers Conference attempt to articulate patterns in fiction that favor their own choices — some of them unexpected.

What novelists say about their work may or may not be true of the work itself. Wharton, for example, felt it necessary to apologize to "the decorous shade of Grace Aguilar . . . for deliberately appropriating, and applying to uses so different" the title of one of Aguilar's most popular books, *The Mother's Recompense*. Wharton's assertion aside, we might argue that her *Mother's Recompense* (1925), published more than seventy years after Aguilar's tale, was less different than she claimed. If Wharton recasts sentimental conventions by having a daughter marry her mother's former lover, she nonetheless brings those conventions into the modern novel. I give this multigenerational example of maternal sacrifice, "the mother's recompense," to suggest that such literary transformations may be less rare and more conscious than novelists intent on arguing their own cases would lead us to believe. We have only to remember F. Scott Fitzgerald's notorious visit to Wharton to see that the "hunger," even the quarrels, of one's successors can come more from a sense of agreement than difference. This view partially accounts for Wharton's contempt for women regional writers, including Jewett and Mary Wilkins Freeman, whom she accused of wearing rose-colored spectacles, or Virginia Woolf's criticism of Wharton's outmoded vocabulary, when London's avant garde had begun to find Bloomsbury old-fashioned.

Given the younger generation's persistent need to disown its elders, what, we might ask, is the legacy of writers like Wharton or Fauset? Clearly some novelists — Sinclair Lewis, John Marquand, Louis Auchincloss, John Cheever, Roxana Robinson, and John Updike among them — write in the tradition of novels of manners, a tradition to which Fitzgerald paid tribute with his courting of Wharton. Whether or not readers forget that he wrote screen dialogue for Wharton's jazz-age novel *The Glimpses of the Moon* (1922), few would deny that his most famous novel, *The Great Gatsby* (1925), defined a class or a generation's view of the failed dream of America itself. For Fitzgerald, no less than Howells, the veneering of America had everything to do with the desiccation of its soul.

But apart from devotees, what about writers whose fiction bears little or no obvious resemblance to those of James and Wharton? There are writers who make manners their implicit or explicit subject without being "novelists of manners." This is true of the African-American novelist Dorothy West, for example, whose study of Boston's black Brahmins in *The Living Is Easy* (1948) might seem a companion to Howells's *The Rise of Silas Lapham* or Fauset's *Comedy: American Style.* Yet West identified Fyodor Dostoyevski as her greatest influence, and her story of obsessive love reflects his passionate sympathy for the dispossessed as well as his preoccupation with morbid psychology. As West herself notes, it would be a disservice to place her only within American traditions of the novel. She felt especially out of touch with black artists in the 1960s — a time, as she described it, "of Rap Brown and other people of that sort who thought that the revolution was on its way and that Martin Luther King was a SoB."[1] West objected to practices that define traditions by single factors such as sex, race, or nationality. Her affinity for Dostoyevski, whose own influences included Gogol and Balzac, circuitously links her to James, the man who called Balzac "the master of us all."

Perhaps few other forms have seemed to exclude minority writers more than novels of manners. But as West makes clear, minority writers inherit a legacy as split and mixed and eclectic as any other American writers, and that legacy includes the novel of manners. While it seems a stretch to connect a Native American writer such as Leslie Silko to studies of manners, a novel like *Ceremony* (1977) moves in two directions, or belongs to two traditions — one specifically Native American, the other whatever constitutes a larger national literature. Its theme (how the continuation of the tribe, of civilization itself, depends upon etiquette or customary practices to regulate social behavior) connects it directly to Louise Erdrich's *Love Medicine* (1984), the story of life on a North Dakota reservation, while its conflicting realities and recursive structure recalls the modernist experiments of Willa Cather. There may not be any such creature as a "naive" reader, to use James's word. Readers come programmed with certain expectations, largely determined by their knowledge of genre or types of novels. For many readers, Silko's book will be forever identified with the so-called "renaissance" of Native American literature. However, *Ceremony* seems another thing entirely when paired with Cather's *The Professor's House* or, perhaps more helpfully, Mary Austin's *Starry Adventure*, which explores an American West peopled by Amerindians and Mexican Americans.[2] For Silko, racial identity grows from a combination of distinctive social practices, structural relationships, and cultural traditions — a view that aligns her with James and Wharton.[3] Our refusal to see minority writers borrowing or developing from "canonical" writers may result from problems of definition or a kind of institutionalized blindness. No matter that Erdrich inverts the usual social hierarchy to give frozen foods and rusting trucks their own cachet, her emphasis is on manners, and she defines identity by social behavior and tribal relationships. The novel of manners has appeared less vital to discussions of contemporary American life and the metamorphoses of the American novel precisely because its form has taken such unexpected trajectories—or maybe because post–World War I writers—Ernest Hemingway, for example—scoffed at its practitioners.

Yet why should Hemingway be the spokesman for his contemporaries (including Fitzgerald, with whom he had a falling out and parodied in "The Snows of Kilimanjaro")? Hemingway may not have been aware that, in his way, he, too, raided a tradition he publicly disowned. How else should we characterize the code that Jake Barnes or Frederick Henry espouse except as a set of manners? The yearning for continuity, which Hemingway associates with peasant life in Spain, his focus on ritualized killing, whether bullfighting or war, and his heroes' obligation to act with grace and dignity under fire make him and Fitzgerald uneasy comrades. No one would confuse Hemingway's jungles with the drawing rooms of old New York—no one except Wharton, who saw every drawing room as a jungle—partly because setting and locale carry their own imperatives. As Wharton's mother once pronounced, "drawing rooms are always tidy," and so, perhaps, is Hemingway's code in such novels as *The Sun Also Rises* (1926) and *A Farewell to Arms* (1929), which position their protagonists in relationship to an outmoded or inadequate set of values. I am not arguing that Hemingway is the same kind of novelist as Wharton or Fitzgerald, nor that he is a novelist of manners, any more than Silko is a novelist of manners, but he does suggest the overlooked centrality of manners to American fiction between the world wars and beyond.

I have tried to show that the novel has responded to the evolving constitution of American life, in its reflection of diverse classes, races, attitudes, and historical periods. Contemporary novelists interested in form and in questions of civilization and national identity, will persist in writing their own versions of social history largely dependent on manners. Wallace Stegner's *Angle of Repose* (1977), for example, incorporates Mary Hallock Foote's correspondence with Helena de Kay Gilder to tell the story of American civilization's trek westward. Like that earlier observer Bayard Taylor, Stegner is fascinated with the manners and mores of a society in the process of defining itself. Toni Morrison's *Beloved* (1987), Sherley Ann William's *Dessa Rose* (1986), and Charles Johnson's *Middle Passage* (1990) pay homage to a tradition of slave narratives as they explore the historically different social realities of blacks and whites. They speak to the enduring obsession of American novelists with questions of human motivation and behavior. When we look at these writers, we recognize the combination of traditions, as well as the mutable boundaries of form that have come to characterize so much recent fiction. They remind us how few traditions can be said to exist wholly in and of themselves.

There are of course obvious differences between contemporary novelists and those I consider. James and Cather did see distinctions, sometimes almost absolute, between high and low culture; and they believed in the transcendent power of art. They did not believe in what Wharton called a "kodak," or strictly representational, reality. Art was, in her words, the "constant," meaning perennially adaptable, "form of human expression,"[4] and we see this in Morrison's borrowing the outlines of Margaret Garner's biography, in Williams's parodying the form of William Styron's *Confessions of Nat Turner* (1967),[5] and in Charles Johnson's spoofing Herman Melville's *Moby-Dick* (1851). As Wharton suggests and writers such as Morrison and Johnson illustrate, worlds of fiction tend to overlap more than replicate. Critics will probably debate James's relationship to fiction for at least another century because the work of the greatest novelists remains on some level as elusive and individual as imagination itself.

This prompts a final question: when many people no longer believe in the reality of things and choose not to recognize distinct times — social and psychological, as well as historical — can there be a "postmodern" novel of manners?[6] I would like to think that postmodernism affects this form as it affects the whole writing of fiction — that when experimental writers such as Thomas Pynchon and Don DeLillo focus on American social reality and reimagine history, they give new meaning to James's observation that we cannot know a culture until we know its manners. We might consider Pynchon's lists of movies and television serials in *Gravity's Rainbow*, oddly reminiscent of Nabokov's cataloging of motel amenities in *Lolita*, a novel that recreates the texture of suburban America. Or DeLillo's stand against "white noise" — the same kind of monologic force that James warned against in his articles on the manners and speech of American women. Although Raymond Carver is best known as a writer of short fiction, we need only to look at a passage from "Why Don't You Dance?" to see that manners serve him no less than they do Willa Cather:

In the kitchen, he poured himself another drink and looked at the bedroom suite in his yard . . . things looked much the way they had in the bedroom — nightstand and reading lamp on his side of the bed, nightstand and reading lamp on her side.

His side, her side.[7]

The parallel belongings of this couple tell their sad history. Carver gives a kind of lettered anguish to the alphabet, "His side, her side," suggesting — by capital and small *h* — the gradual tapering off of love.

To some extent, the current interest in historiography, in narrative patterns, process, and multiplicity, has made manners of more, not less, importance to writers. Something as apparently radical as postmodernism can be conservative in terms of the material of its fiction, as we see in Maxine Hong Kingston's amorphous *The Woman Warrior* (1975). Part fiction, part myth, and subtitled "a memoir," *The Woman Warrior* continues the drama of immigration that intrigued James in *The American Scene*. Kingston's book, with its self-consciously attenuated ties to several genres, highlights one of the ways in which realistic conventions have been modified to integrate social worlds and visions of reality that would have appeared "foreign" to James's readers. Kingston's first chapter, entitled "No Name Woman," opens with an admonition to the narrator (supposedly Kingston herself) not to tell what is about to be revealed: the tale of her Chinese aunt's extramarital affair and resulting pregnancy and suicide. Past and present overlap through analogous, adulterous practices (the aunt's sexual transgression and the niece's rival, "adulterated" versions of her aunt's life). Each disrupts existing codes of etiquette that bind the community. In China, "a nation of siblings,"[8] adultery becomes incest; in the United States, it becomes a metaphor for assimilation.

Again, I am not claiming that *The Woman Warrior* is a novel or that Kingston should be considered a novelist of manners; rather, that Kingston's world, compounded of nuances, grows from codes of etiquette as complicated as those of Balzac's provincial France. The "perpetual interchange of ideas and influences" that Wharton and James saw on both sides of the Atlantic gave rise to "the creation of a new world, ephemeral, shifting but infinitely curious to study" (Wharton, "Great American Novel," 157), and we live with its subsequent impact today.

Perhaps Sigmund Freud was right to say that the unconscious cannot escape the influence of culture.[9] Writing can be a dangerous foray into the public's consciousness of itself. If we can grasp anything from turn-of-the-century novelists, it might be their fearless embrace of process. As Wharton wrote in "Tendencies in Modern Fiction," "the moral and intellectual destruction caused by the war, and by its far-reaching consequences, was shattering to traditional culture. . . . But the natural processes go on."[10] For Wharton, they could go on only by the accumulation of tradition that she thought essential to the nurturing of new art. To her mind, novel writing has a tendency toward "ever-increasing complexity," to the extent that it mirrors "all growth, animal, human, social" ("Great American Novel," 155). Further, it has a recursive quality, the strokes of each writer's "letters" contained and joined.

Each of us tends to live in intersecting worlds. For many that means a larger world composed of customs, politics, and opinions, and a solitary, idiosyncratic world of work, personal struggle, and inward vision. Who can say whether our world confounds us more than Wharton's world confounded her? From the actual and the imagined, from the intersection of the competing and complementary worlds that Wharton and her contemporaries occupied, a vision of America took shape, and it, too, is part of an American literary history when transitions seemed both overwhelming and exhilarating.

The current longing for manners has, I think, little to do with nostalgia and much to do with a desire for truce (Willa Cather thought human relationships "the tragic necessity of human life").[11] When novels of manners are also great novels, they can force us to test the limits of our world as well as ourselves. Whatever the writers in this study may have disagreed about, they had faith that art's engagement with the social and moral complexities of life would allow for as-yet-unimagined variations of their chosen form. And this brings me to a last thought about the relationship between novelists and the larger topic of manners. American novelists did not invent the novel of manners, but in a sense the novel of manners might be said to have invented them. No other form could speak so eloquently to an emerging nation's crises of culture and identity, and none has so shaped a people's understanding of themselves and their society. James thought us condemned to loss, to forget or disown or outlive whatever was most vital to us as human beings. If this is true, it is also true that he and other novelists of manners give us back the histories we would or should want to preserve.

Notes

INTRODUCTION: American Novelists and Manners

1. For discussion of this tension, see Arthur Mizener, introduction to *The Fathers*, by Allen Tate (Chicago: Swallow Press, 1972), ix. See also Norbert Elias, *The Civilizing Process: The Development of Manners*, trans. Edmund Jephcott (New York: Urizen Books, 1978), xiii.

2. Henry James, "The Portrait of a Lady," in *Henry James: Novels, 1881–1886*, ed. Leon Edel (New York: Library of America, 1985), 397.

3. Stephen Gould, *The Mismeasure of Man* (New York: W. W. Norton, 1981), 124.

4. See William James, *Psychology: The Briefer Course*, ed. Gordon Allport (New York: Harper & Row, 1961), 249.

5. See Martha Banta, *Imaging American Women: Idea and Ideals in Cultural History* (New York: Columbia University Press, 1987), 253–57.

6. John F. Kasson, *Rudeness and Civility: Manners in Nineteenth-Century Urban America* (New York: Hill & Wang, 1990), 41, 37.

7. Arthur M. Schlesinger, *Learning How to Behave: A Historical Study of American Etiquette Books* (New York: Macmillan, 1947), 3.

8. Quoted in Frank Luther Mott, *A History of American Magazines* (Cambridge: Harvard University Press, 1957), 3:376.

9. William Dean Howells, *The Rise of Silas Lapham*, intro. and notes by Walter J. Meserve (Bloomington: Indiana University Press, 1971), 182.

10. Catherine Beecher and Harriet Beecher Stowe, *The American Woman's Home* (New York: J. B. Ford, 1869), 14.

11. Ellen Glasgow, *Virginia* (New York: Penguin Books, 1989), 16.

12. *Correct Social Usage: A Course of Instruction in Good Form, Style, and Deportment, by Eighteen Distinguished Authors* (New York: New York Society of Self-Culture, 1906), 52.

13. Charles Darwin, *The Expression of the Emotions in Man and Animals* (New York: Greenwood Press, 1969), v, 364–65. See George W. Stocking Jr., *Victorian Anthropology* (New York: Free Press, 1987), 39. See also Gould, *Mismeasure*, 125. Gould notes that Havelock Ellis accepted the contemporary stereotype that criminals, idiots, and savages rarely blushed.

14. *Oeuvres complètes de Honoré de Balzac: La Comédie Humaine: Scènes de la Vie Privée, I* (Paris: Louis Conard, 1912), xxix. The translation is from *Comédie Humanine*, ed. George Saintsbury (London: J. M. Dent, 1898), 8:5.

15. See Frank Luther Mott, *A History of American Magazines* (Cambridge: Harvard University Press, 1938), 2:32–33, 389–90, 307.

16. Edith Wharton, review of *George Eliot*, by Leslie Stephen, *Bookman* 15 (May 1902): 249, quoted in *Edith Wharton: The Uncollected Writings*, ed. Frederick Wegener (Princeton, N.J.: Princeton University Press, 1996), 76.

17. Letter, William Dean Howells to Joseph A. Howells, Christmas, 1908, in Elsa Nettels, *Language, Race, and Social Class in Howells's America* (Lexington: University Press of Kentucky, 1988), 217 n. 23.

18. Willa Cather, *The World and the Parish: Willa Cather Articles and Reviews, 1893–1902*, ed. William M. Curtin (Lincoln: University of Nebraska Press, 1970), 1:223.

19. Horace Traubel, *With Walt Whitman in Camden* (New York: Mitchell, Kennerly, 1914), 3:400.

20. William Dean Howells, "Editor's Easy Chair," *Harper's Monthly*, 102 (January 1901): 316–17.

21. Herbert Spencer, *Principles of Sociology* (London, 1882), 2:3.

22. Alexis de Tocqueville, *Democracy in America* (New York: Knopf, 1963), 2:60, 35, 57.

23. Lionel Trilling, "Manners, Morals, and the Novel," in *The Liberal Imagination* (Garden City, N.Y.: Anchor Books, 1953), 206.

24. Lionel Trilling, "Art and Fortune," in *The Liberal Imagination*, 252.

25. Henry James, "Hawthorne," in *Henry James: Literary Criticism*, ed. Leon Edel (New York: Library of America, 1984), 1:351–52.

26. For discussion of this point, see William M. Chace, *Lionel Trilling, Criticism and Politics* (Stanford: Stanford University Press, 1980), 3, 4.

27. Percy Lubbock is quoting the historian Gaillard Lapsley, in *Portrait of Edith Wharton* (New York: Appleton-Century-Crofts, 1947), 48.

28. Letter, Henry James to Thomas Sargeant Perry, September 1867, in Leon Edel, *Henry James: A Life* (New York: Harper & Row, 1985), 87.

29. See R. W. B. Lewis, *The American Adam: Innocence, Tragedy, and Tradition in the Nineteenth Century* (Chicago: University of Chicago Press, 1955), 5.

30. Joseph Conrad, "Henry James: An Appreciation," *Notes on Life and Letters* (New York: Doubleday, Page, 1922), 17.

31. Henry James, "The Art of Fiction," in *Henry James: Literary Criticism*, 1:47.

32. Ann Douglas, *The Feminization of American Culture* (New York: Knopf, 1977), esp. 177, but see also 170, 176, 179.

33. C. Hugh Holman, *The Immoderate Past: The Southern Writer and History* (Athens: University of Georgia Press, 1977), 43–44. I am indebted to Holman for emphasizing the impact of change over the force of tradition.

34. Vladimir Nabokov, *Lectures on Literature* (New York Harcourt Brace Jovanovich, 1980), 381.

CHAPTER ONE: William Dean Howells: The Lessons of a Master

1. Charles Chesnutt, "Post-Bellum — Pre-Harlem," in *The Crisis* 40, no. 6 (1931): 194.

2. William Dean Howells, "Novel-Writing and Novel-Reading: An Impersonal Explanation," in *A Selected Edition of William Dean Howells, Selected Literary Criticism* (Bloomington, Indiana University Press, 1993), 3:223.

Howells cited *April Hopes* (1887) as the first time he had a "distinct consciousness" that he was "writing as a realist." See Kermit Vanderbilt, introduction to *April Hopes* (Bloomington: Indiana University Press, 1974), xv.

3. William Dean Howells, in William Cooper Howells, *Recollections of Life in Ohio from 1813–1840* (Gainesville, Fla.: Scholars' Facsimiles and Reprints, 1963), v.

4. William Dean Howells, *Years of My Youth and Three Essays*, ed. David J. Nordloh (Bloomington: Indiana University Press, 1975), 24.

5. William Dean Howells, *The Early Prose Writings of William Dean Howells, 1852–1861*, ed. Thomas Wortham (Athens: Ohio University Press, 1990), 73–74.

6. William Dean Howells, *A Hazard of New Fortunes*, intro. Everett Carter (Bloomington: Indiana University Press, 1993), 49.

7. See William Dean Howells, "The Man of Letters as a Man of Business," *Literature and Life* (New York: Harper & Brothers, 1902), 35.

8. William Dean Howells, *Literary Friends and Acquaintance*, ed. David F. Hiatt and Edwin H. Cady (Bloomington: Indiana University Press, 1968), 100.

9. "As Howells Sees Fiction," in [Howells,] *Interviews with William Dean Howells*, ed. Ulrich Halfmann, *American Literary Realism* 6, no. 4 (1973): 335.

10. See Amy Kaplan, *The Social Construction of American Realism* (Chicago: University of Chicago Press, 1988), 9. Kaplan argues that realists like Howells "engage in an enormous act of construction to organize, re-form, and control the social world," which makes it both static and "tentative" (10). See also Donald E. Pease, introduction to *New Essays on "The Rise of Silas Lapham,"* ed. Donald E. Pease (Cambridge: Oxford University Press, 1991), 1–28. Pease gives a historical overview of the critical response to Howells.

11. Letter, William Dean Howells to John Howells, June 1, 1863, in *Selected Letters of W. D. Howells*, ed. George Arms et al. (Boston: Twayne, 1979), 1:152.

12. Letter, William Dean Howells to John Hay, 22 February 1877, in *John Hay–Howells Letters*, ed. George Monterio and Brenda Murphy (Boston: Twayne, 1980), 24.

13. Letter, William Dean Howells to Charles D. Warner, April 1, 1877, in *Selected Letters*, 2:160.

14. See Alfred Habegger, *Gender, Fantasy, and Realism in American Literature* (New York: Columbia University Press, 1982), 62–62, 233.

15. Henry James, "A Letter to Mr. Howells," *North American Review* 195 (April 1912): 561; published in Michael Anesko, *Letters, Fictions, Lives: Henry James and William Dean Howells* (New York: Oxford University Press, 1997), 452.

16. Thomas Wentworth Higginson, *Short Studies of American Authors* (Boston: Lee & Shepard, 1880), 36–37.

17. See Alfred Bendixen, introduction to *The Whole Family: A Novel by Twelve Authors* (New York: Ungar, 1987), xi, xxxv. *Harper's Bazar* carried the novel from December 1907 to November 1908. See also "Henry James and the *Bazaar* Letters," in *Howells and James: A Double Billing*, ed. Leon Edel and Lyall H. Powers (New York: New York Public Library, 1958), 27–55.

18. Edith Wharton, *A Backward Glance* (New York: Charles Scribner's Sons, 1964), 148.

19. Letter, Henry James to Sara Norton Darwin, September 11, 1907, in *Henry James Letters*, ed. Leon Edel (Cambridge: Harvard University Press, 1984), 4:504 n. 1.

20. William Dean Howells, *My Literary Passions: Criticism and Fiction* (New York: Harper & Brothers, 1895), 15.

21. William Dean Howells, *London Films* (New York: Harper & Brothers, 1905), 63. See James Tuttleton, "Howells and the Manners of the Good Heart," *Modern Fiction Studies* 16 (autumn 1970): 286.

22. Howells, "Editor's Easy Chair," 316–17.

23. William Dean Howells, *Editor's Study*, April 1887, ed. James W. Simpson (Troy, N.Y.: Whitson, 1993), 74.

24. Horace E. Scudder makes this point in his review of *A Modern Instance, Atlantic* 50 (November 1882): 712.

25. Howells, *Editor's Study*, June 1886, 26.

26. See Kaplan, *Social Construction*, esp. 11, 30. Kaplan argues that Hubbard unites different social classes through consumerism and the medium of the media.

27. William Dean Howells, *A Modern Instance*, intro. and notes by George N. Bennett (Bloomington: Indiana University Press, 1977), 159.

28. For responses to Howells's subject, see Kenneth S. Lynn, *William Dean Howells: An American Life* (New York: Harcourt Brace Jovanovich, 1971), 267.

29. See Mott, *American Magazines* (1957), 3:308. From 1874 to 1876, the Beecher-Tilton scandal formed the basis of national debate about marriage.

30. Ibid., 3:312.

31. Thomas Wentworth Higginson, "Howells," in *Short Studies of American Authors*, 32. For Howells's own analysis of his relationship with *Harper's*, see William Dean Howells, "The House of Harper," in *The House of Harper* by J. Henry Harper (New York: Harper & Brothers, 1912), 319–27.

32. William Dean Howells, *The Quality of Mercy* (New York: Harper & Brothers, 1892), 42, 152.

33. Letter, William Dean Howells to James, Oct. 10, 1888, in Anesko, *Letters, Fictions, Lives*, 271. See Gregory L. Crider, "William Dean Howells and the Gilded Age: Socialist in a Fur-lined Overcoat," *Ohio History* 88 (autumn 1979): 416.

34. See Gregory L. Crider, "William Dean Howells and the Antiurban Tradition: A Reconsideration," *American Studies* 19 (spring 1978): 55–64.

35. William Dean Howells, *The Rise of Silas Lapham*, intro. and notes by Walter J. Meserve (Bloomington: Indiana University Press, 1971), 28.

36. William Dean Howells, *A Traveler from Altruria* (New York: Harper & Brothers, 1908), 12.

37. William James, *"Pragmatism" and Four Essays from "The Meaning of Truth,"* (New York: Meridan Books, 1955), 133.

38. For "manufactory," see William Dean Howells, "William James's *Psychology*, 1891," in *W. D. Howells as Critic*, ed. Edwin H. Cady (London: Routledge & Kegan Paul, 1973), 199.

39. For an analysis of Bartley Hubbard's parody of sentimental fiction, see Fred G. See, "The Demystification of Style: Metaphoric and Metonymic Language in *A Modern Instance*," *Nineteenth-Century Fiction* 28 (March 1974): 392–95.

40. Howells shows the product of this thinking in *A Hazard of New Fortunes*'s description of the gas region around Northern Ohio and Indiana. Once bucolic, the small town of Moffitt has become a booming wasteland, identified by the proliferation of suburbs, public buildings, turnpikes, and the smell of benzine. Edith Wharton may have remembered Howells's novel when she was creating Elmer Moffat, also a Midwestern millionaire, in *The Custom of the Country* (1913). For more on Howells's ideas about industrialization, see Howells, *Literature and Life*, 314–15.

41. See Jürgen Habermas, *Structural Transformation of the Public Sphere: An Inquiry into*

a Category of Bourgeois Society, trans. Thomas Burger, in association with Frederic Lawrence (Cambridge: MIT Press; Cambridge, Eng.: Polity Press, 1992), esp. 141–201. See also Kaplan, *Social Construction*, 32–33, 37.

42. Persis, whose plot parallels that of her husband, falters on several occasions: the first has to do with the financial well-being of her family, the second with sexual jealousy, precipitated by an anonymous letter unjustly accusing her husband of infidelity. Howells plays with the dichotomy between man (conscience) and woman (feeling), initially reversing and then restoring these contemporary stereotypes. At last, neither reigns, though feeling, or what seems right, determines.

43. Critics have long debated whether Howells favors the Coreys or the Laphams. For those who side with the Coreys, see Alfred Kazin, "Howells the Bostonian," *Clio* 3 (February 1972): 231; and Ralph Behrens, "Howells' Portrait of a Boston Brahmin," *Markham Review* 3 (October 1972): 71–73. For defenders of the Laphams, see George N. Bennett, *The Realism of William Dean Howells: 1889–1920* (Nashville: Vanderbilt University Press, 1973), 155; and Edwin H. Cady, *The Road to Realism: The Early Years, 1837–1885, of William Dean Howells* (Syracuse: Syracuse University Press, 1956), 231. Critics who think Howells impartial include Habegger, *Gender, Fantasy, and Realism*, 193; and Kermit Vanderbilt, *The Achievement of William Dean Howells: A Reinterpretation* (Princeton: Princeton University Press, 1968), 136.

44. William Dean Howells, *A Chance Acquaintance*, intro. and notes by Jonathan Thomas and David J. Nordloh (Bloomington: Indiana University Press, 1971), 92.

45. Mizener, introduction to *The Fathers*, by Allen Tate, ix.

46. Letter, William Dean Howells to Thomas B. Aldrich, July 3, 1903, in *Selected Letters*, 5:32.

47. William Dean Howells, *The Lady of the Aroostook* (Boston: Houghton, Osgood, 1879), 125–26.

48. Letter, William Dean Howells to William C. Howells, Nov. 6, 1859, in *Selected Letters*, 1:48–49.

49. Robert Price, "The Road to Boston: 1860 Travel Correspondence of William Dean Howells," *Ohio History* 80 (1971): 122.

50. William Dean Howells, "The Pilot's Story," *Atlantic* 6, no. 35 (1860): 323–25.

51. William Dean Howells, introduction to *The Life and Works of Paul Laurence Dunbar* (Nashville: Winston-Derek, 1992), 15. See also William Dean Howells, "Life and Letters," *Harper's Weekly* 40 (June 27, 1896): 630; quoted in Nettels, *Language, Race, Class*, 81.

52. See William L. Andrews, "William Dean Howells and Charles W. Chesnutt: Criticism and Race Fiction in the Age of Booker T. Washington," *American Literature* 48 (November 1976): 327–39. See also Houston A. Baker, *The Journey Back: Issues in Black Literature and Criticism* (Chicago: University of Chicago Press, 1980), 158.

53. For a discussion of Howells and Dunbar, see Nettels, *Language, Race, Class*, 80–86. See also Clare R. Goldfarb, "The Questions of William Dean Howells's Racism," *Ball State University Forum* 12 (1971): 22–24; and James B. Stronks, "Paul Laurence Dunbar and William Dean Howells," *Ohio Historical Quarterly* 67 (April 1958): 95–108.

54. Howells was the earliest of three *Atlantic* editors who wrote novels dealing with race: Bliss Perry wrote *The Plated City* (1895), Walter Hines Page, *The Autobiography of Nicholas Worth* (1921).

55. See Henry B. Wonham, "Howells, Du Bois, and the Effect of 'Common-Sense': Race, Realism, and Nervousness in *An Imperative Duty* and *The Souls of Black Folk*," in *Criticism and the Color Line: Desegregating American Literary Studies*, ed. Henry B. Wonham (New Brunswick, N.J.: Rutgers University Press, 1996), esp. 126–39, 129, 133.

56. W. E. B. Du Bois, *The Souls of Black Folk* (New York: Penguin, 1969), 45.

57. William Dean Howells, *An Imperative Duty*, in *"The Shadow of a Dream" and "An Imperative Duty,"* intro. and notes by Martha Banta (Bloomington: Indiana University Press, 1970), 27. For a less sympathetic reading of this novel, see Jacquelyn Y. McLendon, *The Politics of Color* (Charlottesville: University Press of Virginia, 1995), 17–22. See also Werner Sollors, *Neither Black nor White yet Both: Thematic Explorations of Interracial Literature* (New York: Oxford University Press, 1997), 341, 342; and Martha Banta, introduction to *An Imperative Duty*, iii–xii.

58. For a discussion of this novel, see Robert Mielke, *"The Riddle of the Painful Earth": Suffering and Society in W. D. Howells' Major Writings of the Early 1890s* (Lanham, Md.: Thomas Jefferson University Press, Northeast Missouri State University, 1994), esp. 74–93, 91.

59. See Howells, *Literary Friends and Acquaintance*, 219. Howells regretted his "mean and cruel grudge" against the Irish, whom he characterizes as quick-witted, poetic, greedy, vulgar, and servile in *An Imperative Duty*.

60. See Kevin K. Gaines, *Uplifting the Race: Black Leadership, Politics, and Culture in the Twentieth Century* (Chapel Hill: University of North Carolina Press, 1996), 230. See also Franklin E. Frazier, *Black Bourgeoisie: The Rise of a New Middle Class* (Glencoe, Ill.: Free Press, 1957).

61. See Harrison T. Meserole, "The Dean in Person: Howells' Lecture Tour," *Western Humanities Review* 10, no. 4 (1956): 337–47.

62. William Dean Howells, "The New Historical Romances," in *Selected Literary Criticism*, 3:26.

63. Milan Kundera, *The Art of the Novel* (New York: HarperCollins, 1991), 36.

64. See *William Styron's Nat Turner*, ed. John Henrik Clarke (Boston: Beacon Press, 1968), 4, 32, 36. See also Albert E. Stone, *The Return of Nat Turner: History, Literature, and Cultural Politics in Sixties America* (Athens: University of Georgia Press, 1992), 101–76; James M. Mellard, "The Unquiet Dust: The Problem of History in Styron's *The Confessions of Nat Turner*," in *The Critical Response to William Styron*, ed. Daniel W. Ross (Westport, Conn.: Greenwood Press, 1995), 157–72; Henry Irving Tragle, "Styron and His Sources," *Massachusetts Review* 11 (winter 1970): 135–53; and Tony Horowitz, "A Reporter at Large: Untrue Confessions," *New Yorker*, December 13, 1999, 80–86, 88–89.

65. William Dean Howells, *Editor's Study*, August 1886, 38.

66. James, "Letter to Mr. Howells," 452.

67. William Dean Howells, *Literature and Life*, 75.

68. William Dean Howells, *Editor's Study*, March 1888, 124.

69. See Henry James, entry for October 31, 1895, *The Complete Notebooks of Henry James*, ed. Leon Edel and Lyall H. Powers (New York: Oxford University Press, 1987), 140–41.

70. Mary Austin, tribute to William Dean Howells, bMS Am 1784.4 (43), p. 8, by permission of Houghton Library, Harvard University.

71. Letter, James to Howells, August 10, 1901, in Anesko, *Letters, Fictions, Lives*, 366–67.

CHAPTER TWO: Henry James: The Final Paradox of Manners

1. Edel, *Henry James: A Life*, 588. Biographical information is taken from Edel and from Fred Kaplan, *Henry James: The Imagination of Genius* (New York: William Morrow, 1992).

2. Henry James, October 31, 1895, in *Complete Notebooks*, ed. Edel and Powers, 141. Contemplating the creation, in *The Ambassadors*, of Lambert Strether, a middle-aged editor of a New England literary journal, James observed: "I can't make him a novelist—too like W. D. H. . . . But I want him 'intellectual,' I want him *fine*, clever, literary almost."

3. Letter, Henry James to Edith Wharton, August 17, 1902, in *Henry James and Edith Wharton, Letters: 1900–1915*, ed. Lyall H. Powers (New York: Charles Scribner's Sons, 1990), 34.

4. Henry James, "The Jolly Corner," in *The Complete Tales of Henry James*, ed. Leon Edel (Philadelphia: J. B. Lippincott, 1964), 12:194.

5. For an opposite reading of James's response to the American scene, see Ross Posnock, *The Trial of Curiosity: Henry James, William James, and the Challenge of Modernity* (New York: Oxford University Press, 1991), 141–66, 250–85. Posnock presents James as someone artistically liberated by his confrontation with difference.

6. See Henry James, "The American Scene," in *Collected Travel Writings: Great Britain and America*, ed. Richard Howard (New York: Library of America, 1993), 360.

7. Henry James, *Autobiography: A Small Boy and Others; Notes of a Son and Brother; The Middle Years*, ed. Frederick W. Dupee (New York: Criterion Books, 1956), 94.

8. Wharton, *Backward Glance*, 176.

9. Letter, Elinor M. Howells to Anne T. Howells, November 23, 1871, *If Not Literature: Letters of Elinor Mead Howells*, ed. Ginette de B. Merrill and George Arms (Columbus: Ohio State University Press, 1988), 145.

10. Fragment to E [1904], in letters of William Dean Howells to Elinor M. Howells, Houghton Library.

11. Roland Barthes, *Empire of Signs*, trans. Richard Howard (New York: Hill & Wang, 1982), 3.

12. Henri Bergson, *Mind-Energy, Lectures, and Essays*, trans. H. Wildon Carr (New York: Henry Holt, 1920), 130, 131.

13. I am paraphrasing James. See James, "Hawthorne," 1:435.

14. Albert Camus, *Notebooks, 1935–1942*, trans. Philip Thody (New York: Harcourt Brace Jovanovich, 1978), 13–14.

15. James, "Art of Fiction," 1:64.

16. Letter, Henry James to Edith Wharton, January 16, 1905, in *James and Wharton, Letters*, ed. Powers, 44.

17. See Richard Salmon, *Henry James and the Culture of Publicity* (Cambridge: Cambridge University Press, 1997), 184.

18. See Beverly Haviland, *Henry James's Last Romance: Making Sense of the Past and the American Scene* (New York: Cambridge University Press, 1997), 94–97.

19. Henry James, *The Sense of the Past* (London: W. Collins Sons, 1917), 34.

20. Henry James, preface to *The Golden Bowl*, in *The Art of the Novel: Critical Prefaces by Henry James*, ed. Richard P. Blackmur (New York: Charles Scribner's Sons, 1934), 340.

21. See John R. Commons, *Races and Immigrants in America* (New York: Macmillan,

1908), 217. See also Lawrence Guy Brown, *Immigration: Cultural Conflicts and Social Adjustments* (New York: Arno Press/New York Times, 1969), 151.

22. See letter, W. E. B. Du Bois to Herbert Aptheker, January 10, 1956, in *The Correspondence of W. E. B. Du Bois*, ed. Herbert Aptheker (Amherst: University of Massachusetts Press, 1973), 3:394–96. Du Bois explains: "For two years I studied under William James while he was developing Pragmatism; under [George] Santayana and his attractive mysticism and under [Josiah] Royce and his Hegelian idealism. I then found and adopted a philosophy which has served me since; thereafter I turned to the study of History and what has become Sociology" (394–95). See also letter, James to Du Bois, Aug. 9, 1907, 1:134. James writes to tell Du Bois that he will call on him in London, but Aptheker notes that the two never met. See also Haviland, *Last Romance*, 115–22.

23. See William C. Brownell, *Democratic Distinction in America* (New York: Charles Scribner's Sons, 1927), 42, 199.

24. See Henry James, "The Question of Our Speech," in Peter Buitenhaus, ed., *French Writers and American Women Essays* (Branford, Conn.: Compass, 1960), 19.

25. Letter, Henry James to Thomas Sargeant Perry, September 1867, in *Henry James: A Life*, 87.

26. Letter, Henry James to William James, September 22 [1872], in *The Correspondence of William James*, ed. Ignas K. Skrupskelis and Elizabeth M. Berkely (Charlottesville: University of Virginia Press, 1992–), 1:170.

27. Letter, Edith Wharton to Sara Norton, September 1, 1902, in Susan Goodman, *Edith Wharton's Women: Friends and Rivals* (Hanover: University Press of New England, 1990), 41.

28. Mott, *American Magazines* (1957), 3:308–9.

29. See T. J. Jackson Lears, *No Place of Grace: Antimodernism and the Transformation of American Culture, 1880–1920* (New York: Pantheon, 1981).

30. Henry James, "The Speech of American Women," part 4, *Harper's Bazar* 41, no. 8 (1907): 114. See also Buitenhaus, *French Writers*, 50. For the few discussions of these articles, see Haviland, *Last Romance*, 177; and Salmon, *Culture of Publicity*, 26.

31. Henry James, "The Speech of American Women," part 1, *Harper's Bazar* 40, no. 11 (1906): 980. See also Buitenhaus, *French Writers*, 33.

32. See Linda Dowling, *Language and Decadence in the Victorian Fin de Siècle* (Princeton: Princeton University Press, 1986), xiii–xv.

33. Henry James, "The Manners of American Women," *Harper's Bazar* (1907), part 2: 455. See also idem, *French Writers and American Women Essays*, 64.

34. James, "Manners of American Women," part 3:539, 538. See also idem, *French Writers and American Women Essays*, 68.

35. Aside from his misgivings about the abilities of his collaborators, James so enjoyed writing his chapter that he wanted to write those that remained. "I can't help saying now," he told the book's editor, Elizabeth Jordon, "that I wish I might have been suffered to take upon myself to save the stuff—which would have interested & amused me, & which I would have done ingeniously & —well, *cheap!*" See Alfred Bendixen, introduction to *The Whole Family: A Novel by Twelve Authors* (New York: Ungar, 1987), xxx. See also "Henry James and the *Bazaar* Letters," in *Double Billing*, ed. Edel and Powers, 27–55.

36. James, "Manners of American Women," part 3:538, 539; and part 4:541. See also Buitenhaus, *French Writers*, 73, 78.

37. Joseph Conrad, "Henry James: An Appreciation," in *Notes on Life and Letters* (New York: Doubleday, Page, 1922), 17.

38. Henry James, "The Portrait of a Lady," in *Henry James: Novels*, 612.

39. Henry James, *The Ambassadors* (New York: W. W. Norton, 1964), 281.

40. See Ross Posnock, *Henry James and the Problem of Robert Browning* (Athens: University of Georgia Press, 1985), 10.

41. F. Scott Fitzgerald, *The Great Gatsby* (New York: Macmillan [Collier ed.], 1986), 2.

42. See Gerald E. Myers, "The Influence of William James's Pragmatism in Italy," in *The Sweetest Impression of Life: The James Family and Italy*, ed. James Tuttleton and Agostino Lambardo (New York: New York University Press, 1990), 164.

43. Henry James, *The Notebooks of Henry James*, ed. F. O. Matthiessen and Kenneth B. Murdock (New York: George Braziller, 1955), 298–99.

44. Henry James, *The Sense of the Past*, 288, 291, 289.

45. See Henry James, "The Turn of the Screw," in *"The Aspern Papers" and "The Turn of the Screw"* (New York: Penguin, 1984), 213. The governess has "the baseness to speak," which leads to the corruption that she sees in the children.

46. Letters of Henry James to Edith Wharton, September 10, 1913, and January 31, 1913, in *James and Wharton, Letters* 265, 245.

47. See R. W. B. Lewis, *Edith Wharton: A Biography* (New York: Fromm International, 1985), 342.

48. Henry James, *The Ivory Tower* (London: W. Collins Sons, 1917), 22.

49. Nathaniel Hawthorne, preface to *The House of the Seven Gables: A Romance* (Boston: Ticknor, Reed, & Fields, 1851), iv.

50. Henry James, "Notes of a Son and Brother," in *Henry James: Autobiography*, ed. Frederick W. Dupee (New York: Criterion Book, 1957), 277.

51. See Richard Chase, *The American Novel and Its Tradition* (Garden City, N.Y.: Anchor Books, 1957).

52. Henry James, *Within the Rim and Other Essays, 1914–1915* (London: W. Collins Sons, 1918), 13. See also "Within the Rim" in *Collected Travel Writing*, 329; *Collected Travel Writing* contains three of the five essays that form this volume: "Refugees in England," 319–28, "Within the Rim," 329–40, and "The Long Wards," 341–50.

53. Henry James, "The American Volunteer Motor-Ambulance Corps in France," in *Within the Rim*, 77.

54. Henry James, "France," in *Within the Rim*, 89.

55. Letter, Henry James to Edith Wharton, September 23, 1914, in *James and Wharton, Letters*, 302.

56. *Within the Rim*, 119; see also "The Long Wards," in *Collected Travel Writings*, 350.

57. See Alan Holder, *Three Voyagers in Search of Europe: A Study of Henry James, Ezra Pound, and T. S. Eliot* (Philadelphia: Pennsylvania University Press, 1966), 128.

58. *Within the Rim*, 119; see also "The Long Wards," in *Collected Travel Writings*, 350.

CHAPTER THREE: Edith Wharton: A Backward Glance

1. Letter, Edith Wharton to Sara Norton, March 1 [1906], *The Letters of Edith Wharton*, ed. R. W. B. Lewis and Nancy Lewis (New York: Charles Scribner's Sons, 1988), 105 n. 3.

2. Wharton, *Backward Glance*, 44, 29–30, 128.

3. Lewis, *Edith Wharton: A Biography*, 103.

4. Letter, Edith Wharton to Sara Norton, June 5 1903, in *Letters*, 84–85.

5. Quoted in Percy Lubbock, *Portrait of Edith Wharton* (New York: Appleton-Century-Crofts, 1947), 49, 48.

6. For a discussion of these novels, see Dale Bauer, *Edith Wharton's Brave New Politics* (Madison: University of Wisconsin Press, 1994).

7. Letter, Edith Wharton to Sara Norton, June 5 [1903], in *Letters*, 84.

8. Susan Goodman, *Edith Wharton's Inner Circle* (Austin: University of Texas Press, 1994), 116.

9. Letter, Edith Wharton to Margaret Terry Chanler, March 8 [1903], in *Letters*, 77–78.

10. Edith Wharton, *The Collected Short Stories of Edith Wharton*, ed. R. W. B. Lewis (New York: Charles Scribner's Sons, 1985), 1:14.

11. See Jonathan Morse, *Word by Word: The Language of Memory* (Ithaca: Cornell University Press, 1990), 127.

12. Van Wyck Brooks, "On Constructing a Usable Past," *The Dial*, 64 (1918): 341.

13. Lionel Trilling, "Manners, Morals, and the Novel," in *The Liberal Imagination* (New York: Anchor Books, 1953), 200.

14. Matthew Arnold, "Equality," in *The Portable Matthew Arnold*. ed. Lionel Trilling (New York: Viking, 1949), 587.

15. Edith Wharton, *The Reef* (New York: Charles Scribner's Sons, 1912), 83.

16. Letter, Edith Wharton to Robert Grant, November 19, 1907, in *Letters*, 124. See Katherine Joslin, "Architectonic or Episodic? Gender and *The Fruit of the Tree*," in *Edith Wharton: A Forward Glance*, ed. Clare Colquitt, Susan Goodman, and Candace Waid (Newark: University of Delaware Press, 1999), 62–75. See also Vanessa Chase, "Edith Wharton, *The Decoration of Houses*, and Gender in Turn-of-the-Century America," in *Architecture and Feminism*, ed. Elizabeth Danze and Carol Henderson (New York: Princeton Architectural Press, 1996), 130–60.

17. Edmund, Wilson, "Justice to Edith Wharton," *The Wound and the Bow* (New York: Oxford University Press, 1947), 201, 200.

18. See Lionel Trilling, "The Sense of the Past," in *The Liberal Imagination*, 190–91.

19. See William A. Coles, "The Genesis of a Classic," *The Decoration of Houses* (New York: W. W. Norton, 1997), 256–57. The exact part that either Codman or Wharton had in the writing of *The Decoration of Houses* remains uncertain. After Wharton and Codman had a falling out, he claimed that he wrote the book and that she polished it. Its tone and argument, however, certainly match that of Wharton's other nonfiction books, and a letter that Codman wrote to his mother in January 1897 supports the interpretation that Wharton played a larger role in the writing. Codman states: "She takes my notes and puts them into literary form, and adds a good deal out of her own head." Wharton contacted publishers, did the translating, and composed the index. See Eleanor Dwight, *Edith Wharton: An Extraordinary Life* (New York: Harry N. Abrams, 1994), 58. See also Shari Benstock, *No Gifts from Chance* (New York: Charles Scribner's Sons, 1994), 85. Benstock quotes Wharton's complaint to Codman that she had supposed he would do half the work.

20. Edith Wharton and Ogden Codman Jr., *The Decoration of Houses* (New York: Charles Scribner's Sons, 1897), 18.

21. T. J. Jackson Lears, *Fables of Abundance* (New York: Basic Books, 1994), 115.

22. Herbert Marcuse, *The Aesthetic Dimension: Toward a Critique of Marxist Aesthetics*, trans. and rev. Erica Sherover (Boston: Beacon Press, 1978), ix. See also George Santayana, *The Life of Reason, or The Phases of Human Progress* (New York: Charles Scribner's Sons, 1954), 369.

23. Edith Wharton, "The Daunt Diana," in *Collected Short Stories*, ed. Lewis, 2:57.

24. See Goodman, *Inner Circle*, 96; and Maureen E. Montgomery, *Displaying Women: Spectacles of Leisure in Edith Wharton's New York* (New York: Routledge, 1998), 70–71.

25. See William R. Leach, "Strategists of Display and the Production of Desire," in *Consuming Visions: Accumulation and the Display of Goods in America, 1880–1920*, ed. Simon J. Bronner (New York: W. W. Norton, 1989), 116, 131–32.

26. Edith Wharton, *A Motor-flight through France* (New York: Charles Scribner's Sons, 1908), 178.

27. See Benstock, *No Gifts*, 84. See also Edith Wharton, "Schoolroom Decoration," in *Edith Wharton: The Uncollected Critical Writings* (Princeton: Princeton University Press, 1996), 58–59.

28. Wharton was not alone in this belief. See Stocking, *Victorian Anthropology*, 38.

29. See Scott Marshall, *The Mount: The Home of Edith Wharton* (Lenox, Mass.: Edith Wharton Restoration, 1997), 97.

30. Oscar Wilde, "The Practical Application of the Principles of the Aesthetic Theory to Exterior and Interior House Decoration, with Observations upon Dress and Personal Ornaments," in *Aristotle at Afternoon Tea*, ed. John Wyse Jackson (London: Fourth Estate, 1991), 183–86. See also Mary Warner Blanchard, *Oscar Wilde's America: Counterculture in the Gilded Age* (New Haven: Yale University Press, 1998), 17–19, 86–87.

31. Jules and Edmond de Goncourt, *Journal des Goncourts: Mémoires de la vie littéraire*, 9 vols. [1912], quoted in Montgomery, *Displaying Women*, 174 n. 48.

32. See Gaston Bachelard, *The Poetics of Space* (New York: Orion Press, 1964).

33. Edith Wharton, *Summer* (New York: Penguin, 1993), 130.

34. For a comparison between Balzac and James, see W. Morton Fullerton, "The Art of Henry James," in *Edith Wharton: The Uncollected Critical Writings*, 310–16. Wharton helped Fullerton with the article.

35. Georg Lukàcs, *The Historical Novel* (Boston: Beacon Press, 1963), 61.

36. See letter, Edith Wharton to William Crary Brownell, February 14 [1902], in *Letters*, 18. In *The Valley of Decision*, Wharton included among her characters the poet Count Vittorio Alfieri and gave "glimpses" of the clerical community at Rome and Sir William Hamilton's circle at Naples.

37. Letter, Edith Wharton to Sara Norton, February 13 [1902], in *Letters*, 57.

38. Letter, Henry James to Edith Wharton, August 17, 1902, in *James and Wharton, Letters*, 34.

39. Henry James, preface to *"The Aspern Papers" and "The Turn of the Screw"* (New York: Penguin, 1984), 31.

40. See Alice Payne Hackett, *Fifty Years of Best Sellers, 1895–1945* (New York: R. R. Bowker, 1945). The new century began with historical novels dominating the market.

41. See Amy Kaplan, "Romancing the Empire: The Embodiment of American Masculinity in the Popular Historical Novel of the 1890s," in *American Literary History* 40 (winter 1990): 666.

42. For a discussion of different types of historical novels, see Harry Shaw, *The Forms of Historical Fiction: Sir Walter Scott and His Successors* (Ithaca, N.Y.: Cornell University Press, 1983), 52.

43. Letter, Edith Wharton to William Crary Brownell, February 14 [1902], in *Letters*, 58.

44. Edith Wharton, *The Valley of Decision* (New York: Charles Scribner's Sons, 1902), 636.

45. For information on Arthur Young, see Thomas Okey, introduction to *Travels in France and Italy* (London: J. M. Dent & Sons, 1934), vii–xxi.

46. See Wesley Morris, *Toward a New Historicism* (Princeton: Princeton University Press, 1972), 81.

47. Letter, Edith Wharton to Mary Cadwalader Jones, February 17, 1921, in *Letters*, 440.

48. Edith Wharton, "The Age of Innocence," in *Edith Wharton: Novels*, ed. R. W. B. Lewis (New York: Library of America, 1985), 1050.

49. Lewis, *American Adam*, 5.

50. See Anne MacMaster, "Wharton, Race, and *The Age of Innocence:* Three Historical Contexts," in *Wharton: A Forward Glance*, 188–205.

51. See, for example, George Dekker, *The American Historical Romance* (Cambridge: Cambridge University Press, 1987), 270–71.

52. Quoted in Timothy Bahti's *Allegories of History: Literary Historiography after Hegel* (Baltimore: Johns Hopkins University Press, 1992), 181.

53. Wharton did complete a sentimental novella entitled *The Marne* (1918). Its referent may have been Howard Sturgis's *Tim* (1891), the homoerotic story of a young man's sacrifice.

54. See the epigraph to Wharton's *Son at the Front* (New York: Charles Scribner's Son, 1923).

55. Edith Wharton, *Fighting France: From Dunkerque to Belfort* (New York: Charles Scribner's Sons, 1915), 153.

56. Edith Wharton, *French Ways and Their Meaning* (New York: D. Appleton, 1919), v. See Alan Price, *End of the Age of Innocence: Edith Wharton and the First World War* (New York: Macmillan, 1996), 148, 175.

57. Edith Wharton, "The House of Mirth," in *Edith Wharton: Novels*, 337.

58. For background on *The Book of the Homeless*, see Price, *End of the Age of Innocence*, 60–67, 69, 77–79, 202–3 n. 11.

59. Edith Wharton, "Belgium," *King Albert's Book* (New York: Hearst's International Library, 1915), 165.

60. Edith Wharton, *The Book of the Homeless* (New York: Charles Scribner's Sons, 1916), xxiv, x.

61. Edith Wharton, "You and You; To the American Private in the Great War," *Scribner's Magazine* 65 (Feb. 1919): 152–53.

62. Edith Wharton, "The Great American Novel," in *The Uncollected Writings of Edith Wharton*, 152.

CHAPTER FOUR: Willa Cather: "After 1922 or Thereabout"

1. Sharon O'Brien, *Willa Cather: The Emerging Voice* (New York: Oxford University Press, 1987), 297.

2. Willa Cather, *The Kingdom of Art: Willa Cather's First Principles and Critical Statements, 1893–1896*, ed. Bernice Slote (Lincoln: University of Nebraska Press, 1967), 361.

3. See James E. Miller Jr. "Willa Cather and the Art of Fiction," in *The Art of Willa Cather*, ed. Bernice Slote and Virginia Faulkner (Lincoln: University of Nebraska Press, 1973), 121–48.

4. See, for example, the following essays in *Willa Cather and Her Critics*, ed. James

Schroeter (Ithaca, N.Y.: Cornell University Press, 1967): Edmund Wilson, "Two Novels of Willa Cather," 29; T. K. Whipple, "Willa Cather," 36, 37; and Louise Bogan, "American-Classic," 128.

5. Q. D. Leavis, "Henry James's Heiress: The Importance of Edith Wharton," *Scrutiny* 7 (1938–39): 261–76. See Maxwell Geismar, "Willa Cather: Lady in the Wilderness," in *Willa Cather and Her Critics*, 173. Comparing Cather to other woman writers, he decided that she was "in some ways the most interesting of them all: less restricted than Edith Wharton, more intense than Ellen Glasgow."

6. Willa Cather, "My First Novels," in *Willa Cather on Writing* (Lincoln: University of Nebraska Press, 1988), 94.

7. W. Morton Fullerton, "The Art of Henry James," in *Edith Wharton: The Uncollected Critical Writings*, ed. Frederick Wegener (Princeton: Princeton University Press, 1996), 311. See also William H. Stowe, *Balzac, James, and the Realistic Novel* (Princeton: Princeton University Press, 1983).

8. *The World and the Parish: Willa Cather Articles and Reviews, 1893–1902*, ed. William M. Curtin (Lincoln: University of Nebraska Press, 1970), 2:928.

9. Henry James, "The Lesson of Balzac," *The Atlantic Monthly* (August 1905): 166–80. See also James, preface to *The Golden Bowl*, in *The Art of the Novel: Critical Prefaces by Henry James*, ed. Richard P. Blackmur (New York: Charles Scribner's Sons, 1934), 343–44.

10. Willa Cather, "A Chance Meeting," in *Not under Forty* (New York: Knopf, 1953), 25.

11. James, "Art of Fiction," 53. See also Miller, "Cather and the Art of Fiction," 126.

12. See Otis A. Pease, *Parkman's History: The Historian as Literary Artist* (New Haven: Yale University Press, 1953), 19.

13. Eudora Welty, "The House of Willa Cather," in *The Art of Willa Cather*, 7.

14. Quoted in E. K. Brown, "Willa Cather," in *Willa Cather and Her Critics*, 82.

15. George Santayana, "History," in *Life of Reason*, 395.

16. See Allen Tate, "The New Provincialism," in *Collected Essays* (Denver: Alan Swallow, 1959), 283.

17. Marjorie Kinnan Rawlings, "Regional Literature of the South," in *English Journal* 29, no. 2, part 1 (1940): 93.

18. Carey McWilliams, *The New Regionalism* (New York: Folcroft Library, 1971), 18.

19. For a discussion of the form of the novel, see Joseph R. Urgo, *Willa Cather and the Myth of American Migration* (Urbana: University of Illinois Press, 1995), 35–36.

20. For elaboration on the theme of possession, see Laura Winters, *Willa Cather: Landscape and Exile* (Selinsrove, Pa.: Susquehanna University Press, 1993), 36–52.

21. See Candace Waid, *Edith Wharton's Letters from the Underground* (Chapel Hill: University of North Carolina Press, 1991), 27–30, 37–39, 42–43, 48–49.

22. Willa Cather, *One of Ours* (New York: Vintage, 1991), 312.

23. Douglas, *Feminization*, 177–78.

24. Guy Reynolds, *Willa Cather in Context: Progress, Race, Empire* (Houndsmill, Basingtoke, Eng.: Macmillan, 1996), 140.

25. See Urgo, *Cather and the Myth*, 28; and Winters, *Landscape and Exile*, 45.

26. Willa Cather, "The Professor's House," in *Willa Cather: Later Novels*, ed. Sharon O'Brien (New York: Library of America, 1990), 125.

27. See George Dekker, *The American Historical Romance* (Cambridge: Cambridge University Press, 1987), 15. For a study of Cather's "romantic" imagination, see Susan J.

Rosowski, *The Voyage Perilous: Willa Cather's Imagination* (Lincoln: University of Nebraska Press, 1986).

28. See Reynolds, *Cather in Context*, 128.

29. See Clifton Fadiman, "Willa Cather: The Past Recaptured," *Nation* 135 (December 7, 1932), 563–65. See also Granville Hicks, "The Case against Willa Cather," in *Willa Cather and Her Critics*, 139–47; and Wallace Stegner, "The American Literary West," in *Conversations with Wallace Stegner*, ed. Richard W. Etulain (Salt Lake City: University of Utah Press, 1983), 123. To Stegner, Cather's "innocence" and her affinity for "primitive beginnings" make her a western writer.

30. See Douglas, *Feminization*, 170. One historian wrote that because Ferdinand claimed all new lands for Spain before Columbus set sail, America was conquered before it was discovered.

31. Ralph Waldo Emerson, "History," in *Essays: First Series* (New York: John B. Alden, 1886), 40.

32. Willa Cather, "Shadows on the Rock," in *Willa Cather: Later Novels*, 535.

33. Lionel Trilling, "Willa Cather," *New Republic* 90 (1937), in *Willa Cather and Her Critics*, 152.

34. For a reading of Cather's use of domestic ritual, see Rosowski, *Voyage Perilous*, 178–83, and Gary W. Brienzo, *Willa Cather's Transforming Vision: New France and the American Northeast* (Selinsgrove: Susquehanna University Press, 1994), 68–80.

35. See Karl Lowith, *Meaning in History* (Chicago: University of Chicago Press, 1949), 160–61.

36. Willa Cather, *O Pioneers!* (Boston: Houghton Mifflin, 1976), 48.

37. For a recent exception, see *Willa Cather's Southern Connections: New Essays on Willa Cather and the South*, ed. Ann Romines (Charlottesville: University Press of Virginia, 2000).

38. William Dean Howells, "Novel-Writing and Novel-Reading: An Impersonal Explanation," in *A Selected Edition of William Dean Howells, Selected Literary Criticism* (Bloomington: Indiana University Press, 1993), 3:230.

39. Willa Cather, "Sapphira and the Slave Girl," in *Willa Cather: Later Novels*, 789.

40. *Advice among the Masters: The Ideal in Slave Management in the Old South*, ed. James O. Breeden (Westport, Conn.: Greenwood Press, 1980), xviii.

41. Bertram Wilbur Doyle, *The Etiquette of Race Relations in the South: A Study in Social Control* (Chicago: University of Chicago Press, 1937), xviii.

CHAPTER FIVE: Ellen Glasgow: The Social History of America

1. Upton Sinclair's ten novels of Lanny Budd, which follow world events from 1913 to 1943 through a single character, have a similar scope. See *The World's End* (1940), *Between Two Worlds* (1941), *Dragon's Teeth* (1942), *Wide Is the Gate* (1943), *Presidential Agent* (1944), *Dragon's Harvest* (1945), *A World to Win* (1946), *Presidential Mission* (1947), *One Clear Call* (1948), and *O Shepherd, Speak!* (1948), as well as the sequel *The Return of Lanny Budd* (1953).

2. Letter, Ellen Glasgow to Allen Tate, September 22, 1933, in *Letters of Ellen Glasgow*, ed. Blair Rouse (New York: Harcourt, Brace, 1958), 124.

3. Ellen Glasgow, *A Certain Measure: An Interpretation of Prose Fiction* (New York: Harcourt, Brace, 1943), 9.

4. Lucinda MacKethan, "Plantation Fiction, 1865–1900," in *The History of Southern*

Literature, ed. Louis D. Rubin Jr. et al. (Baton Rouge: Louisiana State University Press, 1985), 212.

5. Ellen Glasgow, *The Woman Within* (New York: Harcourt, Brace, 1954), 104.

6. Ellen Glasgow, tribute to William Dean Howells, bMS Am 1784.4 (43), p. 45, by permission of Houghton Library, Harvard University.

7. Ellen Glasgow, *The Descendant* (New York: Arno Press, 1977), 207.

8. Dorothy M. Scura, ed., *Ellen Glasgow: The Contemporary Reviews*, (New York: Cambridge University Press, 1992), 12.

9. W. J. Cash, *The Mind of the South* (New York: Vintage, 1991), 375.

10. Letter, James Branch Cabell to Ellen Glasgow, August 6, 1941, partly quoted in Susan Goodman, *Ellen Glasgow: A Biography* (Baltimore: Johns Hopkins University Press, 1998), 242.

11. See Ellen Glasgow, "Heroes and Monsters," in *Ellen Glasgow's Reasonable Doubts*, ed. Julius Rowan Raper (Baton Rouge: Louisiana State University Press, 1988), 165.

12. In 1937, Maxwell Perkins approached Glasgow about a Scribner's edition of her novels. Glasgow had already written prefaces for the novels that comprise the Old Dominion Edition, published from 1929 to 1933, but Perkins wanted her to expand these and to add others. See Goodman, *Ellen Glasgow*, 240–46; and Edgar MacDonald, *James Branch Cabell and Richmond-in-Virginia* (Jackson: University Press of Mississippi, 1993), 312–15.

13. James, "Art of Fiction," 64.

14. See Julius Rowan Raper, "*Barren Ground* and the Transition to Southern Modernism," in *Ellen Glasgow: New Perspectives*, ed. Dorothy M. Scura (Knoxville: University of Tennessee Press, 1995), 146–61; see also Linda Wagner-Martin, "Glasgow's Time in *The Sheltered Life*," 196–203.

15. See Edgar MacDonald, "The Last Pleasure," *Ellen Glasgow Newsletter* 14 (March 1981): 12. Glasgow did not give Cabell credit for the insight.

16. Letter, Ellen Glasgow to Bessie Zaban Jones, August 10, 1935, in *Letters*, 194.

17. See Jerome McGann, *The Beauty of Inflections: Literary Investigations in Historical Method and Theory* (Oxford: Clarendon Press; New York: Oxford University Press, 1985), 12.

18. See Lucinda H. MacKethan, "Restoring Order: Matriarchal Design in *The Battle-Ground* and *Vein of Iron*," in *New Perspectives*, 89–105. See also Susan Goodman, introduction to *The Battle-Ground* (University of Alabama Press, 2000), vii–xliv.

19. See Julius Rowan Raper, *Without Shelter: The Early Career of Ellen Glasgow* (Baton Rouge: Louisiana State University Press, 1971), 137–44.

20. Ellen Glasgow, *The Voice of the People* (New York: Doubleday, Doran, 1933), 349.

21. See Ellen Glasgow, *Virginia* (New York: Penguin, 1989), 338–39. Jenny is "dangerous," intellectual, and spinsterish, all possible hints of her covert sexuality.

22. See Francesca Sawaya, "'The Problem of the South': Economic Determination, Gender Determination, and Genre in Glasgow's *Virginia*," in *Ellen Glasgow: New Perspectives*, esp. 132–45, 136.

23. Ellen Glasgow, "'Evasive Idealism' in Literature: An Interview by Joyce Kilmer," in *Ellen Glasgow's Reasonable Doubts*, 122.

24. See William Morton Payne, "Recent Fiction," *Dial* 29 (1 July 1900): 23–24, in Scura, *Contemporary Reviews*, 44–45.

25. Van Wyck Brooks, *The Confident Years: 1885–1915* (New York: E. P. Dutton, 1952), 352.

26. See Raper, "*Barren Ground* and the Transition to Southern Modernism," 160.

27. Letter, Glasgow to Daniel Longwell [probably spring 1932], in *Letters*, 116.

28. Ellen Glasgow, *In This Our Life* (New York: Harcourt, Brace, 1941), 27.

29. See Glasgow, "Heroes and Monsters," 165.

30. See letter, Glasgow to Irita Van Doren, September 8, 1933, in *Letters*, 143.

31. Letter, Glasgow to Allen Tate, March 25, 1933, in *Letters*, 132. See also letter, Glasgow to Tate, April 3, 1933, in *Letters*, 133–34.

32. Letter, Glasgow to Tate, July 14, 1933, in *Letters*, 139–40.

33. See letter, Glasgow to Anice Cooper, August 12, 1932, in *Letters*, 20 (emphasis in the original).

34. Letter, Glasgow to Tate, January 30, 1933, in *Letters*, 127.

35. I am paraphrasing Wharton in *Edith Wharton: The Uncollected Critical Writings*, ed. Frederick Wegener (Princeton: Princeton University Press, 1996), 172–73.

36. Letter, Glasgow to Margaret Mitchell, May 17, 1942, in *Letters*, 297.

37. Letter, Glasgow to Donald C. Brace, May 4, 1942, in *Letters*, 295.

38. "Ellen Glasgow," *Saturday Review of Literature*, December 1, 1945, 26.

39. "Ellen Glasgow," *Woman's Club Bulletin*, Ellen Glasgow papers (#10137-B), the Albert H. Small Special Collections Library, University of Virginia Library.

40. Undated letter, Glasgow to Douglas Southall Freeman, in *Letters*, 195. Freeman tactfully mentioned her deafness in an article he wrote for the *Saturday Review of Literature* (August 31, 1935), entitled "Ellen Glasgow, Idealist."

41. See letter, Glasgow to Bessie Zaban Jones, July 20, 1942, in *Letters*, 302. See also Goodman, *Ellen Glasgow*, esp. 52–56, 61–63, 70–71.

42. Letter, Glasgow to Tate, September 22, 1933, in *Letters*, 124.

43. Irita Van Doren, "Notes for a Biography," Marjorie Kinnan Rawlings Collection, University of Florida Library, Gainesville.

44. Ellen Glasgow, *The Romantic Comedians* (Charlottesville: University of Virginia Press, 1995), 240.

45. See Glasgow, inscription to *Of Ellen Glasgow: An Inscribed Portrait by Ellen Glasgow and Branch Cabell* (New York: Maverick Press, 1938).

46. Emily Clark, *Ingénue among the Lions: The Letters of Emily Clark to Joseph Herge-sheimer*, ed. Gerald Langford (Austin: University of Texas Press, 1965), 166. See also Dorothy M. Scura, afterword to *Romantic Comedians*, 261.

47. See Susan Goodman, "Composed Selves: Ellen Glasgow's *The Woman Within* and Edith Wharton's *A Backward Glance*," in Dorothy Scura, ed., *Ellen Glasgow: Critical Essays* (University of Tennessee Press, 1995), 57–58.

48. Marshall W. Fishwick, *Gentlemen of Virginia* (New York: Dodd, Mead, 1961), 234.

49. Edith Wharton, "Writing a War Story," in *Collected Short Stories*, ed. Lewis, 270

50. Ellen Glasgow, *They Stooped to Folly: A Comedy of Morals* (New York: Literary Guild, 1929), 84.

51. See Rachel Blau DuPlessis, *Writing beyond the Ending: Narrative Strategies of Twentieth-Century Women Writers* (Bloomington: Indiana University Press, 1985).

52. Letter, Allen Tate to Glasgow, May 24, 1933. See Ritchie D. Watson, "The Ellen Glasgow–Allen Tate Correspondence: Bridging the Southern Literary Generation Gap," in *Ellen Glasgow Newsletter* 23 (October 1985): 16.

53. Letter, Glasgow to Stark Young, January 12, 1932, in *Letters*, 112–13.

54. Letter, Allen Tate to Donald Davidson, "The Agrarian Symposium," ed. John Tyree Fain and Thomas Daniel Young, *Southern Review* 8 (October 1972): 872–73. See

also C. Hugh Holman, "The Comedies of Manners," in *Ellen Glasgow: Centennial Essays,* 108–30.

55. Letter, Allen Tate to Stark Young, January 11, 1932, quoted in Goodman, *Ellen Glasgow,* 187.

56. Letter, Isa Glenn to Glasgow, May 7, 1933, in E. Stanly Godbold, *Ellen Glasgow and The Woman Within* (Baton Rouge: Louisiana State University Press, 1972), 192.

57. Letter, Tate to Glasgow, September 9, 1932, *Ellen Glasgow Newsletter* 23 (October 1985): 8.

58. Letter, Glasgow to Tate, September 22, 1932, in *Letters,* 124.

59. Ellen Glasgow, "Dare's Gift," *The Collected Short Stories of Ellen Glasgow,* ed. Richard K. Meeker (Baton Rouge: Louisiana State University Press, 1963), 106.

60. Ellen Glasgow, *The Sheltered Life* (Charlottesville: University Press of Virginia, 1994), 40.

61. For a reading of the novel that emphasizes the development of Jenny Blair, see Pamela R. Matthews, *Ellen Glasgow and a Woman's Traditions* (Charlottesville: University Press of Virginia, 1994), 179–88.

62. Susan Goodman, "Memory and Memoria in *The Sheltered Life,*" *Mississippi Quarterly* (spring 1996), 249.

63. I am paraphrasing James in "Art of Fiction," 1:52.

CHAPTER SIX: Jessie Fauset: The Etiquette of Passing

1. Langston Hughes, *The Big Sea* (New York: Knopf, 1940), 218. See also Abby Arthur Johnson, "Literary Midwife: Jessie Redmon Fauset and the Harlem Renaissance," *Phylon* (June 1978): 143–53.

2. Fauset was literary editor of *The Crisis* (subtitle: "A Record of the Darker Races") from 1919 to 1926. In May 1926 she become a contributing editor. For biographical information on Fauset, see Carolyn Wedin Sylvander, *Jessie Redmon Fauset, Black American Writer* (Troy: N.Y.: Whitson, 1981). See also Cheryl A. Wall, *Women of the Harlem Renaissance* (Bloomington: Indiana University Press, 1995), 33–84; Wall, "Jessie Redmon Fauset," in *The Gender of Modernism: A Critical Anthology,* ed. Bonnie Kime Scott (Bloomington: Indiana University Press, 1990), 155–59; and Elizabeth Ammons, *Conflicting Stories: American Women Writers at the Turn into the Twentieth Century* (New York: Oxford University Press, 1992), 140–60. Ammons compares Fauset and Edith Wharton.

For a history of Fauset's literary editorship of *The Crisis,* see David Levering Lewis, *When Harlem Was in Vogue* (New York: Oxford University Press, 1989), 121–229, 200. Lewis notes that after Fauset left the magazine, less importance was placed on the arts and literature.

3. See Jessie Fauset, "Oriflamme," *The Crisis* 19, no. 3 (1920): 128; and "Looking Backward," *The Crisis* 23, no. 3 (1922): 125–26. Fauset uses a quotation from Sojourner Truth as an epigraph to her poem and recounts the history of Robert Brown Elliott, a U.S. congressman during Reconstruction.

4. Diane Johnson-Feelings, afterword to *The Best of the Brownies' Book* (New York: Oxford University Press, 1996), 338.

5. For information on *The Brownies' Book,* see Sylvander, *Jessie Redmon Fauset,* 115–19. The magazine contained biographies of exceptional people (e.g., Harriet Tubman), as well as games and songs from other countries and cultures.

6. Letter, Du Bois to Herbert Aptheker, January 10, 1956, in *Correspondence of W. E. B. Du Bois*, 3:395.

7. W. E. B. Du Bois, *The Negro* (New York: Henry Holt, 1915), 15.

8. See also Pauline Hopkins, "Of One Blood, Or, the Hidden Self," in *The Magazine Novels of Pauline Hopkins*, ed. Hazel Carby (New York: Oxford University Press, 1988), 521. "What puzzles me is not the origin of the Blacks," a character says, "but of the Whites."

9. Ann Douglas, *Terrible Honesty: Mongrul Manhattan in the 1920s* (New York: Farrar, Straus, & Giroux, 1995), 309.

10. Letter, Jessie Fauset to Du Bois, February 16, 1905, in *Correspondence of W. E. B. Du Bois*, 1:95.

11. See Wall, *Women of the Harlem Renaissance*, 39. The Fauset family, free for several generations before 1865, had lived in Philadelphia since the eighteenth century.

12. Sylvander, *Jessie Redmon Fauset*, 76. See also Thadious M. Davis, introduction to *Comedy: American Style* (New York: G. K. Hall, 1995), xxxv n. 24. According to Davis, Fauset's letter to Locke is misdated 9 January 1933. It should be January 9, 1934.

13. See Hazel Carby, *Reconstructing Womanhood: The Emergence of the Afro-American Woman Novelist* (New York: Oxford University Press, 1987), 176.

14. Pamela L. Caughie, *Passing and Pedagogy: The Dynamics of Responsibility* (Urbana: University of Illinois Press, 1999), 23–26. I am indebted to Caughie for the distinction.

15. Jessie Fauset, *The Chinaberry Tree* (New York: Frederick A. Stokes, 1931), ix.

16. Jessie Fauset, "New Literature on the Negro," in *The Crisis Reader*, ed. Sondra Kathryn Wilson (New York: Random House, 1999), 253.

17. See Lawrence Otis Graham, *Our Kind of People: Inside America's Black Upper Class* (New York: HarperCollins, 1999), 377.

18. Jessie Fauset, *There Is Confusion* (Boston: Northeastern University Press, 1989), 55, 246.

19. W. E. B. Du Bois, "Criteria of Negro Art," *The Crisis*, October 1926, 292. See also *The Crisis Reader*, 320.

20. "The Negro in Art: How Shall He Be Portrayed," in *The Crisis* 32, no. 2 (1926): 71–72.

21. W. E. B. Du Bois, *The Philadelphia Negro* (New York: Benjamin Blom, 1967), 318.

22. Carolyn C. Denard, introduction to *"Mammy": An Appeal to the Heart of the South* and *The Correct Thing to Do — to Say — to Wear* by Charlotte Hawkins Brown (New York: G. K. Hall, 1995), xxxvii.

23. Sandra Smith and Earle West, "Charlotte Hawkins Brown," in *Journal of Negro Education* 51, no. 3 (1982): 195.

24. Willard B. Gatewood, *Aristocrats of Color: The Black Elite, 1880–1920* (Bloomington: Indiana University Press, 1990), 183.

25. E. M. Woods, *The Negro in Etiquette: A Novelty* (St. Louis: Buxton & Skinner, 1899), 24, 14. The book grew out of a lecture entitled "The Gospel of Civility."

26. See Douglas, *Terrible Honesty*, 75–77. See also Eric Lott, "Love and Theft: The Racial Unconscious of Blackface Minstrelry," *Representations* 39 (summer 1992): 23; and Ike Simond, *Old Slack's Reminiscence and Pocket History of the Colored Profession, from 1865 to 1891* (Bowling Green: Popular Press, Bowling Green University, 1974).

27. Thomas Fortune, "Race Absorption," *A.M.E. Church Review* 18, no. 1 (1901): 55.

28. Quoted in Edith Wharton, *French Ways and their Meaning* (New York: D. Appleton, 1919), 65.

29. Kate Chopin, "Désirée's Baby," in *The Storm and Other Stories*, ed. Per Seyersted (New York: Feminist Press, 1974), 116.

30. See *Harlem Heyday: The Photography of James VanDerZee, Portraits of the Harlem Community during the 1920s and 1930s* (New York: Studio Museum in Harlem and New York State Museum, 1982).

31. Sollors, *Neither Black nor White*, 250. For a discussion of passing and gender, see Elaine K. Ginsberg, introduction to *Passing and the Fictions of Identity* (Durham, N.C.: Duke University Press, 1996), 1–18. See also Juda Bennett, *The Passing Figure: Racial Confusion in Modern American Literature* (New York, Peter Lang, 1996).

32. William Faulkner, *Light in August* (New York: Vintage, 1990), 449.

33. Zora Neale Hurston, "The Pet Negro System," in *Zora Neale Hurston*, ed. Cheryl Wall (New York: Library of America, 1995), 914–21.

34. See Jessie Fauset, *The Sleeper Wakes: Harlem Renaissance Stories by Women*, ed. Marcy Knopf (Rutgers, N.J.: Rutgers University Press, 1993), 1–25. The volume also includes "Double Trouble" (26–39) and "Mary Elizabeth" (40–47).

35. Jessie Fauset, "Dark Algiers the White, *The Crisis* 31, no. 6 (1925): 256.

36. *The Crisis* 32, no. 1 (1926): 10. See also Trudier Harris, *Exorcising Black Historical and Literary Lynching and Burning Rituals* (Bloomington: Indiana University Press, 1984). See also Stewart Emory Tolnay, *A Festival of Violence: An Analysis of Southern Lynching, 1882–1930* (Urbana: University of Illinois Press, 1995).

37. W. E. B. Du Bois, "A Matter of Manners," *The Crisis* 19, no. 4 (1920): 170.

38. Letter, Claude McKay to Du Bois, June 18, 1928, in *Correspondence of W. E. B. Du Bois*, 1:375.

39. David Levering Lewis, *When Harlem Was in Vogue* (New York: Oxford University Press, 1989), 298.

40. William Dean Howells, *A Hazard of New Fortunes*, intro. Everett Carter (Bloomington: Indian University Press, 1993), 230.

41. Letter, Sherwood Anderson to Fauset, November 17, 1925, in *Correspondence of W. E. B. Du Bois*, 1:329–30.

42. Letter, Sherwood Anderson to Fauset, New Orleans [1926], in *Correspondence of W. E. B. Du Bois*, 1:342.

43. *The New Negro Anthology*, ed. Alain Locke (New York: Antheneum, 1977), 164.

44. W. E. B. Du Bois, "Criteria of Negro Art," 321.

45. *New Negro Anthology*, 3.

46. Zora Neale Hurston, "How It Feels to Be Colored Me," in *I Love Myself When I Am Laughing*, ed. Alice Walker (New York: Feminist Press, 1979), 153.

47. Mary Helen Washington, preface to Dorothy West's *The Richer, the Poorer* (New York: Doubleday, 1995), xiii.

48. For an analysis of the novel's structure, see Deborah McDowell's introduction to *Plum Bun*, esp. ix–xxxiii, xvi.

49. Jacquelyn Y. McLendon, *The Politics of Color* (Charlottesville: University Press of Virginia, 1995), 9.

50. See Fauset, "The Negro in Art," 71–72; Hurston, "What White Publishers Won't Print," in *The Crisis Reader*, 169; and Katrine Dalsgard, "Alive and Well and Living on

the Island of Martha's Vineyard: An Interview with Dorothy West, October 29, 1988," *Langston Hughes Review* 12, no. 2 (1993): 37.

51. See Joan Rivière, "Womanliness as a Masquerade," *International Journal of Psycho-Analysis* 10 (1929): 303–13.

52. James Weldon Johnson, *Along This Way* (1933; rpt. New York: Viking, 1967), 311.

53. Du Bois organized the First Modern Pan-African Conference in Paris in 1919 to consider the continent's interests following the First World War. The third conference was held in 1923.

54. Jessie Fauset, "Impressions of the Second Pan-African Congress," in *The Crisis* 23, no. 1 (1921): 17–18.

55. Pauline Hopkins, "Winona: A Tale of Negro Life in the South and Southwest," in *Magazine Novels*, 377.

56. W. E. B. Du Bois, "The Problem of the Twentieth Century Is the Problem of the Color Line," in *W. E. B. Du Bois on Sociology and the Black Community*, ed. Dan S. Green and Edwin D. Driver (Chicago: University of Chicago Press, 1978), 281. Reprinted from the *Pittsburgh Courier*, January 14, 1950.

57. See W. E. B. Du Bois, "The Damnation of Women," in *Darkwater* (1920; rpt. New York: Schocken, 1969), 163–86. See also W. E. B. Du Bois, "Criteria of Negro Art," in *The Crisis Reader*, 323–24.

58. Charles Chesnutt, "Post-Bellum — Pre-Harlem," in *The Crisis* 40, no. 6 (1931): 194.

59. Letter, Claude McKay to Du Bois, June 18, 1928, in *Correspondence of W. E. B. Du Bois*, 1:375.

60. Claude McKay, *A Long Way from Home* (1937; rpt. New York: Harcourt, Brace & World, 1970), 112–13.

CONCLUSION: Excursives

1. Dalsgard, "Alive and Well: Interview with Dorothy West," 31.

2. For a critic who takes this approach, see Elizabeth Ammons, *Conflicting Stories: American Women Writers at the Turn into the Twentieth Century* (New York: Oxford University Press, 1992).

3. See Robert Jarvenpa, "The Political Economy and Political Ethnicity of American Indian Adaptations and Identities," *Ethnicity and Race in the U.S.A.*, ed. Richard D. Alba (New York: Routledge, 1988), 39.

4. Edith Wharton, "The Great American Novel," in *The Uncollected Writings*, ed. Frederick Wegener (Princeton, N.J.: Princeton University Press, 1996), 155.

5. See Mae G. Henderson, "(W)riting *The Work* and Working the Rites," in *Black American Literature Forum*, 23, 4 (1989): 631–60. See also Susan Goodman, "Competing Histories: William Styron's *The Confessions of Nat Turner*, and Sherley Ann Williams's *Dessa Rose*," in *The World Is Our Home*, ed. Jeffrey J. Folks and Nancy Summers Folks (Lexington: University of Kentucky Press, 2000), 12–28.

6. Elizabeth Deeds Ermarth, *Sequel to History: Postmodernism and the Crisis of Representational Time* (Princeton: Princeton University Press, 1992), 22. See also Ursula K. Heise, *Chronoschisms: Time, Narrative, and Postmodernism* (Cambridge: Cambridge University Press, 1997).

7. Raymond Carver, "Why Don't You Dance?" in *Where I'm Calling From* (New York: Atlantic Monthly Press, 1988), 111.

8. Maxine Hong Kingston, *The Woman Warrior* (New York: Viking, 1989), 12.

9. See Peter Gay, *Freud: A Life for Our Time* (New York: W. W. Norton, 1988), 338.

10. Edith Wharton, "Tendencies in Modern Fiction," in *Uncollected Critical Writings*, 170.

11. Willa Cather, "Katherine Mansfield," *Willa Cather on Writing* (Lincoln: University of Nebraska Press, 1988), 109.

Selected Bibliography

Anesko, Michael. *Letters, Fictions, Lives: Henry James and William Dean Howells.* New York: Oxford University Press, 1997.

Bahti, Timothy. *Allegories of History: Literary Historiography after Hegel.* Baltimore: Johns Hopkins University Press, 1992.

Barthes, Roland. *Empire of Signs.* Trans. Richard Howard. New York: Hill & Wang, 1982.

Beecher, Catherine, and Harriet Beecher Stowe. *The American Woman's Home.* New York: J. B. Ford, 1869.

Behrens, Ralph. "Howells' Portrait of a Boston Brahmin." *Markham Review* 3 (October 1972): 71–73.

Bell, Michael Davitt. *The Problem of American Realism.* Chicago: University of Chicago Press, 1993.

Bendixen, Alfred. Introduction to *The Whole Family: A Novel by Twelve Authors.* New York: Ungar, 1987.

Bennett, Juda. *The Passing Figure: Racial Confusion in Modern American Literature.* New York, Peter Lang, 1996.

Benstock, Shari. *No Gifts from Chance: A Biography of Edith Wharton.* New York: Charles Scribner's Sons, 1994.

Bentley, Nancy. *The Ethnography of Manners: Hawthorne, James, and Wharton.* Cambridge: Cambridge University Press, 1995.

Blanchard, Mary Warner. *Oscar Wilde's America: Counterculture in the Gilded Age.* New Haven: Yale University Press, 1998.

Breeden, James O., ed. *Advice among the Masters: The Ideal in Slave Management in the Old South.* Westport, Conn.: Greenwood Press, 1980.

Brown, Charlotte Hawkins. *"Mammy": An Appeal to the Heart of the South;* and *The Correct Thing to Do — to Say — to Wear.* New York: G. K. Hall, 1995.

Brownell, William C. *Democratic Distinction in America.* New York: Charles Scribner's Sons, 1927.

———. *French Traits: An Essay in Comparative Criticism.* 1917; reissued New York: Charles Scribner's Sons, 1919.

Budick, Emily Miller. *Fiction and Historical Consciousness: The American Romance Tradition.* New Haven: Yale University Press, 1989.

Buitenhaus, Peter, ed. *French Writers and American Women Essays.* Intro. Peter Buitenhaus. Branford, Conn.: Compass, 1960.

Burckhardt, Jacob. *The Civilization of the Renaissance in Italy.* Vienna: Phaidon Press; London: George Allen & Unwin, 1937.

Cady, Edwin H. *The Road to Realism: The Early Years, 1837–1885, of William Dean Howells.* Syracuse: Syracuse University Press, 1956.

Camus, Albert. *Notebooks, 1935–1942*. Trans. Philip Thody. New York: Harcourt Brace Jovanovich, 1978.

Carby, Hazel. *Reconstructing Womanhood: The Emergence of the Afro-American Woman Novelist*. New York: Oxford University Press, 1987.

Carver, Raymond. *Where I'm Calling From*. New York: Vintage, 1989.

Cather, Willa. "A Chance Meeting." In *Not Under Forty*. New York: Alfred A. Knopf, 1953.

———. *The Kingdom of Art: Willa Cather's First Principles and Critical Statements, 1893–1896*. Ed. Bernice Slote. Lincoln: University of Nebraska Press, 1967, c.1966.

———. *One of Ours*. New York: Vintage Books, 1991.

———. *O Pioneers!* Boston: Houghton Mifflin, 1976.

———. "The Professor's House." In *Willa Cather: Later Novels*, ed. Sharon O'Brien. New York: Library of America, 1990.

———. "Sapphira and the Slave Girl." In *Willa Cather: Later Novels*.

———. "Shadows on the Rock." In *Willa Cather: Later Novels*.

———. *Willa Cather on Writing*. Lincoln: University of Nebraska Press, 1988.

———. *The World and the Parish: Willa Cather Articles and Reviews, 1893–1902*. Ed. William M. Curtin. 2 vols. Lincoln: University of Nebraska Press, 1970.

Chabot, C. Barry. "The Problem of the Postmodern." In *Critical Essays on American Postmodernism*, ed. Stanley Trachtenberg. New York: G. K. Hall, 1995.

Chace, William M. *Lionel Trilling, Criticism and Politics*. Stanford: Stanford University Press, 1980.

Chase, Richard. *The American Novel and Its Tradition*. Garden City, N.Y.: Anchor Books, 1957.

Chase, Vanessa. "Edith Wharton, *The Decoration of Houses*, and Gender in Turn-of-the-Century America." In *Architecture and Feminism*, ed. Elizabeth Danze and Carol Henderson. New York: Princeton Architectural Press, 1996.

Chesnutt, Charles. "Post-Bellum — Pre-Harlem." *The Crisis* 40, no. 6 (1931): 193–94.

Clark, Emily. "Ellen Glasgow." In *Ellen Glasgow: Critical Essays*, ed. Stuart P. Sherman, Sara Haardt, and Emily Clark. Garden City: Doubleday, Doran, 1929.

———. *Ingénue Among the Lions: The Letters of Emily Clark to Joseph Hergesheimer*. Ed. Gerald Langford. Austin: University of Texas Press, 1965.

Coles, William A. "The Genesis of a Classic." In *The Decoration of Houses*. New York: W. W. Norton, 1997.

Conrad, Joseph. "Books." In *Notes on Life and Letters*. New York: Doubleday, Page, 1922.

———. "Henry James: An Appreciation." In *Notes on Life and Letters*. New York: Doubleday, Page, 1922.

———. Preface to *The Nigger of Narcissus*. New York: Norton, 1979.

Correct Social Usage: A Course of Instruction in Good Form, Style, and Deportment, by Eighteen Distinguished Authors. New York: New York Society of Self-Culture, 1906.

Caughie, Pamela L. *Passing and Pedagogy: The Dynamics of Responsibility*. Urbana: University of Illinois Press, 1999.

Dalsgard, Katrine. "Alive and Well and Living on the Island of Martha's Vineyard: An Interview with Dorothy West, October 29, 1988." *The Langston Hughes Review* 12, no. 2 (1993): 28–44.

Davis, Thadious M. Introduction to *Comedy: American Style*, by Jessie Fauset. i–xxxv. New York: G. K. Hall, 1995.

Dekker, George. *The American Historical Romance*. Cambridge: Cambridge University Press, 1987.

Denard, Carolyn C. Introduction to *"Mammy": An Appeal to the Heart of the South* and *The Correct Thing to Do — to Say — to Wear*, by Charlotte Hawkins Brown. New York: G. K. Hall, 1995.

Douglas, Ann. *The Feminization of American Culture*. New York: Alfred A. Knopf, 1977.

———. *Terrible Honesty: Mongrel Manhattan in the 1920s*. New York: Farrar, Straus, and Giroux, 1995.

Dowling, Linda. *Language and Decadence in the Victorian Fin de Siècle*. Princeton, N.J.: Princeton University Press, 1986.

Doyle, Bertram Wilbur. *The Etiquette of Race Relations in the South: A Study in Social Control*. Chicago: University of Chicago Press, 1937.

Du Bois, W. E. B. *The Correspondence of W. E. B. Du Bois*. Ed. Herbert Aptheker. 3 vols. Amherst: University of Massachusetts Press, 1973–78.

———. "Criteria of Negro Art." In *The Crisis Reader*, ed. Sondra Kathryn Wilson. New York: Random House, 1999.

———. *Darkwater*. New York: Schocken, 1969.

———. "A Matter of Manners." *The Crisis* 19, no. 4 (February 1920): 170.

———. *The Negro*. New York: Henry Holt, 1915.

———. *The Philadelphia Negro*. New York: Benjamin Blom, 1967.

———. "The Problem of the Twentieth Century Is the Problem of the Color Line." In *W. E. B. Du Bois on Sociology and the Black Community*, ed. Dan S. Green and Edwin D. Driver. Chicago: University of Chicago Press, 1978.

———. "Review of *Nigger Heaven* by Carl Van Vechten." In *Nigger Heaven*. New York: Harper Colophon, 1971.

———. *The Souls of Black Folk*. New York: Penguin, 1969.

duCille, Ann. *The Coupling Convention: Sex, Text, and Tradition in Black Women's Fiction*. New York: Oxford University Press, 1993.

Dwight, Eleanor. *Edith Wharton: An Extraordinary Life*. New York: Harry N. Abrams, Inc., 1994.

Edel, Leon. *Henry James: A Life*. New York: Harper & Row, 1985.

Elias, Norbert. *The Civilizing Process: The Development of Manners*. Trans. Edmund Jephcott. New York: Urizen Books, 1978.

Emerson, Ralph Waldo. "Behavior." In *Essays and Lectures*, ed. Joel Porte. New York: Library of America, 1983.

———. "History." In *Essays: First Series*. New York: John B. Alden, 1886.

———. "Manners." In *Essays and Lectures*.

———. "Social Aims." In *Letters and Social Aims*. Boston: Houghton Mifflin, 1875.

Fauset, Jessie Redmon. *The Chinaberry Tree*. New York: Frederick A. Stokes, 1931.

———. *Comedy: American Style*. New York: G. K. Hall, 1995.

———. "Dark Algiers the White, *The Crisis* 29, no. 6 (1925): 255–58; *The Crisis* 30, no. 1 (1925): 16–20.

———. "Emmy." *The Crisis* 5, no. 2 (1912): 79–87; *The Crisis* 5, no. 3 (1913): 134–42.

———. "Impressions of the Second Pan-African Congress." *The Crisis* 23, no. 1 (1921): 12–18.

———. "Looking Backward." *The Crisis* 23, no. 3 (1922): 125–26.

———. "The Negro in Art: How Shall He Be Portrayed." *The Crisis* 32, no. 2 (1926): 71–72.

———. "New Literature on the Negro." In *The Crisis Reader*.

———. "Oriflamme." *The Crisis* 19, no. 3 (1920): 128.

————. *Plum Bun: A Novel without a Moral.* Intro. Deborah McDowell. Boston: Beacon Press, 1990.

————. "The Sleeper Wakes." In 3 parts: *The Crisis:* 20, no. 4 (1920): 189–73; 20, no. 5 (1920): 226–29; 20, no. 6 (1920): 267–74.

————. *There Is Confusion.* Boston, Mass.: Northeastern University Press, 1989.

Fullerton, W. Morton. "The Art of Henry James." In Wegener, *Wharton: Uncollected Critical Writings.*

Gaines, Kevin K. *Uplifting the Race: Black Leadership, Politics, and Culture in the Twentieth Century.* Chapel Hill: University of North Carolina Press, 1996.

Gatewood, Willard B. *Aristocrats of Color: The Black Elite, 1880–1920.* Bloomington: Indiana University Press, 1990.

Ginsberg, Elaine K. Introduction to *Passing and the Fictions of Identity.* Durham, N.C.: Duke University Press, 1996.

Glasgow, Ellen. *A Certain Measure: An Interpretation of Prose Fiction.* New York: Harcourt, Brace, 1943.

————. *The Collected Short Stories of Ellen Glasgow.* Ed. Richard K. Meeker. Baton Rouge: Louisiana State University Press, 1963.

————. "'Evasive Idealism' in Literature: An Interview with Joyce Kilmer." In *Ellen Glasgow's Reasonable Doubts: A Collection of Her Writings,* ed. Julius Rowan Raper. Baton Rouge: Louisiana State University Press, 1988.

————. "Heroes and Monsters." In *Ellen Glasgow's Reasonable Doubts.*

————. *In This Our Life.* New York: Harcourt, Brace, 1941.

————. *Letters of Ellen Glasgow.* Ed. Blair Rouse. New York: Harcourt, Brace, 1958.

————. *The Sheltered Life.* Charlottesville: University Press of Virginia, 1994.

————. *They Stooped to Folly: A Comedy of Morals.* New York: Literary Guild, 1929.

————. *Virginia.* New York: Penguin Books, 1989.

————. *The Woman Within.* New York: Harcourt, Brace, 1954.

Glasgow, Ellen, and James Branch Cabell. *Of Ellen Glasgow: An Inscribed Portrait by Ellen Glasgow and Branch Cabell.* New York: Maverick Press, 1938.

Godbold, E. Stanly. *Ellen Glasgow and The Woman Within.* Baton Rouge: Louisiana State University Press, 1972.

Goodman, Susan. "Composed Selves: Ellen Glasgow's *The Woman Within* and Edith Wharton's *A Backward Glance.*" In Scura, ed. *Ellen Glasgow: Critical Essays.*

————. *Edith Wharton's Inner Circle.* Austin: University of Texas Press, 1994.

————. *Edith Wharton's Women: Friends and Rivals.* Hanover: University Press of New England, 1990.

————. *Ellen Glasgow: A Biography.* Baltimore: Johns Hopkins University Press, 1998.

————. Introduction to *The Battle-Ground.* University of Alabama Press, 2000.

————. "Memory and Memoria in *The Sheltered Life.*" *Mississippi Quarterly* (spring 1996): 241–54.

Graham, Lawrence Otis. *Our Kind of People: Inside America's Black Upper Class.* New York: HarperCollins, 1999.

Habermas, Jürgen. *Structural Transformation of the Public Sphere: An Inquiry into a Category of Bourgeois Society.* Trans. Thomas Burger, in association with Frederic Lawrence. Cambridge: MIT Press; Cambridge, Eng.: Polity Press, 1992.

Hackett, Alice Payne. *Sixty Years of Best Sellers, 1895–1955.* New York: R. R. Bowker, 1945.

Hackley, E. Azalia. *The Colored Girl Beautiful.* Kansas City: Burton, 1916.

Haviland, Beverly. *Henry James's Last Romance: Making Sense of the Past and the American Scene*. New York: Cambridge University Press, 1997.

Hawthorne, Nathaniel. Preface to *The House of the Seven Gables: A Romance*. Boston: Ticknor, Reed, & Fields, 1851.

Hay, John, and William D. Howells. *John Hay–Howells Letters*. Ed. George Monterio and Brenda Murphy. Boston: Twayne, 1980.

Hicks, Granville. "The Case Against Willa Cather." In Schroeter, ed., *Willa Cather and Her Critics*.

Higginson, Thomas Wentworth. *Short Studies of American Authors*. Boston: Lee & Shepard, 1880.

Holman, C. Hugh. "The Comedies of Manners." In *Ellen Glasgow: Centennial Essays*, ed. M. Thomas Inge. Charlottesville: University Press of Virginia, 1976.

———. *The Immoderate Past: The Southern Writer and History*. Athens: University of Georgia Press, 1977.

———. *The Roots of Southern Writing: Essays on the Literature of the American South*. Athens: University of Georgia Press, 1972.

———. *Three Modes of Modern Southern Fiction: Ellen Glasgow, William Faulkner, Thomas Wolfe*. Athens: University of Georgia Press, 1966.

Howells, Elinor Mead. *If Not Literature: Letters of Elinor Mead Howells*. Ed. Ginette de B. Merrill and George Arms. Columbus: Ohio State University Press, 1988.

Howells, William Dean. *April Hopes*. Intro. and notes to the text by Kermit Vanderbilt. Bloomington: Indiana University Press, 1974.

———. *A Chance Acquaintance*. Intro. and notes Jonathan Thomas and David J. Nordloh. Text established by Ronald Gottesman, David J. Nordloh, and Johnathan Thomas. Bloomington: Indiana University Press, 1971.

———. *The Early Prose Writings of William Dean Howells, 1852–1861*. Ed. Thomas Wortham. Athens: Ohio University Press, 1990.

———. *Editor's Study*. Ed. James W. Simpson. Troy, N.Y.: Whitson, 1993.

———. *A Hazard of New Fortunes*. Intro. Everett Carter. Notes to the text and text established by David J. Nordloh. Bloomington: Indiana University Press, 1993.

———. "An Imperative Duty." In *"The Shadow of a Dream" and "An Imperative Duty,"* intro. and notes by Martha Banta. Bloomington: Indiana University Press, 1970.

———. *Interviews with Willian Dean Howells*. Ed. Ulrich Halfmann. *American Literary Realism* 6, no. 4 (1973).

———. Introduction to *The Life and Works of Paul Laurence Dunbar*. Nashville: Winston-Derek, 1992.

———. *Literary Friends and Acquaintance*. Ed. David F. Hiatt and Edwin H. Cady. Bloomington: Indiana University Press, 1968.

———. *Literature and Life*. New York: Harper & Brothers, 1902.

———. *London Films*. New York: Harper & Brothers, 1905.

———. *A Modern Instance*. Intro. and notes by George N. Bennett. Bloomington: Indiana University Press, 1977.

———. "Mr. Charles W. Chesnutt's Stories." In *A Selected Edition of William Dean Howells, Selected Literary Criticism*. Ed. Ronald Gottesman. Vol. 3, *1898–1920*. Bloomington: Indiana University Press, 1993.

———. *My Literary Passions: Criticism and Fiction*. New York: Harper & Brothers, 1895.

———. "The New Historical Romances." In *Selected Literary Criticism*, vol. 3.

————. "Novel-Writing and Novel-Reading: An Impersonal Explanation." In *Selected Literary Criticism*, vol. 3.

————. "The Pilot's Story." *Atlantic* 6, no. 35 (1860): 323–25.

————. *The Quality of Mercy*. New York: Harper & Brothers, 1892.

————. *The Rise of Silas Lapham*. Notes by Walter J. Merseve. Text established by Merserve and David J. Nordloh. Bloomington: Indiana University Press, 1971.

————. *Selected Letters of W. D. Howells*. Ed. George Arms, Richard H. Ballinger, Christoph K. Lohmann, John K. Reeves, et al. 6 vols. Boston: Twayne, 1979–83.

————. *A Traveler from Altura*. New York: Harper & Brothers, 1908.

————. *Years of My Youth and Three Essays*. Ed. David J. Nordloh. Bloomington: Indiana University Press, 1975.

————. "William James's *Psychology*, 1891." In *W. D. Howells as Critic*, ed. Edwin H. Cady. London: Routledge & Kegan Paul, 1973.

Hughes, Langston. *The Big Sea*. New York: Alfred A. Knopf, 1940.

Hughson Lois. *From Biography to History: The Historical Imagination and American Fiction, 1880–1940*. Charlottesville: University Press of Virginia, 1988.

Hurston, Zora Neale. "How It Feels to Be Colored Me." In *I Love Myself When I Am Laughing*, ed. Alice Walker. New York: Feminist Press, 1979.

————. "The Pet Negro System." In *Zora Neale Hurston*, ed. Cheryl Wall. New York: Library of America, 1995.

————. "What White Publishers Won't Print." In *The Crisis Reader*, ed. Sondra Kathryn Wilson. New York: Random House, 1999.

James, Henry. *The Ambassadors*. New York: W. W. Norton, 1964.

————. "The American Scene." In *Collected Travel Writings: Great Britain and America*, ed. Richard Howard. New York: Library of America, 1993.

————. "The Art of Fiction." In *Henry James: Literary Criticism*, vol. 1, ed. Leon Edel with Mark Wilson. New York: Library of America, 1984.

————. *The Art of the Novel: Critical Prefaces by Henry James*. Ed. Richard P. Blackmur. New York: Charles Scribner's Sons, 1934.

————. *Autobiography: A Small Boy and Others; Notes of a Son and Brother; The Middle Years*. Ed. Frederick W. Dupee. New York: Criterion Books, 1956.

————. *The Complete Notebooks of Henry James*. Ed. Leon Edel and Lyall H. Powers. New York: Oxford University Press, 1987.

————. *The Complete Tales of Henry James*. Ed. Leon Edel. 12 vols. Philadelphia: J. B. Lippincott, 1962–65.

————. "Hawthorne." In *Henry James: Literary Criticism*, vol. 1.

————. *Henry James Letters*. 4 vols., ed. Leon Edel. Cambridge: Harvard University Press, 1974–84.

————. *Italian Hours*. New York: Horizon Press, 1968.

————. *The Ivory Tower*. London: W. Collins Sons, 1917.

————. "The Lesson of Balzac." *Atlantic Monthly* (August 1905): 166–80.

————. "A Letter to Mr. Howells." *North American Review* 195 (April 1912): 558–62.

————. *The Letters of Henry James*. 2 vols., ed. Percy Lubbock. New York: Charles Scribner's Sons, 1920.

————. "The Manners of American Women." In 4 parts, *Harper's Bazar* (April–July 1907): 41, no. 4: 355–59; 41, no. 5: 453–58; 41, no. 6: 537–41; 41, no. 7: 646–51.

————. *The Notebooks of Henry James.* Ed. F. O. Matthiessen and Kenneth B. Murdock. New York: George Braziller, 1955.

————. "The Portrait of a Lady." In *Henry James: Novels, 1881–1886,* ed. Leon Edel. New York: Library of America, 1985.

————. Preface to *"The Aspern Papers" and "The Turn of the Screw."* New York: Penguin, 1984.

————. "The Question of Our Speech." In *French Writers and American Women Essays,* ed. and intro. Peter Buitenhaus. Branford, Conn.: Compass, 1960.

————. *The Sense of the Past.* London: W. Collins Sons, 1917.

————. "The Speech of American Women." In 4 parts, *Harper's Bazar* (November 1906–February 1907): 40, no. 11: 979–82; 40, no. 12: 1101–6; 41, no. 1: 17–21; and 41, no. 2: 113–17.

————. "The Turn of the Screw." In *"The Aspern Papers" and "The Turn of the Screw."* 143–262. New York: Penguin, 1984.

————. *Within the Rim and Other Essays, 1914–1915.* London: W. Collins Sons, 1918.

James, William. *The Correspondence of William James.* 6 vols., ed. Ignas K. Skrupskelis and Elizabeth M. Berkely. Charlottesville: University of Virginia Press, 1992–.

————. *"Pragmatism" and Four Essays from "The Meaning of Truth."* New York: Meridan Books, 1955.

Jarvenpa, Robert. "The Political Economy and Political Ethnicity of American Indian Adaptations and Identities." In *Ethnicity and Race in the U.S.A.,* ed. Richard D. Alba. New York: Routledge, 1988.

Johnson, Abby Arthur. "Literary Midwife: Jessie Redmon Fauset and the Harlem Renaissance." *Phylon* (June 1978): 143–53.

Johnson, James Weldon. *Along This Way.* 1937; rpt. New York: Viking Press, 1967.

Johnson-Feelings, Diane. Afterword to *The Best of the Brownies' Book.* New York: Oxford University Press, 1996.

Jones, Howard Mumford. "The Earliest Novels." In *Ellen Glasgow: Centennial Essays.*

————. "Northern Exposure: Southern Style." In *Ellen Glasgow: Centennial Essays.*

Joslin, Katherine. "Architectonic or Episodic? Gender and *The Fruit of the Tree.*" In *Edith Wharton: A Forward Glance,* ed. Clare Colquitt, Susan Goodman, and Candace Waid. Newark: University of Delaware Press, 1999.

Kaplan, Amy. "Romancing the Empire: The Embodiment of American Masculinity in the Popular Historical Novel of the 1890s." *American Literary History* 40 (winter 1990): 659–90.

————. *The Social Construction of American Realism.* Chicago: University of Chicago Press, 1988.

Kaplan, Fred. *Henry James: The Imagination of Genius.* New York: William Morrow, 1992.

Kasson, John F. *Rudeness and Civility: Manners in Nineteenth-Century Urban America.* New York: Hill & Wang, 1990.

Kazin, Alfred. "Howells the Bostonian." *Clio* 3, no. 2 (1974): 219–34.

Kennedy, J. Gerald and Daniel Mark Fogel. *American Letters and the Historical Consciousness: Essays in Honor of Lewis P. Simpson.* Baton Rouge: Louisiana State University Press, 1987.

Kingston, Maxine Hong. *Conversations with Maxine Hong Kingston.* Ed. Paul Skenazy and Tera Martin. Jackson: University Press of Mississippi, 1998.

Leach, William R. "Strategists of Display and the Production of Desire." In *Consuming Visions: Accumulation and the Display of Goods in America, 1880–1920*, ed. Simon J. Bronner. New York: W. W. Norton, 1989.

Lears, T. J. Jackson. *Fables of Abundance*. New York: Basic Books, 1994.

———. *No Place of Grace: Antimodernism and the Transformation of American Culture, 1880–1920*. New York: Pantheon, 1981.

Leavis, Q. D. "Henry James's Heiress: The Importance of Edith Wharton." *Scrutiny* 7 (1938–39): 261–76.

Lewis, David Levering. *When Harlem Was in Vogue*. New York: Oxford University Press, 1989.

Lewis, R. W. B. *The American Adam: Innocence, Tragedy, and Tradition in the Nineteenth Century*. Chicago: Chicago University Press, 1955.

———. *Edith Wharton: A Biography*. New York: Fromm International, 1985.

Locke, Alain, ed. *The New Negro Anthology*, New York: Antheneum, 1977.

Lubbock, Percy. *Portrait of Edith Wharton*. New York: Appleton-Century-Crofts, 1947.

Lukàcs, Georg. *The Historical Novel*. Boston: Beacon Press, 1963.

Lynn, Kenneth S. *William Dean Howells: An American Life*. New York: Harcourt Brace Jovanovich, 1971.

MacDonald, Edgar. *James Branch Cabell and Richmond-in-Virginia*. Jackson: University Press of Mississippi, 1993.

MacKethan, Lucinda. "Plantation Fiction, 1865–1900." In *The History of Southern Literature*, ed. Louis D. Rubin Jr., Blyden Jackson, Rayburn S. Moore, Lewis P. Simpson, and Thomas Daniel Young. Baton Rouge: Louisiana State University Press, 1985.

Marcuse, Herbert. *The Aesthetic Dimension: Toward a Critique of Marxist Aesthetics*. Trans. Erica Sherover. Boston: Beacon Press, 1978.

Marshall, Scott. *The Mount: The Home of Edith Wharton*. Lenox, Mass.: Edith Wharton Restoration, 1997.

McGann, Jerome. *The Beauty of Inflections: Literary Investigations in Historical Method and Theory*. Oxford: Clarendon Press; New York: Oxford University Press, 1985.

McKay, Claude. *A Long Way from Home*. New York: Harcourt, Brace & World, 1970.

McLendon, Jacquelyn Y. *The Politics of Color*. Charlottesville: University Press of Virginia, 1995.

Michaels, Walter Benn. *The Gold Standard and the Logic of Naturalism*. Berkeley: University of California Press, 1987.

Miller, James E., Jr. "Willa Cather and the Art of Fiction." In *The Art of Willa Cather*, ed. Bernice Slote and Virginia Faulkner. Lincoln: University of Nebraska Press, 1974.

Mizener, Arthur. Introduction to *The Fathers*, by Allen Tate, vii–xvii. Chicago: Swallow Press, 1972.

Montgomery, Maureen E. *Displaying Women: Spectacles of Leisure in Edith Wharton's New York*. New York: Routledge, 1998.

Morgan, Charlotte E. *The Rise of the Novel of Manners: A Study of English Prose Fiction between 1600 and 1740*. New York: Russell & Russell, 1963.

Morris, Wesley. *Toward a New Historicism*. Princeton, N.J.: Princeton University Press, 1972.

Mott, Frank Luther. *A History of American Magazines*. 5 vols. Cambridge: Harvard University Press, 1930–68.

Muhlenfeld, Elisabeth. "The Civil War and Authorship." In Rubin et al., *The History of Southern Literature*. Baton Rouge: Louisiana State University Press, 1985.

"Mulattoes, Negroes and the Jamestown Exhibit." In *Colored American Magazine* 13 (August 1907): 87–88.

Myers, Gerald E. "The Influence of William James's Pragmatism in Italy." In *The Sweetest Impression of Life: The James Family and Italy*, ed. James Tuttleton and Agostino Lambardo. New York: New York University Press, 1990.

Nabokov, Vladimir. *Lectures on Literature*. New York: Harcourt Brace Jovanovich, 1980.

Nettels, Elsa. *Language, Race, and Social Class in Howells's America*. Lexington: University Press of Kentucky, 1988.

Newton, Sarah E. *Learning to Behave: A Guide to American Conduct Books Before 1900*. (Westport, Conn.: Greenwood Press, 1994).

O'Brien, Sharon. *Willa Cather: The Emerging Voice*. New York: Oxford University Press, 1987.

Pease, Donald E., ed. *New Essays on "The Rise of Silas Lapham."* Cambridge: Oxford Univesity Press, 1991.

Posnock, Ross. *Henry James and the Problem of Robert Browning*. Athens: University of Georgia Press, 1985.

———. *The Trial of Curiosity: Henry James, William James, and the Challenge of Modernity*. New York: Oxford University Press, 1991.

Powers, Lyall H., ed. *Henry James and Edith Wharton, Letters: 1900–1915*. New York: Charles Scribner's Sons, 1990.

Price, Alan. *End of the Age of Innocence: Edith Wharton and the First World War*. New York: Macmillan, 1996.

Raper, Julius Rowan. "*Barren Ground* and the Transition to Southern Modernism." In Scura, ed., *Ellen Glasgow: New Perspectives*.

———. *From the Sunken Garden: The Fiction of Ellen Glasgow, 1916–1945*. Baton Rouge: Louisiana State University Press, 1980.

———. *Without Shelter: The Early Career of Ellen Glasgow*. Baton Rouge: Louisiana State University Press, 1971.

Reynolds, Guy. *Willa Cather in Context: Progress, Race, Empire*. Houndsmills, Basingtoke, Eng.: Macmillan, 1996.

Salmon, Richard. *Henry James and the Culture of Publicity*. Cambridge: Cambridge University Press, 1997.

Santayana, George. *The Life of Reason, or The Phases of Human Progress*. New York: Charles Scribner's Sons, 1954.

Schroeter, James, ed. *Willa Cather and Her Critics*. Ithaca: Cornell University Press, 1967.

Scudder, Horace E. Review of *A Modern Instance*. *Atlantic* 50 (November 1882): 709–13.

Scura, Dorothy M. Afterword to *The Romantic Comedians*. Charlottesville: University of Virginia Press, 1995.

———, ed. *Ellen Glasgow: The Contemporary Reviews*. New York: Cambridge University Press, 1992.

———. *Ellen Glasgow: Critical Essays*. Knoxville: University of Tennessee Press, 1995.

———. *Ellen Glasgow: New Perspectives*. Knoxville: University of Tennessee Press, 1995.

Sollors, Werner. *Neither Black nor White yet Both: Thematic Explorations of Interracial Literature*. New York: Oxford University Press, 1997.

Sylvander, Carolyn Wedin. *Jessie Redmon Fauset, Black American Writer.* Troy, N.Y.: Whitson, 1981.

Tate, Allen. "The New Provincialism." In *Collected Essays.* Denver: Alan Swallow, 1959.

Tocqueville, Alexis de. *Democracy in America.* 2 vols. New York: Alfred A. Knopf, 1963.

Tolnay, Stewart Emory. *A Festival of Violence: An Analysis of Southern Lynching, 1882–1930.* Urbana: University of Illinois Press, 1995.

Trachtenberg, Alan. *The Incorporation of America: Culture and Society in the Gilded Age.* New York: Hill & Wang, 1982.

Tragle, Henry Irving. "Styron and His Sources." *Massachusetts Review* 11 (winter 1970): 135–53.

Traubel, Horace. *With Walt Whitman in Camden.* Vol. 3. New York: Mitchell, Kennerly, 1914.

Trilling, Lionel. "Art and Fortune." In *The Liberal Imagination.* Garden City, N.Y.: Anchor Books, 1953.

———. "Manners, Morals, and the Novel." In *The Liberal Imagination.*

———. "The Sense of the Past." In *The Liberal Imagination.*

Tuttleton, James. "Howells and the Manners of the Good Heart." *Modern Fiction Studies* 16 (autumn 1970): 271–88.

———. *The Novel of Manners in America.* Chapel Hill: University of North Carolina Press, 1972.

Wall, Cheryl A. "Jessie Redmon Fauset." In *The Gender of Modernism: A Critical Anthology,* ed. Bonnie Kime Scott. Bloomington: Indiana University Press, 1990.

———. *Women of the Harlem Renaissance.* Bloomington: Indiana University Press, 1995.

Watson, Ritchie D. "The Ellen Glasgow–Allen Tate Correspondence: Bridging the Southern Literary Generation Gap." In *Ellen Glasgow Newsletter* 23 (October 1985): 3–23.

Wegener, Frederick, ed. *Edith Wharton: The Uncollected Critical Writings.* Princeton, N.J.: Princeton University Press, 1996.

Wharton, Edith. "The Age of Innocence." In *Edith Wharton: Novels,* ed. R. W. B. Lewis. New York: Library of America, 1985.

———. *A Backward Glance.* New York: Charles Scribner's Sons, 1964.

———. "Belguim." In *King Albert's Book.* New York: Hearst's International Library, 1915.

———. *The Book of the Homeless.* New York: Charles Scribner's Sons, 1916.

———. *The Collected Short Stories of Edith Wharton.* 2 vols., ed. R. W. B. Lewis. New York: Charles Scribner's Sons, 1968.

———. *The Custom of the Country.* New York: Penguin Books, 1987.

———. *Fighting France: From Dunkerque to Belfort.* New York: Charles Scribner's Sons, 1915.

———. *French Ways and Their Meaning.* New York: D. Appleton, 1919.

———. "The Great American Novel." In Wegener, *Wharton: Uncollected Critical Writings.*

———. "Henry James in His Letters." *Quarterly Review* 234 (1920): 188–202.

———. "The House of Mirth." In *Edith Wharton: Novels.* Ed. R. W. B. Lewis. New York: Library of America, 1985.

———. *The Letters of Edith Wharton.* Ed. R. W. B. Lewis and Nancy Lewis. New York: Charles Scribner's Sons, 1988.

———. *The Mother's Recompense.* New York: D. Appleton, 1912.

———. *A Motor-flight through France.* New York: Charles Scribner's Sons, 1908.

———. "Mr. Paul on the Poetry of Matthew Arnold." In Wegener, *Wharton: Uncollected Critical Writings.*

———. "The Other Two." In *Collected Short Stories.*

———. "Permanent Values in Fiction." In Wegener, *Wharton: Uncollected Critical Writings.*

———. *The Reef.* New York: Charles Scribner's Sons, 1912.

———. "Schoolroom Decoration." In Wegener, *Wharton: Uncollected Critical Writings.*.

———. *A Son at the Front.* New York: Charles Scribner's Sons, 1923.

———. *Summer.* New York: Penguin, 1993.

———. "Tendencies in Modern Fiction." In Wegener, *Wharton: Uncollected Critical Writings.*

———. *The Valley of Decision.* New York: Charles Scribner's Sons, 1902.

———. "William C. Brownell." In Wegener, *Wharton: Uncollected Critical Writings.*

———. "Writing a War Story." In *Collected Short Stories.*

———. "You and You; To the American Private in the Great War." *Scribner's Magazine* 65 (Feb. 1919): 152–53.

Wharton, Edith, and Ogden Codman Jr. *The Decoration of Houses.* New York: Charles Scribner's Sons, 1897.

Whipple, T. K. "Willa Cather." In Schroeter, ed., *Willa Cather and Her Critics.*

Wilde, Oscar. "The Practical Application of the Principles of the Aesthetic Theory to Exterior and Interior House Decoration, with Observations upon Dress and Personal Ornaments." In *Aristotle at Afternoon Tea,* ed. John Wyse Jackson. London: Fourth Estate, 1991.

Wilson, Edmund. "Two Novels of Willa Cather." In Schroeter, ed., *Willa Cather and Her Critics.*

———. *The Wound and the Bow.* New York: Oxford University Press, 1947.

Winters, Laura. *Willa Cather: Landscape and Exile.* Selinsgrove: Susquehanna University Press, 1993.

Wonham, Henry B. "Howells, Du Bois, and the Effect of 'Common-Sense': Race, Realism, and Nervousness in *An Imperative Duty* and *The Souls of Black Folk.*" In *Criticism and the Color Line: Desegregating American Literary Studies,* ed. Henry B. Wonham. New Brunswick, N.J.: Rutgers University Press, 1996.

Woods, E. M. *The Negro in Etiquette: A Novelty.* St. Louis: Buxton & Skinner, 1899.

Index

Abbott, John S. C., 7
About Paris (Richard Harding Davis), 7
Adams, Henry, 10–11, 45, 73
Adventures of Huckleberry Finn (Twain), 36
The Age of Innocence (Wharton), xiii, 4, 30, 62, 74–78, 79, 83, 84, 89, 114
Aguilar, Grace, 151
Alexander's Bridge (Cather), 83
The Ambassadors (James), 45, 52, 62, 163n. 2
The American (James), 45, 52, 58, 74
The American Scene (James), 40, 41–48, 50, 53, 54, 55, 155
The American Woman's Home (Catherine Beecher and Harriet Beecher Stowe), 3–4, 68
The Ancient Law (Glasgow), 107
Anderson, Henry, 115, 116
Anderson, Sherwood, 112, 140–41
Angle of Repose (Stegner), 153
Arnold, Matthew, 8, 9, 41, 64
"The Art of Fiction" (James), 44, 85, 102–3
Auchincloss, Louis, 151
Auden, W. H., 9
Austin, Mary Hunter, 86, 152
The Awakening (Chopin), 148

Babbit (Lewis), 81
Bakhtin, Mikhail, 5
Baldwin, James, 149
Balzac, Honoré de, 6–7, 12, 20, 69, 84, 104, 115, 152, 155
Bancroft, George, 10, 88
Barren Ground (Glasgow), 108–9, 111, 112, 114, 122
Barthes, Roland, xiii, 1
The Battle-Ground (Glasgow), 105, 107, 110, 111

Beecher, Catherine, 3–4, 68
Beecher, Henry Ward, 23
Beerbohm, Max, 81
Beloved (Morrison), 154
Bennett, Arnold, 120
Bentley, Nancy, xiii
Berenson, Bernard, 67, 78
Björnson, Björnstjerne, 14
Blanche, Jacques-Émile, 81
Bontemps, Arna, 130
The Book of the Homeless (Wharton), 80–81
Bourget, Paul, 81
Brawley, Benjamin, 134
Brooke, Rupert, 81
Brooks, Van Wyck, 111
Broughton, Rhoda, 58
Brown, Charlotte Hawkins, 134
Brownell, William Crary, 7–8, 48, 71
The Builders (Glasgow), 107, 115
Burke, Edmund, 1, 8

Cabell, James Branch, 106, 107, 114, 116, 119–20
Caldwell, Erskine, 113, 132
Camus, Albert, 44
Carver, Raymond, 154–55
Cather, Willa, xv, 1, 6–7, 9, 17, 27, 37, 53, 83–103, 141, 148, 150, 152, 154, 156, 169n. 5, 170n. 29; *Alexander's Bridge*, 83; *Death Comes for the Archbishop*, 102; and form, 8, and France, 7, 93–97; and history, 85, 88, 90–93, 97, 101–2; and Henry James, 83–86; *A Lost Lady*, 85; and manners, 89; and memory, 85; *My Àntonia*, 83, 85, 98; and nationalism, 94; "The Novel Démeublé," xiv, 53, 84, 86, 88, 98; *One of Ours*, 88, 114; *O Pioneers!*, 7, 83, 86, 95,

Cather (*cont.*)
  113; *The Professor's House*, 85, 86–93, 152; and Pulitzer Prize, 114; and race, 11, 98–100, 101–2, 127; and realism, 84–85, 86, 95; and regionalism, 85–86, 97–98, 99, 102; *Sapphira and the Slave Girl*, 85, 86, 97–102; *Shadows on the Rock*, 85, 93–97, 122; *The Song of the Lark*, 83; and spirituality, 94, 95–97; and time, 94–95; and World War I, 88, 92–93
Ceremony (Silko), 152
Cheever, John, 151
Chesnutt, Charles, 13–14
The Children (Wharton), 61
The Chinaberry Tree (Fauset), 4, 132, 133–34
Chopin, Kate, 136, 148
Civilization and Its Discontents (Freud), 117
Claudel, Jean, 81
Claudel, Paul, 81
Clemens, Samuel L. *See* Twain, Mark
Codman, Ogden Jr., 64, 166n. 19
Comedy: American Style (Fauset), 7, 132, 133, 148–49, 152
Confessions of Nat Turner (Styron), 36, 154
The Conjure Woman (Chesnutt), 14
Conrad, Joseph, 81, 102, 123, 130
Cooper, James Fenimore, 86, 150
Correct Social Usage, 4, 8
Cox, Palmer, 131
Crane, Stephen, 16
Crawford, Francis Marion, 71
Crévecoeur, St. Jean de, 9
The Crisis (magazine), 130–31, 133–34, 138–41, 140, 173n. 2
"Criteria of Negro Art" (Du Bois), 133
Cullen Countee, 130, 140
The Custom of the Country (Wharton), 21, 56, 62, 67, 74, 160n. 40

"Daisy Miller" (James), 19, 40, 49
"Dare's Gift" (Glasgow), 124
"Dark Algiers the White" (Fauset), 139
Darwin, Charles, 6, 73, 76, 106, 111
"The Daunt Diana" (Wharton), 67–68
David Copperfield (Dickens), 35
Davis, Rebecca Harding, 7, 16
Davis, Richard Harding, 7

Death Comes for the Archbishop (Cather), 102
The Decoration of Houses (Wharton), xiv, 63, 64–70, 73, 74, 75, 76, 84, 166n. 19
DeLillo, Don, 154
The Deliverance (Glasgow), 105
Democracy (Tocqueville), 9
Democracy: An American Novel (Henry Adams), 10
The Descendant (Glasgow), 105–6, 107, 111
The Descent of Man (Wharton), 6
"Désirée's Baby" (Chopin), 136
Dessa Rose (Sherley Ann Williams), 154
Dickens, Charles, 20–21, 23, 36, 47
Dixon, Thomas, 111
Dos Passos, John, 21
Dostoyevski, Fyodor, 152
Doyle, Bertram Wilbur, 100
Dreiser, Theodore, 7, 28, 45, 56, 141
Du Bois, W. E. B., 32, 48, 164n. 22, 176n. 53; and Jessie Fauset, 130–31, 133, 134, 139, 140, 141, 144, 146, 148, 149
Du Bos, Charles, 76
Dunbar, Paul Laurence, 14, 139

El Dorado (Bayard Taylor), 6
Ellison, Ralph, 33, 137
Emerson, Ralph Waldo, 8, 13, 85, 93, 106
"Emmy" (Fauset), 138
English Hours (James), 46
Erdrich, Louise, 152–53

A Farewell to Arms (Hemingway), 153
Faulkner, William, 32, 98, 109, 113, 129, 132, 137–38
Fauset, Arthur Huff, 140
Fauset, Jessie, xii, 1, 6–7, 19, 130–49, 150–51, 173n. 3; and Africa, 145, 149; and African American literature, 131–34, 140–43, 147, 149; and audience, 134, 135, 142; and *The Brownies' Book*, 130–31, 173n. 5; *The Chinaberry Tree*, 4, 132, 133–34; and class, 132–34, 149; *Comedy: American Style*, 7, 132, 133, 148–49, 152; and *The Crisis*, 130–31, 133–34, 138–41, 173n. 2; and W. E. B. Du Bois, 130–31, 133, 134, 139, 140, 141, 144, 146, 148, 149; and France, 148–49; and gender, 130, 134,

136, 143, 146–47; and history, 132–34, 144, 149; and manners, 143; and passing, 132, 136–37, 141–49; *Plum Bun*, 132, 136, 137, 138, 139, 141–49; and race, 11–12, 131–34, 139–49; *There Is Confusion*, 34, 132, 133, 139; and war, 133; and Edith Wharton, 130, 131, 132, 133, 140, 142, 148, 149

Fenollosa, Ernest, 5

Ferber, Edna, 140

Fichte, Johann, 11

Fighting France (Wharton), 79

The Financier (Dreiser), 56

The Finer Grain (James), 51

Fiske, John, 91, 111

Fitzgerald, F. Scott, 37, 53, 82, 151, 153

Flaubert, Gustave, 84–85

Foote, Mary Halleck, 153

A Foregone Conclusion (Howells), 19

Fortune, T. Thomas, 144

Foucault, Michel, xiii

France, 7–8, 40, 47, 59, 65, 76–77, 79–82, 117, 137, 145, 148–49

Franklin, Benjamin, 15

Freeman, Douglas Southall, 109

Freeman, Mary Wilkins, 18, 151

French Traits (Brownell), 8

French Ways and Their Meaning (Wharton), 7, 79–80

Freud, Sigmund, 2, 117, 155

"The Fullness of Life" (Wharton), 63

Galsworthy, John, 81, 120, 130

Gardiner, Isabella Stewart, 67

Garland, Hamlin, 11, 105–6

Garner, Margaret, 154

Gay, Walter, 81

Gilder, Helena de Kay, 153

Glasgow, Ellen, xii, 1, 6–7, 19, 37, 53, 104–29, 98, 132, 133, 142, 150–51, 169n. 5; *The Ancient Law*, 107; and *Barren Ground*, 108–9, 111, 112, 114, 122; *The Battle-Ground*, 105, 107, 110, 111; *The Builders*, 107, 115; and James Branch Cabell, 106, 107, 114, 116, 119–20; and Calvinism, 106, 113; and Civil War, 105, 124–28; and class, 11, 105, 109, 110, 111, 125; "Dare's

Gift," 124; and Charles Darwin, 106; and deafness, 115, 116–17, 122, 172, 172n. 40; *The Deliverance*, 105; *The Descendant*, 105–6, 107, 111; and "evasive idealism," 111, 118, 121; and gender, 104–5, 109–11, 113, 115, 117–22, 127; and history, 11, 107, 109, 113, 123–25, 127–29; *In This Our Life*, 107, 111, 112–13, 114; *Life and Gabriella*, 111; and manners, 107, 113, 117–19, 121–25, 127–28; *The Miller of Old Church*, 111; and modernism, 106, 112, 126; and mysticism, 106; and naturalism, 105; *Old Dominion Edition*, 171n. 12; *One Man in His Time*, 107, 115; *Phases of an Inferior Planet*, 107; prefaces of, 105–6; and process, 8, 107, 127; and Pulitzer Prize, 114; and race, 109, 110, 111, 112–13, 125; and realism, 104, 106, 108–9, 128; and romance, 104; *The Romance of a Plain Man*, 7; *The Romantic Comedians*, 112, 114, 116–19; "Sharp Realities," 105; *The Sheltered Life*, 53, 111, 112, 115, 116, 122, 123–28; and social history, 105, 107, 109–15, 123, 128–29; and the South, 104, 106, 110, 111, 112, 113–14, 128–29; and southern literature, 109, 113–14; and Southern Writers Conference, 112, 123, 151; *They Stooped to Folly*, 112, 114–15, 116, 119–23; *Vein of Iron*, 105, 109, 111, 112, 128; *Virginia*, 4, 110–11, 112, 124, 171n. 21; *The Voice of the People*, 106, 107, 110, 111; *The Wheel of Life*, 105, 107; and World War I, 112, 115–16, 118, 120, 124, 126

Glenn, Isa, 112

The Glimpses of the Moon (Wharton), 61, 151

Godey's Lady's Book, 3

The Gods Arrive (Wharton), 132

Gogol, Nicolai, 152

The Golden Bowl (James), 40, 52, 53

Goldsmith, Oliver, 120

Goncourt, Edmond de, 69

Gordon, Caroline, 109

Gravity's Rainbow (Pynchon), 154

The Great Gatsby (Fitzgerald), 151

Hale, Sarah Josepha, 3

Hardy, Thomas, 74, 81, 129

Harper, Frances, 32, 136

Hawthorne, Nathaniel, 11, 13, 36, 57–58, 64, 150

Hayes, Roland, 140

A Hazard of New Fortunes (Howells), 18, 20, 23, 24, 56, 140

Heidegger, Martin, 93

Hemingway, Ernest, 53, 88, 153

Higginson, Thomas Wentworth, 18, 19

History of California (Royce), 37

Holmes, Oliver Wendell, 13

Hopkins, Pauline, 136, 146

The House of Mirth (Wharton), 3, 67, 141 (Lily Bart), 143, 145–46

The House of the Seven Gables (Hawthorne), 57

Howells, Elinor, 42

Howells, William Cooper, 14–16, 24, 31

Howells, William Dean, xii, 1, 7, 9, 13–42, 66, 72, 81, 85, 91, 98, 105–6, 136, 150–51, 163n. 2; *April Hopes*, 158n. 1; and *Atlantic Monthly*, 13–14, 23–25; childhood of, 14–15; and class, 11, 15–16, 19, 20–21, 22–23, 25–26, 30–34; and Jessie Fauset, 131, 132, 145; *A Foregone Conclusion*, 19; and *Harper's Monthly*, 7, 13, 24; *A Hazard of New Fortunes*, 18, 20, 23, 24, 56, 140; *An Imperative Duty*, xiv, 18, 30–35, 36, 55, 98, 101, 133; and Henry James, 18, 33, 37, 39, 54, 59; *The Landlord at Lion's Head*, 36; *Literary Friends and Acquaintance*, 19; *London Films*, 19; and manners, 17–20; *A Modern Instance*, 20–25, 36; "Novel-Writing and Novel-Reading," 18, 35–36; *The Quality of Mercy*, 23; and race, 31–35, 98; and realism, 16–18, 23; *The Rise of Silas Lapham*, xiv, 3, 19, 20, 23, 25–30, 36, 152, 161nn. 42, 43; *Roman Holidays and Others*, 5, 19; as social observer, 8, 11, 18–20; *Their Wedding Journey*, 19; *The Undiscovered Country*, 36; *Venetian Life*, 19; and Edith Wharton, 39, 49, 53; *The Whole Family*, 18, 159n. 17, 164n. 35

Howells, Winifred, 17

Hudson River Bracketed (Wharton), 132

Hughes, Langston, 130, 132, 149

Hunt, William, 57

Hurston, Zora Neale, 130, 138, 142, 146

Ibsen, Henrik, 14, 105

An Imperative Duty (Howells), xiv, 18, 30–35, 36, 55, 98, 101, 133

In Our Time (Hemingway), 53

In This Our Life (Glasgow), 107, 111, 112–13, 114

The Invisible Man (Ellison), 33

Iola Leroy, or Shadows Uplifted (Frances Harper), 32, 136–37

Irving, Washington, 150

Italian Backgrounds (Wharton), 64

Italian Gardens and Villas (Wharton), 5

Italian Hours (James), 5, 46

The Ivory Tower (James), 40, 41

James, Henry, xii, xv, 39–60, 62, 64, 70, 71, 77, 113, 123, 142, 150–51, 152, 154, 156, 164n. 35; *The Ambassadors*, 45, 52, 62, 163n. 2; *The American*, 7, 45, 52, 58, 74; *The American Scene*, 40, 41–48, 50, 53, 54, 55, 155; "The Art of Fiction," 44, 85, 102–3; and Willa Cather, 83–86; and culture, 1, 5, 9–12, 16, 50; "Daisy Miller," 19, 40, 49; *English Hours*, 46; *The Finer Grain*, 51; and form of the novel, 40–42; *The Golden Bowl*, 40, 52, 53; and history, 46–47; and William Dean Howells, 18, 33, 37, 38, 39, 54; and immigrants, 47–48; *Italian Hours*, 5, 46; *The Ivory Tower*, 40, 41, 57–58; "The Jolly Corner," 43; *A Little Tour of France*, 46; "The Manners of American Women," 49–50, 51–52; New York Edition, 50; *Notes of a Son and Brother*, 56, 58; *The Portrait of a Lady*, xiv, 2, 45, 49, 50, 87, 88; and race, 46, 47–48; *Roderick Hudson*, 35, 52; *The Sense of the Past*, 40, 54–56, 57; *A Small Boy and Others*, 56; "The Speech of American Women," 49–52; "The Turn of the Screw," 54; *The Wings of the Dove*, 52; and World War I, xiv, 40, 53–54, 58–59

James, William, 26, 32, 36, 48, 49, 53, 54, 57, 131, 164n. 22

Jewett, Sarah Orne, 95–96, 150, 151

Johnson, Charles, 154

Johnson, Charles S., 130

Johnson, James Weldon, 140, 144

"The Jolly Corner" (James), 43
Jurgen (Cabell), 116, 119–20

Kaplan, Amy, xiii, 159n. 10, 160n. 26
King, Grace, 105
Kingston, Maxine Hong, 37, 155

LaFarge, John, 45, 57
The Landlord at Lion's Head (Howells), 36
Lapsley, Gaillard, 60
Larsen, Nella, 130, 136
Lears, T. J. Jackson, 50
Leatherstocking Tales (Cooper), 150
Leavis, Q. D., 83
The Leopard's Spots (Dixon), 111
Lewis, Sinclair, 82, 114, 151, 170n. 1
Life and Gabriella (Glasgow), 111
Life in the Iron Mills (Davis), 16
Light in August (Faulkner), 32, 137–38
Literary Friends and Acquaintance (Howells), 19
A Little Tour of France (James), 46
The Living Is Easy (West), 152
Locke, Alain, 130, 132, 141
Lolita (Nabokov), 154
London Films (Howells), 19
A Lost Lady (Cather), 85
Love Medicine (Erdrich), 152
Lowell, James Russell, 13, 22–23, 131, 132
Lowell, Percival, 5
Lyrics of Lowly Life (Dunbar), 31

Maggie: A Girl of the Streets (Crane), 16
manners, xii–xv, 1–12, 42–44, 50–53, 56, 69, 70–71, 74, 78–80, 84, 99–102, 152–59; and class, 2–4, 7, 135–36; and eugenics, 2; and gender, 3–4, 50–52, 136; globalization of, 66, 59; manuals, 2–4, 66, 69, 133–36; and passing, 135–38; and race, 6–10, 99–102. *See also* novel of manners
"Manners, Morals, and the Novel" (Trilling), 9
"The Manners of American Women" (James), 49–50, 51–52
Marcuse, Herbert, 66
The Marne (Wharton), 79
Marquand, John, 151

"A Matter of Manners" (Du Bois), 139
McKay, Claude, 130, 140, 149
Melville, Herman, 150, 154
Mencken, Sarah Haardt, 109
Middle Passage (Johnson), 154
Miller, Arthur, 91
The Miller of Old Church (Glasgow), 111
Mitchell, Margaret, 109, 114
Mitchell, S. Weir, 71
Moby-Dick (Melville), 154
A Modern Instance (Howells), 20–25, 36
Monet, Claude, 81
Morrison, Toni, 154
The Mother's Recompense (Wharton), 61, 151
My Àntonia (Cather), 83, 85, 98

NAACP, xii, 131
Nabokov, Vladimir, 12, 154
The Negro (Du Bois), 131
The Negro in Etiquette (Woods), 134–36, 139, 147–48, 174n. 25
Nigger Heaven (Vechten), 141
Norris, Frank, 7
Norton, Robert, 62
Norton, Sara, 61, 62
Notes of a Son and Brother (James), 56, 58
"The Novel *Démeublé*" (Cather), xiv, 53, 84, 86, 88, 98
novel of manners, 37, 87–88, 90, 97, 107, 150–56; and civilization, xiv–xv, 1, 4–5, 59, 117, 119, 126; and class, xi, xiii, xv, 4–5, 11; definition of, xi–xiii, xiv–xv, 9, 11–12, 58; and etiquette books, xii, 2–4, 6, 26, 27, 29, 69, 136; and farm journals, 100; and film, xiii; and gender, 3–5, 11; and history, xii–xiii, xiv, 10–11, 36; and minority writers, 11, 152–53; and narrative strategies, 3–4, 25; and national identity, xi, xiii, xiv, 5, 7, 8–10, 20, 51, 61, 96–97; and place, xiv, 9, 12, 41, 60–65, 85–86; and postmodernism, 72, 154–55; and race, xiv, 11; and travel literature, 5–6
"Novel-Writing and Novel-Reading" (Howells), 18, 35–36

Of One Blood Or, the Hidden Self (Hopkins), 136

Omoo (Melville), 150
One Man in His Time (Glasgow), 107, 115
One of Ours (Cather), 88, 114
"On the Art of Fiction" (Cather), 85
O Pioneers! (Cather), 7, 83, 86, 95, 113
Our Mutual Friend (Dickens), 21

Page, Thomas Nelson, 105, 150
Page, Walter Hines, 131
Parkman, Francis, 10, 85
passing, 132–49
Passing (Nella Larsen), 136
Patten, Simon Nelson, 66
Peterkin, Julia, 141
Phases of an Inferior Planet (Glasgow), 107
Phelps, Elizabeth Stuart, 18, 148
Phillips, David Graham, 23
"The Pilot's Story" (Howells), 31
Plum Bun (Fauset), 132, 136, 137, 138, 139,
    141–49
The Portrait of a Lady (James), xiv, 2, 45, 49,
    50, 87, 88
Post, Emily, 3
Prescott, William, 10, 88, 91
"The Present Crisis" (Lowell), 131
The Professor's House (Cather), 85, 86–93,
    127, 152
Proust, Marcel, 151
Puddn'head Wilson (Twain), 32, 137
Pynchon, Thomas, 154

The Quality of Mercy (Howells), 23

Raper, Julius Rowan, 112
Rawlings, Marjorie Kinnan, 86, 109
The Reef (Wharton), 75
Richardson, Samuel, xii, 120
The Rise of Silas Lapham (Howells), xiv, 3, 19,
    20, 23, 25–30, 36, 152
Rivière, Joan, 143
Robeson, Paul, 141
Robinson, Roxana, 151
Roderick Hudson (James), 35, 52
The Romance of a Plain Man (Glasgow), 7
Roman Holidays and Others (Howells), 5, 19
The Romantic Comedians (Glasgow), 112,
    114, 116–19

A Room of One's Own (Woolf), 41, 73, 81
Roosevelt, Theodore, 23
Royce, Josiah, 36–37, 164n. 22
Ruskin, John, 68

Saint-Gaudens, Augustus, 45
Santayana, George, 11, 78, 164n. 2
Sapphira and the Slave Girl (Cather), 85, 86,
    97–102
Sargent, John Singer, 81
The Scarlet Letter (Hawthorne), 36, 150
Scarlet Sister Mary (Peterkin), 141
Scott, Sir Walter, 3, 10
Scribner, Charles, 57
Sedgwick, Catharine Maria, 3
The Sense of the Past (James), 40, 54–56
Shadows on the Rock (Cather), 85, 93–97,
    122
"Sharp Realities" (Glasgow), 105
The Sheltered Life (Glasgow), 53, 111, 112,
    115, 116, 122
Silko, Leslie, 37, 152–53
Sinclair, Upton, 170n. 1
"The Sleeper Wakes" (Fauset), 138–39
A Small Boy and Others (James), 56
Smith, John, 9
"The Snows of Kilimanjaro" (Hemingway),
    153
Something about Eve (Cabell), 119–20
A Son at the Front (Wharton), 79, 80
The Song of the Lark (Cather), 83
Spacks, Patricia Meyer, xiii
"The Speech of American Women" (James),
    49–52
Spencer, Herbert, 8, 111
Springarn, Joel, 140
Stanton, Elizabeth Cady, 23
Starry Adventure (Mary Austin), 152
Stegner, Wallace, 27, 98, 153–54, 170n. 29
Stein, Gertrude, 46
Stevenson, Robert Louis, 22
The Story of Avis (Elizabeth Stuart Phelps),
    148
Stowe, Harriet Beecher, 3–4, 36, 68
Styron, William, 36, 154
Summer (Wharton), 79
The Sun Also Rises (Hemingway), 153

Tarkington, Booth, 28
Tate, Allen, 109, 114, 122–24
Taylor, Bayard, 6, 153
"Tendencies in Modern Fiction" (Wharton), 156
Their Wedding Journey (Howells), 19
There Is Confusion (Fauset), 34, 132, 133, 139
They Stooped to Folly (Glasgow), 112, 114–15, 116
Tocqueville, Alexis de, xi, 9, 41
Tolstoy, Leo, 14, 36, 70, 90
Toomer, Jean, 130
To the Lighthouse (Woolf), 53, 128
travel literature, xiv, 5–6
Trilling, Lionel, xi, xiii, xv, 9, 64
Trollope, Anthony, 70
Trollope, Frances, 9
Turgenev, Ivan, 14
Turner, Nat, 147
"The Turn of the Screw" (James), 54
Tuttleton, James, xiii
Twain, Mark, 16, 32, 36, 86, 97, 137
Twilight Sleep (Wharton), 61
Tyler, Elisina, 81

Uncle Tom's Cabin (Stowe), 36
The Undiscovered Country (Howells), 36
Updike, John, 151

The Valley of Decision (Wharton), 62, 63, 64, 70–74, 77, 107, 167n. 36
VanDerZee, James, 137
Van Doren, Carl, 114
Van Doren, Irita, 112
Van Vechten, Carl, 140–41
Veblen, Thorstein, 67
Vein of Iron (Glasgow), 105, 109, 111, 112, 128
Venetian Life (Howells), 19
Virginia (Glasgow), 4, 110–11, 112, 124, 171n. 21
The Voice of the People (Glasgow), 105, 107, 110, 111

Wells, Ida B., 139
Welty, Eudora, 85, 86

West, Dorothy, 142–43, 149, 152
Wharton, Edith, xv, 1, 37, 60–82, 113, 125, 150–51, 154, 155, 169n. 5; *The Age of Innocence*, xiii, 4, 30, 62, 74–78, 79, 83, 84, 89, 114; *A Backward Glance*, 75; *The Book of the Homeless*, 80–81; *The Children*, 61; and civilization, 60–62, 63, 64, 75, 76–77, 80–82; and culture, xi, 7, 9, 11, 64, 65, 67, 73, 77, 80–82, 94; *The Custom of the Country*, 21, 56, 62, 67, 74, 160n. 40; "The Daunt Diana," 67–68; *The Decoration of Houses*, xiv, 63, 64–70, 73, 74, 75, 76, 84, 166n. 19; *The Descent of Man*, 6; and expatriation, 60–61, 77; and Jessie Fauset, 130, 131, 132, 133, 140, 142, 148, 149; *Fighting France*, 79; *French Ways and Their Meaning*, 7, 79–80; "The Fullness of Life," 63; *The Glimpses of the Moon*, 61, 151; *The Gods Arrive*, 132; and historical novels, 62, 65, 71, 74–75, 78–79; and history, 60–64, 65, 70–71, 72–74, 78; *The House of Mirth*, 3, 67, 141 (Lily Bart), 143, 145–46; on Howells, 18–19; *Hudson River Bracketed*, 132; and international novel, 12, 62, 69, 87; *Italian Backgrounds*, 64; *Italian Gardens and Villas*, 5; and Henry James, 39, 49, 53; *The Marne*, 79; *The Mother's Recompense*, 61, 151; and place, 62–63, 64–65, 74; and Pulitzer, 114; and race, 65, 80; *The Reef*, 75; *A Son at the Front*, 79, 80; *Summer*, 79; "Tendencies in Modern Fiction," 156; *Twilight Sleep*, 61; *The Valley of Decision*, 62, 63, 64, 70–74, 77, 167n. 36; and World War I, 76, 78–82; "You and You," 82
The Wheel of Life (Glasgow), 105, 107
White, Walter, 140
Whitman, Walt, 79, 105
The Whole Family (Howells), 18, 159n. 17, 164n. 35
"Why Don't You Dance?" (Raymond Carver), 154–55
Wilde, Oscar, 69, 113
Williams, Sherley Ann, 100, 154
Wilson, Edmund, 65
The Wings of the Dove (James), 52
Wister, Owen, 71

Woman Warrior (Kingston), 155

Woodhull & Caflin's Weekly, 24

Woods, E. M., 134–36, 138, 147–48, 149, 174n.25

Woolf, Virginia, 41, 53, 73, 81, 84, 128, 132, 151

The Writing of Fiction (Wharton), 151

Yeats, William Butler, 41, 81

"You and You" (Wharton), 82

Young, Arthur, 72

Young, Stark, 109

Zangwill, Israel, 140

Zola, Émile, 14